FORD MADOX FORD

a study of his novels

FORD MADOX FORD

A STUDY OF HIS NOVELS

BY RICHARD A. CASSELL

The Johns Hopkins Press • Baltimore

Library of Congress Catalog Card Number 61–17069
This book has been brought to publication with the
assistance of a grant from The Ford Foundation.

TO HARRIET

"Yet looking back in days of snow
Unto this olden day that's now,
We'll see all golden in these hours
This memory of ours."

> —*The Face of the Night*

PREFACE

THE REPUTATION OF FORD MADOX FORD AS A NOVELIST
rests primarily on *The Good Soldier* (1915) and the
Christopher Tietjens tetralogy, *Some Do Not . . .* (1924),
No More Parades (1925), *A Man Could Stand Up—*
(1926), and *The Last Post* (1928). Since his death, the
reissue of *The Good Soldier* (1951) and of the Tietjens
novels under the title *Parade's End* (1950) has revived
interest in him among a considerable number of critics,
though not among the general reading public.[1] A prolific
writer who wrote nearly every day of his life from the

---

[1] *Parade's End* (New York: Knopf, 1950), and *The Good Soldier* (New
York: John Lane, 1915 and New York: Knopf, 1951; reprinted as a Vintage
Book in 1957). Mark Schorer's " The Good Novelist in *The Good Soldier*,"
Horizon, xx (August, 1949), 132-138, and Robie Macauley's " The Good
Ford," *Kenyon Review*, xi (Spring, 1949), 269-288, helped to create the new
critical interest in Ford, whose fame had steadily declined since *The Last Post*
was published as a Literary Guild selection in 1928. Schorer's essay appears
in revised form as an introduction to the 1951 Knopf edition of *The Good
Soldier*; Macauley's essay, also revised, appears as the introduction to the 1950
Knopf edition of *Parade's End*.

A promotional brochure printed by Knopf in 1950 includes laudatory
comments on Ford by Graham Greene, Granville Hicks, Arthur Mizener,
Allen Tate, Lionel Trilling, William Troy, Carl Van Doren, and William
Carlos Williams. See also " Homage to Ford Madox Ford," *New Directions:
1942* (Norfolk, Connecticut: New Directions, 1942), pp. 443-494.

time he was in his late teens, Ford published fairy tales, critical biographies of artists and writers, poetry, novels, travel books, critical essays, and reminiscences. Including his collaborations with Joseph Conrad and Violet Hunt, he wrote seventy-five books. Of these, thirty were novels, and the best of them are instructive to students of contemporary fiction.

Critical interest in Ford's fiction has been focused largely on the techniques of his major novels. Mark Schorer says of *The Good Soldier* that " it can tell us more about the nature of the novel than most novels or books about them: the material under perfect control, the control resulting in the maximum meaning, the style precisely evaluating that meaning." [2] The Tietjens novels, according to William Carlos Williams, " together constitute the English prose masterpiece of their time." [3] These are typical assessments of those who admire Ford's work. R. P. Blackmur represents those among responsible critics who approach Ford with more reserve. Ford belongs, he says, " to that race of novelists whose facility for the mere act of writing is so great that their minds never quite catch up with the job under way, and whose writing seldom stops on the difficulties that make the job worth doing." [4]

It has not been until recently that attention has been paid to Ford's subject matter. A few critical essays and histories of contemporary fiction offer certain valuable but general evaluations of the relation between Ford's art and his life or remark, without much elaboration, on the

[2] "An Interpretation," which serves as an introduction to the 1951 and 1957 editions of *The Good Soldier*, p. xv. All future references from *The Good Soldier* are taken from the 1957 edition.

[3] " *Parade's End*," *Sewanee Review*, LIX (January–March, 1951), 155.

[4] " The King Over the Water: Notes on the Novels of F. M. Hueffer," *The Princeton University Library Chronicle*, IX (April, 1948), 123.

connection between his techniques and themes.[5] Douglas
Goldring, in *South Lodge* and *Trained For Genius*, gives
a valuable record of the years of his close relationship
to Ford (1908-1924), but he offers only perfunctory criticism of Ford's art. To these must be added the revelations
of the two individualistic, fascinating artistic women with
whom Ford, at different times, spent several years of his
life: Violet Hunt's *The Flurried Years* and Stella Bowen's
Drawn From Life. Most of the other accounts of Ford
in books are anecdotal and either tributes or complaints
by those who met or knew him as a literary figure.

Except for occasional brief references by critics to the
Katherine Howard trilogy, to *Ladies Whose Bright Eyes*,
and to the collaborations with Conrad, most of Ford's
novels, other than *The Good Soldier* and *Parade's End*,
have been ignored. The eighteen less well-known novels
are out of print, and most of them may not deserve to be
revived, but it is curious that Ford, prolific as he was,
could manage only twice to create fiction of any apparently
permanent interest. " When I really analyze my thoughts,"
he once wrote, " I find I am writing all the while with an
eye to posterity." [6] Today the prospect is not clear; one
critic has suggested he should be remembered for his
memoirs, not his fiction.[7] But no one seems to have

[5] See in particular the essay by Macauley, Edward Crankshaw's " Ford
Madox Ford," *The National Review*, cxxxi (August, 1948), 160-167, and
Morton Dauwen Zabel's " Ford Madox Ford: Yesterday and After " in his
Craft and Character in Modern Fiction (New York: Viking, 1957), pp. 253-
263. The best treatments of Ford's subject matter in histories of contemporary fiction appear in Walter Allen's *The English Novel* (New York:
Dutton, 1957), pp. 394-399, and John McCormick's *Catastrophe and Imagination: An Interpretation of the Recent English and American Novel* (London
and New York: Longmans, Green, 1957), pp. 217-221.

[6] Ford Madox Ford, *Memories and Impressions* (New York: Harper, 1911),
p. 212.

[7] Hugh Kenner, " He Wrote of Giants," *Kenyon Review*, xi (Autumn,
1949), 699.

questioned that *The Good Soldier* and *Parade's End* are his fictional masterpieces. It is probable that they did not just happen or spring spontaneously from his imagination. It would seem, at least in their themes and techniques, that his early novels somehow prepared him for his major work.

There are at least two reasons why the greater number of Ford's novels have not been extensively considered. His death only twenty-two years ago has allowed little time for critics and scholars to examine all of his work or to gain the saving critical detachment that Ford particularly requires because of his controversial life, his proximity to Conrad and James, and the strong loyalties or antagonisms he inspired among his contemporaries. The other reason arises from a conviction that Ford was an able technician, but that, except in his major novels, he too often lacked both self-discipline and a significant subject matter. " Style, technique, manner, and method were kept grinding away," Morton Dauwen Zabel remarks, " half the time saying little and producing what can be, for long and desperate stretches, a garrulously tiresome parody of his intentions." [8]

My study will try to place Ford's major novels in the context of his lesser fiction. By reviewing his representative novels from 1892 to 1936 in the light of his literary background and fictional theory, I want to describe his major themes and to suggest the developing technical methods by which he rendered them. The materials are almost exclusively Ford's published criticism, reminiscences, and novels. The first chapter is a brief look at Ford the man, the second reviews the main aesthetic formulations in fictional craftmanship which he gathered from his Pre-Raphaelite background, from his years of intimacy and

[8] " Ford Madox Ford: Yesterday and After," p. 260.

collaboration with Joseph Conrad, and from other writers he considered to be his literary models. The third chapter summarizes his conceptions of the function of the novel, the obligations of the artist, and the requirements he set for the novel so that the examination of several of his novels in the chapters which follow can be seen in a clearer and more reasonable perspective.

The value of such a study is that, at the least, it begins to give attention to all of Ford's novels, to his major themes, and to the excellence of his techniques, and to pay tribute to a brilliant technician with a fascinating mind whose art at its best is instructive to other novelists and to students of contemporary fiction, whose analysis of society from the age of Victoria to the eve of World War II is incisive and revealing, and whose message may still have appeal for those who read today in the context of our tradition.

The book is frankly not an exhaustive analysis, but a survey that considers Ford's novels on their own terms without extensive comment upon their relationship to other novels written before or during his lifetime, except as they affected either his theory or his practice. Such a critical examination should help to clear the field for those who wish to pursue particular problems more thoroughly or to place Ford more exactly among his contemporaries.

For guidance, criticism, and encouragement I want particularly to thank Professors Morton Dauwen Zabel and Richard Stern of The University of Chicago, and my wife, Harriet, whose acuteness of mind is fortunately equaled by a warm and generous understanding. I am also grateful to Dakota Wesleyan University, which gave me several opportunities during my tenure there to pursue this study.

RICHARD A. CASSELL

Butler University, Indianapolis, June, 1961

CONTENTS

FORD MADOX FORD

a study of his novels

I

THE STORYTELLER

" GOOD LETTERS, IN THE FLAUBERTIAN SENSE," VIOLET HUNT
wrote of Ford, " were to him more important than king
or country, wife or mistress." [1] Ford liked to refer to
himself, in a phrase adapted from Hokusai, as " an old
man mad about writing." [2] He was indeed born to letters,
to painting, and to music. His father was music critic
on the London *Times*, a librettist, and the author of
books on Wagner and Provence. His maternal grandfather was Ford Madox Brown, and Christina Rossetti was
his " courtesy aunt." He spent his youth in the company
of a large group of writers, musicians, and painters, including Dante Gabriel Rossetti, William Morris, Ruskin,
Swinburne, Holman Hunt, Edward Burne-Jones, Joseph
Joachim, and perhaps Liszt.

Ford was to complain that " [I] came out of the hothouse
atmosphere of Pre-Raphaelism where I was being trained
for a genius." [3] Since the " Great Figures " of the Victorian

[1] *The Flurried Years* (London: Hurst and Blackett, 1926), p. 139.
[2] *The March of Literature* (New York: Dial, 1938), p. vi.
[3] *Memories and Impressions*, p. 216.

Age were held by his family as models to emulate, he was expected to be brilliant and artistic. As Ford tells his story, his youth had more than its share of frustration, apparently because he did not always come up to the mark and was sometimes made to feel like " a very small, a very sinful, a very stupid child." [4] He never forgot that his father was once led to call him " the patient but extremely stupid donkey." [5] He seemed, however, to have a relatively happy childhood. He found escape in " penny dreadfuls " like *Dick Harkaway* and *Sweeney Todd, the Demon Barber*, played with the Richard Garnett children, and helped his Rossetti cousins with their anarchistic journal, *The Torch*, which they printed for a time in the basement of William Michael Rossetti's home. His first poem was published in *The Torch*, probably in 1891, when he was seventeen.

Ford spent eight years at Praetoria House, a private school of liberal discipline and education, and a short time at the University College School in London studying music, a field which interested him for a brief period. Though somewhat aimless in his ambitions, he read widely. Other than the penny dreadfuls, which he preferred to " the three-volume novels of William Black, Besant, and Rice and other purveyors of the nuvvle," [6] he read, under his mother's direction, such novels as *Silas Marner, The Mill on the Floss, Wuthering Heights, Sidonia the Sorceress, Diana of the Crossways, Far From the Madding Crowd*, and the two most famous novels by Wilkie Collins. His father, who was less advanced in his literary tastes, cautioned him against Dickens, whom he thought vulgar, and Robert

---

[4] *Ibid.*, p. xiii.

[5] *Ibid.*, p. xi.

[6] Ford, *The English Novel* (Philadelphia and London: Lippincott, 1929), p. 118. The following list of Ford's early reading comes from the same book, pp. 115-116.

Louis Stevenson. Ford Madox Brown introduced him to French fiction ("when I was about seventeen"), recommending *Madame Bovary* and Daudet's *Tartarin de Tarascon* and *Tartarin sur les Alpes*. Ford also mentions reading at this time Smollett, Watertown's *Wanderings in South America*, *The Castle of Otranto*, *Caleb Williams*, *Frankenstein*, and among American writers, Mark Twain, Artemus Ward, Sam Slick, and Will Carleton. He remarks that his reading in poetry was that of the usual schoolboy and young man interested in letters.[7]

In late 1891, when his first book, a fairy tale titled *The Brown Owl*, appeared, Ford claims that he had no literary pretensions but was thinking rather of the Indian Civil Service, the Army, or, it seems, of any job to escape the stultifying Pre-Raphaelite atmosphere.[8] He had not intended to have *The Brown Owl*, published, but Ford Madox Brown had given it to Edward Garnett, then a reader for T. Fisher Unwin. Even though the book sold thousands of copies, Ford received only ten pounds for the copyright.[9] This success must have given him a certain measure of confidence and direction, for in the following year he published another children's book, *The Feather*, and his first novel *The Shifting of the Fire*. These were followed shortly after by a volume of poems, under the pseudonym of Fenil Haig, and a third fairy story, *The Queen Who Flew*.

He could be said to have had something of a career by 1894, when, as a fitting end to this period in his life, he eloped with Elsie Martindale, a friend of his school days,

[7] Ford was fond of claiming that during his youth he could not read poetry. See his *Thus to Revisit* (London: Chapman & Hall, 1921), pp. 132-135, where in later years he analyzes his youthful reaction as a protest against poets being "purely childish" people who considered poetry "as something aloof from life, art, form and language."

[8] Ford, *Portraits from Life* (Boston: Houghton Mifflin. 1937), pp. 92-93.

[9] *Ibid.*

in the face of her parents' disapproval but with Ford
Madox Brown's energetic assistance. The young couple
moved to the country in Kent, where they remained almost
uninterruptedly until 1903. Ford worked on and completed the biography of his grandfather, who had died
shortly after the marriage. The book had been started by
Mrs. W. M. Rossetti, Brown's daughter by his first wife,
but upon her death Ford had been chosen by William
Michael Rossetti to complete it.[10] It was published in
1896, two years before Edward Garnett introduced Ford
to Joseph Conrad.

By the time Conrad and Ford agreed to collaborate in
the autumn of 1898, Ford had completed his Pre-Raphaelite
apprenticeship. In addition to his six books, he had written
a few articles on the Pre-Raphaelites and apparently had
already acquired his reputation as an excellent stylist.[11]
But Ford at this time of his life gives the impression of
still being a dilettante, not, as he says, seriously interested
in writing as a career. H. G. Wells remarks in his *Experiment in Autobiography* that

> Ford is a long blond with a drawling manner, the very spit
> of his brother Oliver, and oddly resembling George Moore,
> the novelist, in prose and person. What he is really, or if
> he is really, nobody knows now and he least of all; he has
> become a great system of assumed personas and dramatized
> selves. His brain is an exceptionally good one and when
> first he came along he had cast himself for the rôle of a
> very gifted scion of the pre-Raphaelite stem, given over to
> artistic purposes and a little undecided between music,

[10] Douglas Goldring, *Trained for Genius* (New York: Dutton, 1949), p. 60.
[11] The articles were: "D. G. Rossetti and His Family Letters," *Living
Age*, CCIX (April 4, 1896), 53-59; "Millais and Rossetti Exhibitions," *Fortnightly*, LXIX (February, 1898), 189-196; "Sir Edward Burne-Jones," *Living
Age*, CCXIX (October 8, 1898), 110-121.

poetry, criticism, the Novel, Thoreauistic horticulture and the simple appreciation of life.[12]

Ford's " assumed personas and dramatized selves " may have been poses acquired in order to assert his personality or to reassure himself after the frustrations and admonitions he experienced as a youth. When Ford was with James, he was " *le jeune homme modeste.*" [13] Those he deeply admired, like James, Conrad, Crane, and Hudson, he patronized.[14] With boors he became an arrogant pontificator, and with sweet American ladies he could play the role of the gallant baron. He was always the kind counselor and " *doyen* of letters " to young writers. Emulating his friend Arthur Marwood, he sometimes assumed the role of the country gentleman: the cricket-playing, fox-hunting, benevolent lord of the manor. He also liked to give the impression that he was listened to in the councils of the Liberal party.[15] Ford was often to complain with some bitterness of writers who thought more of appearing as gentlemen than as artists.[16] He may have gone through the stage himself. In dress he varied between that of the Chelsea Bohemian, wearing a thirty-three-year-old overcoat of Rossetti's, and that of the gallant with a black

[12] (New York: Macmillan, 1934), pp. 526-527.

[13] Hugh Walpole also claims that James used the same epithet for him. Edgar Jepson, *Memoirs of an Edwardian* (London: Richards, 1937), pp. 122-123.

[14] Stephen Crane once wrote a Canadian friend: " You must not be offended by Mr. Hueffer's manner. He patronizes Mr. James. He patronizes Mr. Conrad. Of course he patronizes me and he will patronize Almighty God when they meet, but God will get used to it, for Hueffer is all right. . . ." Quoted in *Portraits from Life*, p. 34.

[15] Douglas Goldring, *South Lodge* (London: Constable, 1943), pp. 15-16; and Jepson, *Memoirs of an Edwardian*, p. 176. Ford gave Jepson the impression that Asquith and Grey conferred with him before declaring war on Germany. Ford was a good friend of C. F. G. Masterman, who for a time was an Undersecretary of State.

[16] See, for example, *The English Novel*, pp. 96-97.

coat and a cape which " floated out a little way behind " over his shoulders.[17] He was sometimes the Kentish farmer in his smock; sometimes the dandy with wing collar, bowler, and cane. Most of the photographs of him show him wearing baggy tweeds.

Ford, above all, was an inveterate storyteller. In conversation and in reminiscences he wove elaborate impressions about himself. Because his anecdotes were often more imaginative than factual, he irritated those he could not amuse or impress. " He could lie most pleasantly," Norman Douglas once wrote. " No doubt he thought a good deal of himself, as do many others and with less reason. Later on, in Paris, he grew so fat and Buddhistic and nasal that a dear friend described him as an animated adenoid. Adenoid or no, he remained good company." [18] David Garnett was assured that Ford was genuinely moved by his own stories and the songs he was fond of singing. " I have never known anyone else behave in such a way— but I can imagine Dickens doing so." [19] Sometimes Ford merely sought to fool others. Ferris Greenslet met him during the war in a railway compartment. Ford was wearing his captain's uniform and was surrounded by papers. He told Greenslet that he was working on " the proofs of an erotic novel he had written in French for publication in Paris, to eke out his captain's pay. . . ." [20]

Ford admitted that he had " a most profound contempt " for literal facts if they did not contribute to the impressions he sought to convey.[21] Goldring remarks that Ford

[17] Goldring, *Trained for Genius*, pp. 52-53.

[18] Norman Douglas, *Late Harvest* (London: Drummond, 1946), p. 45.

[19] David Garnett, *The Golden Echo* (London: Chatto and Windus, 1954), p. 129.

[20] Ferris Greenslet, *Under the Bridge* (Boston: Houghton Mifflin, 1943), pp. 161-162.

[21] *Memories and Impressions*, p. xviii.

regarded words as a painter regards his paints and that " the sort of Truth he was concerned with could be revealed by the artist only by the creation of precise and striking images and the modern equivalent of parables." [22] Ford's imaginative fictions and his poses may have been not only the result of his attempts to create exact impressions, but also artful devices to conceal his true self from the world.[23]

Having a strong distaste for gossip, he tried to keep his private life to himself. Goldring emphasizes that in his periods of mental and marital crises and during the last hectic months of his connection with Violet Hunt he maintained his composure and genial good nature. Only a few of his closest friends ever knew when he was ill or troubled. And yet for several years his private life was aired in the public press. His business and personal affairs he often seemed to complicate beyond repair. " Ford had all the virtues," Pound says, " but on any given occasion he would manage to use the wrong one. I once told Fordie that if he were placed naked and alone in a room without furniture, I could come back in an hour and find total confusion." [24] But through all the grief, confusion, and muddlement in his life Ford continued to write and was able to shape out of his personal trials much of the content of his writing and even the methods of his craft.

Ford was a collection of all his personas and more complex than any single one of them. Essentially, he was always a storyteller and an actor who lived the roles he

[22] Goldring, *Trained for Genius*, p. 251.

[23] Ford, in *Portraits from Life*, p. 34, writes that Stephen Crane " would assert that he had been in all sorts of improbable spots and done all sorts of things, not vaingloriously lying, but in order to spin around his identity a veil behind which he might have some privacy. A writer needs privacy, and people talked so incessantly about poor Steevie that he had to keep his private life to himself."

[24] Interview, February 5, 1951, at St. Elizabeth's Hospital, Washington, D. C.

narrated or assumed. This quality, apparently developed rather early, was later to stand him in good stead by allowing him to be sympathetic to those unlike himself and to achieve in his novels a depth in his characters which gives them an objectivity while at the same time they keep reminding us of Ford at one period or another of his life.

From the evidence of his life and of several of his poems and fictional characters, it is probable that underneath every trait, controlling all, was his life-long search in both art and life for serenity. Christopher Tietjens, for example, achieves it; Ford probably never did, at least fully. Living on high hills commanding broad views in Surrey or Provence, being a market gardener, he could escape the stultifying Pre-Raphaelite literary environment of Chelsea and the disapproving gaze of the public eye. His later decision to leave post-war England was another attempt to find the serenity he cherished. He may have found a measure of it, shortly before his death, at Olivet College in Michigan, where he wrote, taught, and gratefully received an honorary doctorate.

From the time he met Conrad, Ford's public career can be described in terms of those writers he met, knew, encouraged, and published. Remarkably responsive to the demands and aims of several artistic and literary groups, he became a significant transitional figure between the Pre-Raphaelites and the experimental British, French, and American writers of the nineteen-twenties and nineteen-thirties. Of Conrad's generation he knew James, Wells, Crane, Bennett, Galsworthy, Hardy, Hudson, and others. During his editorship of *The English Review* (December 1908 to February 1910) and the years he spent with Violet Hunt (1908 to 1915 and for a short, strained period after World War I), he was the first publisher of D. H. Lawrence, a staunch supporter of Pound, an ally of the

Imagists, and something of an elderly mentor to Wyndham Lewis, the Vorticists, and later to Glenway Wescott and other young American writers. After the war and during the years he spent mostly in Paris (1922 to 1927), he knew Joyce, Gide, and Gertrude Stein, championed the novels of René Béhaine, and was associated with a large group of young expatriates including Pound, Hemingway, Cecil Maitland, Mary Butts, and Robert McAlmon, many of whom he published in *The Transatlantic Review* (1924). Writing and traveling between the United States and France, he spent the last ten to fifteen years of his life in relative obscurity. Nevertheless, he was cordially received by several American writers like Katherine Anne Porter, Allen Tate, Caroline Gordon, John Peale Bishop, William Carlos Williams, and Eudora Welty. A tireless guide to younger writers throughout his life, at the time of his death " he had about two hundred MSS. in his possession . . . and his last energies were spent on them." [25]

The collaboration with Conrad had permanently centered Ford's creative talents on writing and led to his years of intense literary activity. Until his death he turned out at least one book almost every year, and sometimes as many as five. " I am not proud of the record," he writes in 1931. " If I had written less I should no doubt have written better." [26] But he could receive some solace for his creative haste and carelessness from the fact that he had remained faithful to a lesson he had learned from Ford Madox Brown. " My grandfather," he writes to his two daughters in the " Dedication " to *Memories and Impressions*, " was not only perpetually giving; he was perpetually enjoining upon all others the necessity of giving never-endingly." He warns them that " such a rule of life will expose you

[25] Goldring, *Trained for Genius*, pp. 276-277.
[26] *Return to Yesterday* (New York: Liveright, 1932), p. 348.

9

to innumerable miseries, to efforts almost superhuman, and to innumerable betrayals "; and then he adds:

> For the past generosities of one's life are the only milestones on that road that one can regret leaving behind. Nothing else matters very much, since they alone are one's achievement. And remember this, that when you are in any doubt, standing between what may appear right and what may appear wrong, though you cannot tell which is wrong and which is right, and may well dread the issue—act then upon the lines of your generous emotions, even though your generous emotions may at the time appear likely to lead you to disaster. So you may have a life full of regrets, which are fitting things for a man to have behind him, but so you will have with you no causes for remorse (pp. xiv-xv).

Ford Madox Brown seems to have been the strongest influence in shaping Ford's temperament and in encouraging the practice of his " generous emotions." [27] Brown was an inveterate storyteller, was unable to handle his money or business affairs, and was immoderately generous with help and praise to other artists, especially those who were young and promising—all characteristics of Ford, who seemed to give always of his time and talents for the glory of the kingdom of letters. It was a dedication which often must have compensated for the miseries, the efforts, the betrayals he lived through.

[27] Goldring, *Trained for Genius*, pp. 43-50.

II

FROM
PRE-RAPHAELITE
TO IMPRESSIONIST

1

FROM FORD MADOX BROWN AND FROM HIS MANY YEARS
of close association with the Pre-Raphaelite group, Ford
acquired an ardent devotion to the life of art and to his
fellow artists, whom he always defended as a group even
when he did not care for some of them individually. It was
because the Pre-Raphaelites spoke out for the right of the
artist to represent life as he saw it that Ford most admired
them. He also gained from them his emotionalism and his
intensely personal evaluations of art and life. Ultimately
a good deal of his social idealism grew out of their medievalism. And from them he acquired his lifelong interest
in music and painting, his love of conversation and soci-
ability, and his distrust of politicians.

Ford was primarily a man of letters, and his Pre-
Raphaelite apprenticeship served him best by offering him

a basis for criticism of art and life. Although his fairy stories, his early poetry, and even his first novel might easily identify him as a young Pre-Raphaelite, his early critical appreciations of artists and writers show an independence of mind that would allow for no slavish devotion to the group. The criteria by which he discovered their weaknesses and their virtues laid the foundations for his later criticism of fiction and for his own fictional theory and practice.

His book on Ford Madox Brown, though more of an appreciation than a criticism, does illustrate that early in his career Ford had, if only abstractly and tentatively, established a critical viewpoint. Ford indicates that his purpose is to be documentary, that he prefers to " the Scylla of a relative's emotional praise the Charybdis of a simple chronicle." [1] Although he holds remarkably well to his documentary intention, the book is more than a simple chronicle, since he does offer some critical evaluations in the last chapter as he summarizes Brown's artistic development.

Ford sees most of Brown's work as reflecting his naive, imaginative, sympathetic, humorous personality, not only in the subjects he chose but also in his techniques and use of materials. He was more original than most of the Pre-Raphaelites, who, Ford charges, were apt to be imitative, to suppress individuality. They " wished their work to exhibit minuteness of finish and a certain Early Italian sentiment—the first as young men wanting in technical skill; the second as persons drawing from the Early Italian masters their sentiment of what nature-inspired art should be." Significantly, Ford most admires Brown's realistic work, inspired by Holbein rather than by the Italian

---

[1] *Ford Madox Brown: A Record of His Life and Work* (London: Longmans, Green, 1896), p. 402. The following references are to pp. 402-421.

primitives, and thinks much less of his " aesthetic period " when he paid more attention to the " sensuous side of his art," to decoration for its own sake, to " balanced masses as opposed to pictures of combined details." But Ford finds that even the works he likes best from Brown's realistic period, *The Last of England* and *Work*, are aesthetically unsuccessful. He finds too much art with too much formlessness, too many " combined details " lacking a focus. In both of these paintings a great deal of attention is paid to such technical matters as *chiaroscuro* and composition. Although *The Last of England*, he thinks, is comparatively successful, in *Work* the spectator has difficulty in finding any center to the picture, any point for the eye to settle on. The whole painting lacks " harmoniousness " and is " disturbing and whatnot." What is valuable in such a painting as *The Last of England* is its " dramatic motive," a quality which Ford praises in all of Brown's later work, even when he is being more or less consciously decorative. This painting " pays its tribute to the stern force of irresistible, slow-brooding Destiny quite as unmistakably as any of the great tragedies have done."

Already to be noted is Ford's concern with technique and with the shaping influence of temperament upon the artist's work. He is aware of the danger in an overelaborate manner inappropriate to content, or in a technique which fails to focus or arrange the composition clearly for the viewer. Here is established his preoccupation with the " harmoniousness " of " combined details " and with the dramatic quality of a work of art, by which he apparently means not merely the telling or suggesting of a story or action. As the remark on Destiny implies, the total impression of a given work moves the spectator into a particular mood of self-forgetfulness and into a special train of thought. These views, so typically Pre-Raphaelite, prepare for the impressionistic theory and practice Ford later developed with Conrad.

On the other hand, one of the results of the collaboration with Conrad appears to have been the finding of surer ground on which to be critical of the Pre-Raphaelites, a tendency already evident in his book on Brown. The best sources for Ford's evaluations of the Pre-Raphaelites are his books *Rossetti* (1902), *The Pre-Raphaelite Brotherhood* (1907), and *Memories and Impressions* (1911), along with certain essays and chapters or comments from his other books. His admiration for Holbein, evident in his grandfather's biography, led him to a full study which he published in 1905. In Holbein Ford found a healthy antidote to the excesses of the Pre-Raphaelites as well as an example of a man who embodied the artistic qualities dear to him. That is, Holbein was a keen observer of men, a dispassionate renderer, instead of a moralizer, and a craftsman unencumbered by mystical ideals of the function of the artist.[2]

Ford continued to state his objections to the Pre-Raphaelite tendencies toward overelaborate detail, formlessness, and slavish imitation of the primitivists in both their writing and painting. He added to these a distaste for their verbal excesses, for their miguided devotion to medievalism, and for their propensity for moralizing, for being " priests," which opened them to the charge of establishing a kind of " intellectual tyranny." [3]

Ford objects to their inability to blot a line, their " backboneless " sentences, their overuse of similes, and to their disassociating themselves from the life and language of their day.[4] He sees several of the Pre-Raphaelite writers,

[2] *Hans Holbein the Younger* (London: Duckworth. [1905]), pp. 27-36 and *passim.*
[3] *Memories and Impressions*, pp. 265-278.
[4] *The March of Literature*, pp. 773-774.

especially the later ones, as responsible for the decline of public interest in literature.

> For those young men from whom I fled into the country invented later, or had already invented, the dreary shibboleth that literature must be written by those who have read the " Cuchullain Saga " or something dull and pompous, for those who have read similar works. Literature, these people say, is of necessity abstruse, esoteric, farfetched and unreadable. Nothing is less true, nothing more fatal. Great literature always is and always has been popular.[5]

Even Dante Gabriel Rossetti, the most representative of the Pre-Raphaelites, " came to paint and write for a limited circle of men well read in a certain type of work." [6] Though Ford believed that Rossetti was a genius in the arts of both painting and poetry, he felt that he was a master of neither one. Rossetti's emotionalism and his lack of a highly developed technical skill weakened the lasting value of his work. He often failed, as in " The Blessed Damozel," which was a " numbing blow " to the English art of writing by virtue of its overelaborate language and obsolete words.[7] These complaints against the Pre-Raphaelite mannerisms in style and against their literary allusiveness look forward to Ford's plea for the reform in poetic language which he expounded in his significant preface to his *Collected Poems* (1914) .

His objections to the Pre-Raphaelites' medievalism were

[5] *Memories and Impressions*, pp. 275-276. Ford recalls here Homer, Virgil, Chaucer, Dante, Shakespeare (who " deliberately ' wrote down ' in order to catch the ear of the multitude "), Goethe, and Maupassant (" the most popular author of today or anytime ").

[6] *Rossetti: A Critical Essay on His Art* (Chicago: Rand, McNally, [1915]), p. 86. Originally published in London by Duckworth and in New York by Dutton in 1902.

[7] *Memories and Impressions*, p. 59.

less to its use than to the service to which it was put.
He was contemptuous of that variety of medievalism he
felt to be championed by William Morris, " who had never
looked medievalism, with its cruelties, its filth, its stenches,
and its avarice, in the face." [8] The statement is inaccurate,
but in any event Ford thought that Morris and Burne-
Jones, who along with Rossetti were the " true Aesthetics,"
dangerously idealized anything that was medieval.[9] Their
productions could be " symbolized by the words, ' long
necks and pomegranates.' " [10] Even so, Ford was himself
fascinated by the Middle Ages, sometimes turned to them
for the subjects of his poems and novels, and saw the
feudal state and the feudal frame of mind as possessing
the positive values of an orderly society.[11] His own
attempts at being a cottage farmer and the return of his

---

[8] *Ibid.*, p. 18.

[9] Rossetti, Burne-Jones, and Morris " gave aestheticism to the western
world." The lily-bearing group Ford felt to be marginal. *Memories and
Impressions*, pp. 3-4. See pp. 9-10 for an amusing portrait, more typical than
real, of one of the lily-bearers.

Ford is not always too clear in his use of the term " aestheticism," although
he generally refers to Morris, Rossetti and Burne-Jones and their medievalism
in theory and in practice. In the first part of *Memories and Impressions* he
tries to prove that the real Aesthetics were lusty, hard-working people who
did not have time for antics. Wilde he did not like (pp. 164-170). Sometimes
he uses the term " Pre-Raphaelite " when a more careful historian would use
"Aesthetic ": " The writer, indeed, begs the reader not to consider that we
Pre-Raphaelites were the depressed beings that Gilbert and Sullivan ridiculed,
or that Mr. Oscar Wilde, dining on the smell of a lily, represented us, *les
jeunes* of the movement." *The March of Literature*, p. 773. In 1898, however,
he distinguishes between the two movements by noting that Pre-Raphaelism
had less effect than Aestheticism, which was " a plant of stronger growth."
" Millais and Rossetti Exhibitions," p. 195. In 1910 he writes that Henley
and his circle " took, as it were, the place of Pre-Raphaelism after Pre-
Raphaelism had degenerated into a sort of aestheticism and aestheticism into
a sort of mawkish flapdoodle." *Memories and Impressions*, p. 194. In spite
of this confusion of terms, it appears to be that for Ford the Pre-Raphaelites
and the Aesthetics are of the same sturdy plant and that those such as
Wilde are decadent offshoots.

[10] *Memories and Impressions*, p. 169.

[11] See, for examples of his literary use of medievalism, one of his adaptations

characters like Christopher Tietjens to the simple life, by suggesting the serf tiller of the soil, have no less the flavor of medievalism than do Morris' craftsmen of the earth who made their own furniture, wove tapestries, and printed books.

The defender of the Pre-Raphaelites, Ruskin, is Ford's special target, for he represents one of the " Victorian Great " so distasteful to Ford because they were essentially moralizers and priests. Ford calls Ruskin and the older Pre-Raphaelites the " last of the Romantics " and complains that they had less care for precision of language than for preaching.

> Pre-Raphaelism in itself was born of Realism. Ruskin gave it one white wing of moral purpose. The Aestheticists presented it with another, dyed all the colors of the rainbow, from the hues of mediaeval tapestries to that of romantic love. Thus it flew rather unevenly and came to the ground. The first Pre-Raphaelites said that you must paint your model exactly as you see it, hair for hair, or leaf-spore for leaf-spore. Mr. Ruskin gave them the added canon that the subject they painted must be one of moral distinction. You must, in fact, paint life as you see it, and yet in such a way as to prove that life is an ennobling thing. How one was to do this one got no particular directions. Perhaps one might have obtained it by living only in the drawing-room of Brantwood House, Coniston, when Mr. Ruskin was in residence.[12]

---

of the ballad form, " The Old Lament," and " St. Aethelburga: For a Picture," and his " Little Play " *Perseverance D'Amour* in his *Collected Poems* (London: Max Goschen, 1914). *Ladies Whose Bright Eyes, The Young Lovell,* and *Great Trade Route* offer other important views of Ford's medievalism.

[12] *Memories and Impressions,* p. 65. My copy of the English edition of this work, published under the title *Ancient Lights and Certain New Reflections* (London: Chapman and Hall, 1911), appears to have W. M. Rossetti's signature on the flyleaf. In the same handwriting in the margin by the sentence " How one was to do this one got no particular directions " these words are written: " By choice of ennobling subjects."

Their assuming the priestly function was a betrayal of the artist's duty to look at life rather than to share it. It is the artist's " calamity " and " curse," but he cannot, like Morris or the " Henley Gang," be a man of action or a missionary idealist and also an artist.[13]

Ford's objections to the priestly function of literature as well as his complaints against the medievalism of the Pre-Raphaelites he never tired of repeating, but it is clear that he adapted the priestly function as he did their medievalism to his special purpose. In each case his objections seem sincere. As we shall see, Ford himself hoped for a better world, and more and more for him the artist could be the most powerful and effective instrument in achieving it. In his nonfiction, from his book on Rossetti and the essays in *The English Review* to *Great Trade Route* and *The March of Literature*, Ford, as much as Arnold before him, was trying to open the eyes of middle-class England and America to the salvation that works of art could offer to mankind. In his fiction and poetry the priestly function was not embodied in the sermon but rather in dramatized action or sometimes in the parable or the allegorized tale. According to Ford, the end of art is to make mankind better by bringing each person closer to an understanding of his fellows.[14] It is not achieved by moralizing or choosing an ennobling subject but rather by the artist's rendering dispassionately the life of his day and doing it not haphazardly but as one disciplined in the arts of his craft.

By being so in arms against elaborate diction and prose-lytizing idealism, Ford places most of the Victorian writers (especially the poets) in the enemy camp. Only Christina Rossetti is left on Ford's battlements. For lesser service there are her brother Dante Gabriel and Robert Browning.

[13] *Ibid.*, p. 268.   [14] *Ibid.*, pp. 277-278.

It was for Christina of all the Pre-Raphaelites that Ford had the greatest admiration and respect. Ford defends her as both a stylist and a temperament. She and Browning are the only " artists in words " in the nineteenth century.[15] " Her verse at its best is as clean in texture and as perfect in the choice of epithet as any of Maupassant's short stories "; within her limited range of subjects " she expressed herself consummately." Her language was conversational and, though limited, was truly " non-poetic " and her own. He saw her as one of the first modern minds, one of those for whom the little things count in a world which is " losing more and more the sense of a whole." Amid " all the romantic generalizers who surrounded her, who overwhelmed her, who despised and outshouted her," she lived her inner life torn, as Ford sees it, between " a pagan desire for life, the light of the sun and love " and a " Calvinistic restraint." [16] Her real value was that she held aloof from the problems of the day and was a poet who faithfully " rendered " the sufferings of her soul.[17] Ford admired her for the same reasons he admired Holbein. He was to require similar qualities of temperament and artistry from the novelist.

2

Although Ford has popularly and with some justification been called " the last Pre-Raphaelite," his fictional theory and methods are more nearly allied to those of

[15] *The March of Literature*, p. 774.

[16] *Memories and Impressions*, pp. 60-69.

[17] " Collected Poems of Christina Rossetti," *Living Age*, ccxli (April 16, 1904), 167.

the Impressionists. Ford always willingly accepted the Impressionist label, the transition from Pre-Raphaelite to Impressionist being a relatively simple one for him.

Inasmuch as most of Ford's fiction and criticism of fiction was written during or after his collaboration with Conrad (1898 to 1903 and intermittently thereafter until 1907), that phase of his career and those conceptions about technique which evolved from that association deserve primary consideration, because they are the foundation of Ford's impressionistic theory and lead us towards a clearer definition of his kind of impressionism. I do not intend to examine the intricate, at times agonizing, personal relationships between Ford and Conrad. Douglas Goldring, using the available data, has discussed these at some length.[18] I do want to suggest the importance of their immediate literary environment and of their devotion to the aims and ideas formulated by the French Realists and Impressionists.

Conrad by 1898 had published three novels and a book of tales, none of which had been greatly popular.[19] He had already established the core of his aesthetic theory, elaborated in his 1897 preface to *The Nigger of the " Narcissus."* Although Ford in his published writings up to this time had never stated so fully or compactly his view, he had developed criteria and attitudes similar and sympathetic to those of Conrad's. " That message," Ford writes, " that the province of written art is above all things to make you see was given before we met: it was because that same belief was previously and so profoundly held by the writer that we could work for so long together.

---

[18] See in particular, *South Lodge*, pp. 165-177, and *Trained for Genius*, pp. 60-90.

[19] *Almayer's Folly* (1895); *An Outcast of the Island* (1896); *The Nigger of the " Narcissus "* (1897); *Tales of Unrest* (1898).

We had the same aims and we had all the time the same aims." [20] Written some twenty-six years after he and Conrad met, these sentences may be retrospective over-statements, but readers familiar with Ford's earlier works (and Conrad's), especially the book on F. M. Brown, can see that the two would more or less agree on fundamental matters.

From their numberless conversations, peregrinations (Pent Farm, London, Belgium), and readings of Flaubert and of each other's manuscripts, Conrad and Ford developed techniques which were to help revitalize the serious novel written in English. According to Ford, it was actually his and Conrad's devotion to Flaubert and Maupassant which brought them together.[21] They found in these French writers and in Turgenev a means of strengthening and even revolutionizing the English novel. Like the Pre-Raphaelites fifty years earlier, they were revolting against typical and standardized art forms. Whereas the Pre-Raphaelites had protested against the traditional painting and poetry of their day, Ford and Conrad protested against the traditional novel of theirs, which was a " more or less arbitrary tale so turned as to ensure a complacent view of life and carried on by charac-ters that as a rule are—six feet high and gliding two inches above the ground! " [22]

A number of " foreigners "—Conrad, James, Crane, Hudson, Cunninghame Graham, Ford—along with Gals-worthy and, for a time, Wells, represented the relatively

[20] *Joseph Conrad: A Personal Remembrance* (London: Duckworth, 1924), p. 168.

[21] *Ibid.*, p. 36.

[22] *The English Novel*, p. 109. Ford goes on to say here that Trollope, Rutherford, Gissing, and Austen, among a few others, give the reader " some attempts at rendering English life that are above the attention of adults with the mentality of French boys of sixteen."

close-knit group that brought to England the insights of fictional art initiated by the French Realists and Turgenev. The methods of Continental realism had, of course, been introduced earlier into Engish fiction. George Eliot and George Meredith, although probably not directly influenced by the French writers, were nevertheless a part of a similar current and

> the counterparts of new growing points already visible in European fiction generally . . . looking back we can see that the English writers [Eliot and Meredith] belonged to the same broad movement that was shaping the novel anew in Europe, and henceforward, for English novelists younger than they, the usable past of fiction was to include, besides the traditional English novel from Defoe onwards, nineteenth century French and Russian fiction. The result, so far as England was concerned, was the mutation of which the modern English novel was the product.[23]

George Gissing worked within the tradition of Zola and the Naturalists, and George Moore was thoroughly schooled in the French writers, Turgenev, and the Impressionist painters. Arnold Bennett, more familiar in his youth with contemporary French novels than with English, followed the foreign models more closely in his early work than he did later.

But it is essentially true, as Ford says with his characteristic exaggeration, that the English writers of the nineties " avoided writers; there remained no perceptible Literary Life in England. Books were written, but the problems of how best to treat a given subject, or how most exactly to render an Affair—these problems were banned and remained undiscussed." There were other novelists concerned with methods, but they, like Hardy,

[23] Allen, *The English Novel*, pp. 253-254.

Meredith, and Moore, "lived each apart on his little hill." [24] But the foreign horde, as H. G. Wells somewhere refers to the group centering around James and Conrad, were artistically remarkably close.[25] Crane, Hudson, Cunninghame Graham lived near them or often met with them. Ford and Conrad, "buried deep in rural greenesses," wrought together the disciplines of their art, while nearby lived James, who "was performing the miracles after whose secret we were merely groping. I don't know why—but we rather ignored that fact." [26]

All these writers from Gissing to Ford acknowledged their debt to the Continental Realists. Ford saw their tradition stemming from Richardson and Jane Austen, then shifting to the France of Diderot and the Encyclopedists, to Chateaubriand, Stendhal, Flaubert, Maupassant, and the Goncourts, Gautier, and Turgenev.[27] Among English novelists he largely ignores George Eliot and barely mentions Gissing. He admired Moore's mastery of technique, but did not like him or his books and seldom mentions him in his many lists of the traditions of his kind of English novel, although he does admit in his last

[24] *Thus to Revisit,* p. 39.

[25] Ford refers to Wells's statement in *The English Novel,* p. 143.

[26] *Thus to Revisit,* pp. 39 and 46. Although Conrad and Ford knew James, it seems that their personal relationships with James were never close. However, James speaks of Conrad with the respect due a fellow craftsman in his essay "The New Novel," where he refers to him as "a votary of the way to do a thing that shall make it undergo most doing." Apparently James felt for Ford a kind of distant affection until their relations cooled after the public scandal of Ford's "divorce." Conrad admired James as "the historian of fine consciences." James never, and Conrad seldom, referred to Ford in their public writings. But within the limits of their devotion to their art they were all genuinely sympathetic to each other. See Henry James, *The Art of Fiction and Other Essays,* ed. Morris Roberts (New York: Oxford, 1948), pp. 202-203; and Conrad's essay on James included in *Notes on Life and Letters* (London: Dent, 1921), p. 21.

[27] *Henry James: A Critical Study* (New York: Albert and Charles Boni, 1915), p. 55. For one of his fuller treatments see *The English Novel,* pp. 121-141.

book that Moore is " the father of Anglo-Saxon impressionism." [28] Of the great French Realists, Balzac is brushed aside as having no " aesthetic ideal "; the *Comédie Humaine* was a fairy tale about the author rather than a serious treatment of his subject matter.[29] There is a certain justification for Ford's belief that the English novel had no tradition comparable to the French in the sense of a pattern developing through the ages. The great English novelists, Ford says, arrive at " peaks," but each one is " absolutely without inter-relation with any other." [30] Ford's concept of his tradition was limited to those writers who gave their complete attention to their art and approached their subject matter aloofly. Authors like Fielding or Thackeray, who intrude upon the reader, or those like George Eliot or Dickens, who act as priests, though excellent writers in individual passages, must be ruled out. Any thorough study of Ford's heritage would naturally have to include Balzac and George Eliot (if only for her influence on James) and Moore.

Ford cannot be considered apart from the tradition in which he worked. In view of his fictional theory and of the techniques he was to develop in his novels in order to project his themes, it may help to review briefly certain aesthetic assumptions held in common by both the Pre-Raphaelites and the Impressionists. I want particularly to suggest how from these assumptions writers like Ford justified their fascination with the fictional point of view and the time-shift. These and related techniques proved extremely fruitful for the impressionistic and later novelists

[28] *The March of Literature*, p. 840. For other evaluations of Moore, see *The Critical Attitude* (London: Duckworth, 1911), p. 94, and *It Was the Nightingale* (Philadelphia and London: Lippincott, 1933), pp. 35-42.

[29] *The March of Literature*, pp. 810-811. The charge is similar to that made by James in his essay on Balzac.

[30] *The English Novel*, p. 11.

by helping to shape their novels—by helping to create, in effect, a new form for the novel.

Generally, among the Pre-Raphaelites and Impressionists, there was a distrust of inspiration without the guidance of skill in art. Rossetti speaks of the agonies of writing, of the " fundamental brainwork " that must go with the " music " to make up a poem.[31] Flaubert struggled endlessly to achieve *le mot juste*,[32] Conrad wracked his nerves and sharpened his temper over every book, and James, as is witnessed by his notebooks, calculated long and carefully to achieve his intended effects. For all of them art was a way of life, and the life of art offered a legitimate and noble contribution to humanity. They were not men whose central passion was to make a living, or to preach, or to reform. The Pre-Raphaelites, to be sure, sought ennobling subjects more consciously than, say, Wilde or Remy de Gourmont, but then they all felt, although in varying degrees of intensity, that a faithful rendering of reality, by presenting us with a picture of things as they are, gave to their art a moral atmosphere or sense from which the reader could infer as much in the nature of a sermon as he would.[33]

---

[31] W. M. Rossetti, ed., *Family Letters with a Memoir* (Boston: Roberts, 1895), I, 416-417.

[32] " One must distrust anything looking like inspiration," Flaubert writes to Louise Colet; " it is often a mere self-deception, a factitious exaltation with nothing spontaneous about its origin, something, in fact, deliberately fostered. Besides, one does not live on inspiration." Flaubert, *Letters*, ed. Richard Rumbold; trans. J. M. Cohen (London: George Weidenfeld and Nicolson, 1950), p. 37.

[33] See, for example, Flaubert's speaking of the " moral effect of Art." " [Art's] intrinsic sublimity, like nature's, will lead to a higher morality; by virtue of its very superiority it will serve a useful purpose." *Letters*, p. 85. W. M. Rossetti says of his brother: " In all poetic literature, anything of a didactic, hortatory, or expressly ethical quality was alien from my brother's liking. That it should be more or less implied was right, but that it should be propounded and preached was wrong." D. G. Rossetti, *Works*, ed. W. M. Rossetti (London: Ellis, 1911), p. 671.

After necessary qualifications, certain other similarities
might fairly be noted among these serious and self-con-
scious writers in England and France from 1850 to 1900,
for, despite their differences, the principles these writers
held in common take us to the very heart of their aesthetic
concerns. First there is their view of the relationship of art
to nature, which is easy to oversimplify. Basically it is
expressed by Flaubert when he says "Art is not Nature!" [34]
Coventry Patmore, closely allied with the Pre-Raphaelites
at one time, reviewing favorably an exhibition of Pre-
Raphaelite paintings in 1857, speaks of Rossetti's work and
denies, like Rossetti, Ruskin, and Hunt before him, that
the painter needs to make a mere copy of nature. He
praises Rossetti's work because it is

> more simply and devotedly true to that, in his mind's eye,
> which is more beautiful than nature—to a nature not to be
> adequately expressed in words or art at all, and only
> approximately rendered by non-natural and symbolic re-
> arrangements of the elements of natural effect—form, sound,
> color, etc.[35]

By the time of the later Aesthetics the conviction that
art is more beautiful than nature had shifted to the conviction that nature imitates art. But the key term in
Patmore's statement is " mind's eye," the vision of the
artist. For the Pre-Raphaelites, the Aesthetics, the Impressionists, reality is as we perceive it to be, not as the
" masters " or the public or anyone else thinks it is.
Holman Hunt tells us in his history of the Pre-Raphaelite
Brotherhood that he and Rossetti, despite their many
differences, agreed that a " man's work must be the reflex
of a living image in his own mind and not the icy double

[34] *Letters*, p. 228.
[35] " Pre-Raphaelite Exhibition," *Saturday Review*, IV (July 4, 1857), 11-12.

of the facts themselves." [36] Although they often failed in their objective because their intellectual bias was founded more on literature than on life, the primary *raison d'être* of the brotherhood had been to study nature (the subject matter of art) freshly, not according to any rules but to what the artist actually saw.[37]

> When whoso merely hath a little thought
>   Will plainly think the thought which is in him,—
>   Not imaging another's bright or dim,
> Not mangling with new words what others taught . . .[38]

The idea is reflected in Arnold's and Pater's concern with the " object as it really is," [39] and for Pater, " the first step towards seeing one's object as it really is, is to know one's own impression as it really is, to discriminate it, to realise it distinctly." [40] Henry James in 1888 expressed his adaptation of this assumption in his famous and significant statements that " a novel is in its broadest definition a personal, a direct impression of life: that, to begin with, constitutes its value, which is greater or lesser

---

[36] William Holman Hunt, *Pre-Raphaelitism and the Pre-Raphaelite Brotherhood* (New York: Macmillan, 1905), I, 150.

[37] Holbrook Jackson, *The Eighteen Nineties* (Middlesex: Hammondsworth, 1950), p. 277. Jackson here tries to explain the disparity between Pre-Raphaelite theory and practice in art. Their paintings, he says, were romantic, literary, and unnatural because " they were not inspired by physical reality at all," but rather by the intellectual and literary tradition of the Bible, medieval legends, Shakespeare and Dante. " The Pre-Raphaelites brought with them a fine aesthetic sense and high purpose . . . but . . . it must be admitted that they never succeeded in doing more than represent in paint what had already been realised in literature."

[38] The poem from which these lines are taken is by W. M. Rossetti and appeared on the front cover of all four issues of *The Germ*. See Thomas B. Mosher's reprint, Portland, Maine, 1898.

[39] Geoffrey Tillotson, *Criticism and the Nineteenth Century* (London: Athlone, 1951), pp. 82-94 and 104-111, compares and contrasts Arnold's and Pater's conceptions of this precept.

[40] Quoted in Tillotson, p. 104 from the introduction to *Studies in the History of the Renaissance*, 1873 edition, p. viii.

according to the intensity of the impression," and his corollary of this that " the deepest quality of a work of art will always be the quality of the mind of the producer." [41] For Ford, strongly influenced and deeply convinced of these words of James, the artist " is a sensitized instrument, recording to the measure of the light vouchsafed him what is—what *may* be—the Truth." [42]

Remy de Gourmont in describing the doctrine of impressionism, which he saw as a revolution in aesthetics, gives a clear if somewhat extreme expression to this controlling assumption about the artistic nature of truth. A " new truth," he says, has been introduced into the fields of art and literature.

This truth . . . is the principle of the ideality of the world. In relation to man the thinking subject, the world and all that is external to the *ego*, exists only according to the idea of it which he forms for himself. We know only phenomena, we reason only concerning the appearances; all truth in itself escapes us; the essence of things is unassailable by us. It is what Schopenhauer popularized in the very clear and simple formula: The world is my representation. I do not see what is; that which is, is what I see. There are as many diverse and perhaps different worlds as there are thinking men. . . . The capital crime of a writer is conformity, imitation, submission to rules and teachings. The work of a writer should be not only the reflection, but the enlarged reflection of his personality. The only excuse that a man has for writing is that he express his own self, that he reveal to others the kind of world that is reflected in his individual mirror; his only excuse is that he be original; he must say things not said before and say them in a form not formulated before. He must create his own aesthetic—and we

[41] " The Art of Fiction " in *The Art of Fiction and Other Essays*, pp. 8 and 21.
[42] *Thus to Revisit*, p. 49.

must admit as many aesthetics as there are original minds, and judge them according to what they are and not according to what they are not.[43]

Whatever the author's vision of reality, "*il faut intéresser*," as Flaubert said; and of the later English writers, James, Conrad, and Ford sought to adhere exactly to this restrictive principle which allowed no compromise with any desire the author might have to preach or reform. The artist has to learn, as Ford phrased it, " that he is not a man to be swayed by the hopes, fears, consummations or despairs of a man." [44] A work of art was for them undeniably an expression of temperament—" the enlarged reflection " of the artist's personality—but it must always be a detached one. Flaubert perhaps felt this most strongly of them all. " The artist must stand to his work as God to his creation, invisible and all powerful; he must be everywhere felt but nowhere seen." [45] In theory, he was searching for a " pitiless method [with] the precision of the physical sciences," [46] an idea which Zola later expanded into a theory of art based upon the laboratory method, with his plea for a " dissection " of life, of life laid on the table like a corpse on the dissecting board of Claude Bernard. This notion also prefigured Joyce's ambition to be like " the God of the creation " sitting on a cloud " paring his fingernails " and watching his characters be fools or saints as they will.[47] Few of these writers would go so far as Zola did in reducing art into a science, and

[43] From " The Self and the World " from *Le Livre des Masques*, selections from which are translated and printed in Ludwig Lewisohn (ed.), *A Modern Book of Criticism* (New York: Modern Library, 1919), pp. 28-29.

[44] *Thus to Revisit*, p. 49.

[45] *Letters*, p. 98.

[46] *Ibid.*, p. 99.

[47] James Joyce, *A Portrait of the Artist as a Young Man* (New York: Modern Library, 1928), p. 252.

many would not agree fully with Gourmont's injunction that the only excuse for a writer is to be original, for it is too open to the danger of the author directly entering in.[48] However, from Rossetti with his belief in the value of " fundamental brainwork " to the novelists who paid such close attention to manner we see writers who sought an objective, intellectual control over undisciplined inspiration.

One characteristic control, they discovered, was made possible through a new concept of perceived experience. It was to affect their methods of representing reality and, in particular, to create a profound interest in the technique of the writer's point of view. If reality is as we perceive it to be, then in representing reality the artist should present the action or emotion precisely as it strikes the consciousness, and not literally or completely, but rather through careful selection to reproduce the *pattern* of stimuli as they reach the conscious mind.

The consequences of this attitude towards representing reality, strengthened in time by the studies of psychologists like Freud and of philosophers like Bergson and William James, were significant for artists in expanding their subject matter and in suggesting new and effective methods. These new concepts made them aware of the fragmentary nature of conscious experience and of the fact that the mind orders events according to its own laws. Writers, especially poets, became interested in trying to capture and immobilize these fragments. In English poetry the evidence was first seen clearly in Rossetti's attempts to sustain the " spiritual ecstasy "

[48] See, for example, Conrad's statement in his review of George Bourne's *The Ascending Effort*: " In the same way a poet hears, reads, and believes a thousand undeniable truths which have not yet got into his blood . . . ; he writes, therefore, as if neither truths nor book existed. Life and the arts follow dark courses, and will not turn aside to the brilliant arc-lights of science." *Notes on Life and Letters*, p. 99.

of fleeting moments.[49] So for him a " sonnet is a moment's monument," and " some basis of special momentary emotion " was one of the stimuli he needed for poetic creation.[50] Pre-Raphaelite paintings and poems characteristically captured dramatic moments. Christina Rossetti, Ford realized, avoided abstraction and generalized statement in her verse and brought to her poetry intimacy and precision, and in many of her poems illustrated a single emotion, an instance of heightened feelings.[51] The Imagists offer the best later example of this habit of transcribing impressions of the fleeting moment, although they would certainly draw up short of " spiritual ecstasy."

This desire to capture moments of time with all of their implications and complexities reflected the growing intellectual interest of these writers, as products of their times, in avoiding generalities and pursuing the particulars of human experience. Naturally each writer discovered his own method. Rossetti's search for the suspended moment became for others an attempt to recreate the flow of momentary impressions upon the consciousness. Ford understood the vital difference in this respect between the Pre-Raphaelites and the Impressionists.

They [the Pre-Raphaelites] never convey to us, as do the Impressionists [. . .] the sense of fleeting light and shadow. Looking at Millais' nearly perfect *Blind Girl*, or at Mr. Hunt's nearly perfect *Hireling Shepherd*, one is impelled to think, " How lasting all this is! " One is, as it were, in the mood in which each minute seems an eternity. Nature is grasped and held with an iron hand. There is not in any of the landscapes that delicious and delicate sense of swift

[49] Paull Franklin Baum, " Introduction " to D. G. Rossetti, *House of Life* (Cambridge, Massachusetts: Harvard University Press, 1928), pp. 27-28.
[50] W. M. Rossetti, *Family Letters and a Memoir*, I, 418.
[51] *The Critical Attitude*, p. 179.

change, that poetry of varying moods, of varying lights, of varying shadows that gives to certain moods and certain aspects of the earth a rare and tender pathos.[52]

In the novel a more remote but similar shift is observable. Flaubert's elaborations of particular scenes (a succession of moments) were attempts to portray every separate perception of himself or his characters relevant to the effect to be created. By a careful selection of numerous details of setting and consciousness, Flaubert wanted to reproduce the full impact of a given event, as, for example, in *Madame Bovary* in the scene at the county fair where the speeches and the announcements of agricultural awards function as an ironic counterpoint to Emma and Rodolphe's declaration of love. A more strictly impressionistic novelist like Remy de Gourmont placed sensual response alongside sensual response in attempts to create from these separate perceptions a total impression. In *A Night in the Luxembourg* he seemed to pursue evanescence, the effect is so vague and difficult to grasp. The pursuit of a similar kind of effect is discernible in the work of Pater, Wilde, and other English Aesthetics.

Conrad added substance to the impressionistic novel by the demands of his artistic conscience. In his significant and suggestive preface to *The Nigger of the "Narcissus,"* he explains that the fragmenting of experience into illusive moments becomes the means by which the novelist achieves the kind of nonscientific truth he seeks. He appeals to our emotions, as art must do, by a synthesis of the total impressions from his "rescued fragment."

[52] *The Pre-Raphaelite Brotherhood* (London: Duckworth [1907]), pp. 164-165. Since Ford uses the ellipsis so frequently, and particularly in his later work, I will enclose *in brackets* my own omissions from quotations of Ford's work. With my omission from quotations of other writers I will follow the standard practice of spaced periods *without* brackets.

The difficulty is in achieving the task through language to make us " hear," " feel," and " see."

> To snatch in a moment of courage, from the remorseless rush of time, a passing phase of life, is only the beginning of the task. The task approached in tenderness and faith is to hold up unquestioningly, without choice and without fear, the rescued fragment before all eyes in the light of a sincere mood. It is to show its vibration, its colour, its form; and through its movement, its form, and its colour, reveal the substance of its truth—disclose its inspiring secret: the stress and passion within the core of each convincing moment.

The effect upon the reader of this " moment of vision, a sigh, a smile " is an awakened sense of " that feeling of unavoidable solidarity . . . which binds men to each other and all mankind to the visible world." [53]

The implications for the novel of the search to explore significant moments and " rescued fragments " of experience were manifold.[54] More often than not, novelists turned to themselves, to their familiar surroundings and perceptions, and hence to contemporary subjects and usually to middle-class life. But of more importance was the effect this search had on the novelist's handling of point of view. Though defending the freedom of the writer to present his subject as he saw and felt it, the novelists since Flaubert have none the less favored the submerged novelist,

[53] Joseph Conrad, *Prefaces to His Work*, with an essay by Edward Garnett (London: Dent, 1937), p. 52.

[54] Zola and the Naturalists like him I do not believe are to be included among those writers influenced by a concern for the momentary sensation, which always for writers like Maupassant, James, and Conrad implied the necessity of selection and often of viewing the recorded instance through a many-sided glass. James objected to what he called the Naturalists' " saturation," their catalogues of unselected observations. See his essays on Zola and " The New Novel."

who gives to the reader as fully as possible the world of his stories through the limited consciousness of one or a few of his characters, as in *Madame Bovary* we " see " primarily through the eyes of its heroine and her husband and never explicitly through those of Flaubert himself. " Intelligences " James called them, and he utilized them to maintain his detachment and to help create his particular illusion of reality. Conrad often used Marlow as a narrator for the same purpose. By the complicated time schemes of many of his works he attempted, like Ford, to reproduce events as they came to the mind either of his narrator or of himself as narrator from the memories of the past.

James, Conrad, and Ford dealt primarily with the conscious mind and in a highly selective fashion, while other novelists, such as Dorothy Richardson, Joyce, Gertrude Stein, and Virginia Woolf, explored the subconscious world and its intrusions into the consciousness. Eschewing the complexities of traditional romantic plots and extended psychological analysis of character, many of them—Flaubert, Conrad, James, and Woolf in particular—steadily captured moment upon moment of daily existence as lived by unexceptional people until plot of the traditional type practically disappeared and character took over the center of their novels.[55] The shift in emphasis from action to character in serious novels showed a steady evolution from Flaubert to Joyce, and, considered in their totality, little of what man has learned or imagined of the mind and its

---

[55] E. K. Brown, " James and Conrad," *Yale Review*, xxxv (Winter, 1945), 265-285. Mr. Brown writes (p. 285): " It is certainly too soon to say whether fiction of this kind, in which the reverberations of events within the consciousness of the principal characters are more important than the happening of the events themselves, will continue to satisfy critical taste. The art of James and Conrad is cunning and intricate beyond that of any earlier novelist in England. In the extreme is danger."

various levels of consciousness has been left out of these works.

Since narrative methods adapted to the clock and the calendar were inadequate for representing the associative sequences of the mind, these writers sought new approaches and initiated a revolution in narrative techniques. It was their concern for techniques which was probably one of their greatest contributions to the modern novel. Their experiments expanded and enriched the traditional concept of form for the novel. They sought tirelessly, as Flaubert had, to achieve for fiction the dignity and complexity of poetry.[56]

The numerous concerns of Flaubert and his followers for techniques were of enormous value to James, Conrad, and Ford. Ford has made clear the significance of Flaubert's literary set and their preoccupation with the manner of their art. Flaubert, the Goncourts, Turgenev, Gautier, Maupassant, Zola, James, he writes, all

> discussed the *minutiae* of words and their economical employment; the *charpente*, the architecture, of the novel; the handling of dialogue; the rendering of impressions; the impersonality of the author. They discussed these things with the passion of politicians inciting to rebellion. And in these *coenaculae* the modern novel—the immensely powerful engine of our civilization—was born.[57]

These matters were the special concerns of Conrad and Ford. During the collaboration the two writers talked endlessly about the numerous practical problems of their

[56] Allen Tate believes that it was "through Flaubert that the novel has at last caught up with poetry." "Techniques of Fiction," *Forms of Modern Fiction*, ed. William Van O'Connor (Minneapolis: University of Minnesota Press, 1948), pp. 30-45.

[57] "Techniques," *Southern Review*, i (July, 1935), 23-24.

craft. They were working as in a laboratory and were searching for a new form in the novel, a form which no longer could be served by intricate plots worked out as skillfully as crossword puzzles and in a high-flown language divorced from real life. The principles which they had argued and then partially tested in their collaborative novels Ford accepted as the criteria for his theory of fiction. He formulated a method compatible with the high aesthetic ideals and artistic dedication of his Pre-Raphaelite inheritance.

IIII

FORD'S THEORY
OF FICTION

1

FORD'S THEORY OF THE NOVEL CAN BE DRAWN FROM ALL
his books of criticism and reminiscence, in which he was
in the habit of rephrasing and repeating his ideas.[1]
Although he modified or altered some early views, especially about individual writers, he consistently maintained
the fundamental criteria he had formulated before and
during the collaboration with Conrad. As an Impressionist, Ford's criticism is extremely personal, and often
idiosyncratic, but at the same time it is more objective
than it might at first appear to be in his deceptively casual
and rambling memoirs and literary essays. He understood

---

[1] Ford's repetitions bothered him, but, as he says, he was seeking " after a
final clarity of expression. It is all one that one may have already printed the
matter of the theme; the mind continues to work at the phraseology until
one, finally, isn't certain that one has or hasn't sought the crystallization of
the press." *No Enemy* (New York: Macaulay, 1929), p. 118. Very often,
however, Ford's repetitions are word for word, or almost so.

the discoverable methods of James, Conrad, and those writers he studied, and he was lucid about his own intentions and practice. According to Hugh Kenner, " it was Ford who was able to disengage technique from intuition sufficiently to make useful statements about narrative procedures." [2] A brief glance at Ford's critical method will help explain the terms in which he dealt with the technique and temperament of the novelist, both touchstones of his fictional theory.

James's " The Art of Fiction " and Conrad's preface to *The Nigger of the " Narcissus "* might not unreasonably be taken as the immediate texts from which Ford shaped the outlines of his fictional theory. For instance, his remarks about the artistic temperament, his handling of problems of morality, and his attitudes towards traditional plots can be found in James. His views about art as a way to a special kind of truth, his distrust of facts, his insistence upon the creation of atmosphere in a work of art, and his interest in recreating the complex methods by which the mind operates, all suggest Conrad. He probably reflects their views oftener than they reflect those of Flaubert, Turgenev, Maupassant, and the whole group of writers they admired.

This is not to say that Ford lacked individuality as a critic. His critical sensitivity was particularly responsive to matters of technique and to the qualities of the artistic temperament. He believed that the critic could be objective only when discussing techniques. Comments on a writer's personality and subject matter are motivated by personal likes and dislikes and are only as valuable as the critic's perceptions.[3] The critic's function is then twofold.

---

[2] *The Poetry of Ezra Pound* (Norfolk, Connecticut: New Directions, n. d.), p. 264.

[3] *Henry James*, pp. 149-151.

He must first perceive the exact nature of a writer's contribution to the art of fiction. Novelists are judged according to the degree of attention they pay to techniques. When evaluating techniques, the critic must be both impersonal and logical. He must " look things in the face." [4] In *The Critical Attitude*, Ford notes that " logic is unhuman and that criticism, though it need not be actively inhumane, must, as far as possible, put aside sympathy with human weaknesses." [5] Thirty years later, defining literature as " that which men read and continue to read for pleasure or to obtain that imaginative culture which is necessary for civilizations," he affirms that it is foolish to set up one's private judgment against that of mankind, except when dealing with contemporaries, when taste is the only criterion.[6]

Ford's assumption that the artist's primary devotion must be to techniques imposes limitations upon his critical evaluations. He relegated to the second-rate not only the novels of commerce and escape (the " nuvvle," as he terms them) but also several major novels which fail in whole or in part to follow the disciplines demanded by Flaubert, Maupassant, or James. This view arose logically from Ford's assumptions. He could always admit the historical importance of novels he did not like and could admire passages in them, but he chastized their authors for being the villains who had perpetrated the worst excesses of English fiction. Because of their intrusions and digressions, Fielding and Sterne, for example, did much to ruin writers like Thackeray and Dickens.[7] The earlier heroes of English fiction were for him, naturally, Richardson and Jane Austen.

---

[4] *The Critical Attitude*, p. 8.
[5] *Ibid.*, p. 21.
[6] *The March of Literature*, pp. 10-11.
[7] *Ibid.*, pp. 580-586.

Although the critic ideally reaches his evaluations by means of a rigorous logical process, he must also convey to his readers an impression of what the man behind the work is like, of how his personal, moral, and intellectual qualities of temperament helped to shape his work. The critic's method here is the same as that of the novelist. Particularly when dealing with his contemporaries, or with the collaboration, or with literary movements, Ford writes criticism as though it were fiction. He prefaces most of his nonfiction books from *Memories and Impressions* through *The March of Literature* with the statement that he is writing a novel, not history. As in a novel, the person about whom you are writing must be " projected," must gradually be revealed as he was revealed to the writer. " For [. . .] a novel should be the biography of a man or of an affair, and a biography whether of a man or of an affair should be a novel, both being, if they are efficiently performed, renderings of such affairs as are our human lives." [8] When treating movements, like impressionism, he deals with the writers " as if they were natural objects bringing in a touch from one here and from another there so that there may result not a picture of men, but an impression of a world movement." [9] His numerous reminiscences are also calculated efforts to create an impression. He says early in *It Was The Nightingale* that " I have employed every wile known to me as novelist— the time-shift, the *progression d'effet*, the adaptation of rhythms to the pace of action." [10]

Such a commitment plays havoc with facts. " My business in life, in short, is to attempt to discover and to try to let you see where you stand. I don't really deal

[8] *Joseph Conrad*, pp. 5-6.
[9] *The March of Literature*, p. 802.
[10] *It Was the Nightingale*, p. 6.

in facts; I have for facts a most profound contempt. I try to give you what I see to be the spirit of an age, of a town, of a movement. This cannot be done with facts." [11] Critics, especially those who dislike Ford, have spent a good deal of time pointing out his errors and distortions of fact.[12] Undeniably they are there throughout his work. If we read literally, we have to approach a good many of Ford's statements with extreme caution and admit that his prevarications, whether intentional or not, are an annoyance to many readers and a hindrance to the acquisition of accurate information. When writing books like *The English Novel* or *The March of Literature*, it was Ford's practice to use a literary manual for checking names and dates but to rely on his wide knowledge and excellent memory for the content of his reading. Often he liked to make sweeping categorical statements in order, as he says, to excite the reader into thinking for himself.[13] Sometimes he would not even correct what he knew to be errors in fact.[14] Art had become life; facts gave way to impressions. In his anecdotes and in his books, critical, fictional, or autobiographical, he created atmospheres in which he saw what was for him the truth.

Ford's critical methods follow quite naturally from the assumption that the artist must present the world as he sees it. Particularly for the Impressionists, the functions

---

[11] *Memories and Impressions*, p. xviii.

[12] Goldring, *Trained for Genius*, p. 99, mentions Archibald Marshall as one such critic. See Marshall's *Out and About* (New York: Dutton, 1934) for several references to Ford's inaccuracies. G. Jean-Aubry in his *The Sea Dreamer: A Definitive Biography of Joseph Conrad* (Garden City, New York: Doubleday, 1957), p. 232, calls Ford a "pathological liar."

[13] *The English Novel*, p. 32.

[14] Ford writes in the "preface" to *Joseph Conrad*, p. 6: "Where the writer's memory has proved to be at fault over a detail afterwards out of curiosity looked up, the writer has allowed the fault to remain on the page; but as to the truth of the impression as a whole the writer believes that no man would care—or dare—to impugn it."

of the artist and critic merged, as is witnessed by Oscar Wilde, who thought " criticism of the highest kind " was that which " treats the work of art simply as the starting-point for a new creation." [15] James, more demanding, saw the critic's job as that of showing the temperament behind the work of art, the critic serving " as the real helper of the artist, a torch-bearing outrider, the interpreter, the brother." For, " just in proportion as he is sentient and restless, just in proportion as he reacts and reciprocates and penetrates, is the critic a valuable instrument; for in literature assuredly criticism *is* the critic, just as art is the artist." [16] Ford accepted, in principle, this charge to the critic. He appears to have thought that bringing fictional techniques to his criticism would appeal to a larger audience than more academic criticism and literary history would, and that a fictional method might be especially useful in educating the English-speaking world to the salvation of humane letters.

Most readers, once they grant Ford his approach and understand it, can accept the reminiscences and criticism more readily. These writings reveal a complex, subtle temperament that has its fascinations, and they have a good deal to say to us about techniques, about the personalities of the great and near-great he knew or admired, and about how a sensitive, unique, often wise mind reacted to art and life.[17] On the other hand, writing criticism as fiction places many of Ford's judgments beyond criticism.

[15] " The Critic as Artist," *Works* (New York: Walter S. Black, 1927), p. 566.

[16] " Criticism " in *The Art of Fiction and Other Essays*, p. 218.

[17] Janice Biala writes: "Read in their proper order, the body of his work, fiction, general and critical, forms a landscape of modern civilization, seen through one man's eyes, and that man one of great knowledge and great maturity of mind, that must be very nearly unique in modern literature." In a letter to me, dated July 4, 1951.

One accepts the atmospheres Ford has created, or one does not.

2

As Ford states the Impressionist creed, its purpose is amoral, and the goal of its writers is " to leave behind them a creative record of their time " from which the audience can draw its own morals. He adds that " the important thing is that the World should have an *aperçu* of itself as it is . . . a passionless reconstitution, not passionate fakings of aspects and of evidence by widows past marriage and eunuchs " (he refers here to Carlyle and Ruskin).[18] Literature provides " Something or Other " necessary to existence:

> And that something or other can only be the knowledge of what song the Syrens sang; or, if you prefer it, of the Sermon on the Mount. . . . For such things alone can give you knowledge of the hearts, the necessities, the hopes and the fears of your fellow men; and such knowledge alone can guide us through life without disaster.[19]

The function of imaginative literature is " to record life in terms of the author—to stimulate thought." [20] The artist's temperament, then, is the " sensitised instrument " through which we see life.[21] The artist must know the heart of man. "And one's own heart is the heart that one knows best." [22] " The artist, is, as it were, the eternal

---

[18] *Portraits from Life*, pp. 207-209.
[19] *Thus to Revisit*, p. 7.
[20] *The Critical Attitude*, p. 32. On the other hand, " the functions of inventive literature are to divert, to delight, to tickle, to promote appetites."
[21] *Return to Yesterday*, p. 214.
[22] *Thus to Revisit*, p. 212.

mental prostitute who stands in the marketplace crying:
' Come into contact with my thought, with my visions,
with the sweet sounds I cause to arouse—with my personality.' " [23] As James had perceived earlier, the better
the artist's temperament, the better and more valuable
his work.[24] Since a nation can be saved only by its art,
the function of the artist is messianic. Like his Pre-
Raphaelite forebears, Ford champions the divine right of
the artist; the rest of humanity is merely the " stuff to
fill graveyards." [25] The artist brings thought to the un-
thinking, a voice to the voiceless.[26]

Subject matter is relatively unimportant, for the *how* is
more significant than the *what*. A novelist's subject is
chosen because of his temperament, is limited only by
what he must write, what he can write. This does not
mean, Ford warns, that he can necessarily write what he
wants to.[27] Actually each novelist finds his own natural
pattern. According to Ford, James found his in moral
scruple, and Crane

> in physical life, in wars, in slums, in western saloons, in a
> world where the " gun " was the final argument. The life
> that Conrad gives you is somewhere halfway between the
> two; [. . .] But the approach to life is the same with all
> these three; they show you that disillusionment is to be
> found alike at the tea-table, in the slum and on the tented
> field. That is of great service to our Republic.[28]

[23] *The Critical Attitude*, p. 64.

[24] " The Art of Fiction," p. 21.

[25] *It Was the Nightingale*, p. 85. Harriet Monroe writes in *A Poet's Life*
(New York: Macmillan, 1938), p. 434: " In Mr. Ford's opinion, the arts
alone *are* civilization; and I tried in vain to get in a word for science, mathe-
matics, pioneer audacities, and other manifestations of man's spiritual energy
in the search for truth."

[26] *The Critical Attitude*, p. 64.

[27] *Henry James*, p. 122.

[28] *Return to Yesterday*, pp. 210-211.

Like other realistic novelists, Ford believed that the author should present life as he viewed it but at the same time be detached. The task is " simply an affair of getting down to one's least rhetorical form of mind, and expressing that." He must avoid poetic moods when the desire to preach takes command, " for no man's views are worth very much." [29] As a " sensitised instrument," the novelist must not plead a cause, or project what he thinks of himself, or what he wants others to think of him as a private citizen. The ideal enjoins the discipline earlier stated by Flaubert, the discipline that is a technique based upon a study of what interests and what has interested the reader in the past.[30] Since what has always interested the reader is to become so engrossed in a story that he forgets the storyteller, it is only by an absolute suppression of the author himself that the reader can be tempted to enter the life of a story.[31]

Ford and Conrad worked out a method they felt would imitate life and engross the reader. They " agreed that the general effect of a novel must be the general effect that life makes on mankind." They " saw that Life did not narrate, but made impressions on our brains. We in turn, if we wished to produce on you an effect of life, must not narrate but render . . . impressions." [32] The word " general " is important, suggesting that stories were to be *montages*, or like carefully edited films of words, images, and ideas as they appear to the mind, past blending into future. Yet, the aim is to achieve a precision of effect, an effect so precise that, like the swifts that fly at sixty miles per hour into the holes of their nests, the artist always hits exactly the right mark, tone, or atmosphere

---

[29] *Thus to Revisit*, pp. 211-212.
[30] *Ibid.*, pp. 9-10.
[31] *Ibid.*, p. 139.
[32] *Joseph Conrad*, pp. 180-182.

for his story.[33] They sought a form and method which would give "a sense of the complexity, the tantalisation, the shimmering, the haze, that life is." [34]

The "New Form," as Ford calls it, was new, they realized, only in the English novel. It was a discovery shared by James, and possibly by Moore and Bennett.[35] Ford describes it in a significant statement which serves as an illuminating definition of psychological realism in the novel.

> We considered a Novel to be a rendering of an Affair. We used to say, I will admit, that a Subject must be seized by the throat until the last drop of dramatic possibility was squeezed out of it. I suppose we had to concede that much to the Cult of the Strong Situation. Nevertheless, a Novel was the rendering of an Affair: of one embroilment, one set of embarrassments, one human coil, one psychological progression. From this the Novel got its Unity. No doubt it might have its caesura—or even several; but these must be brought about by temperamental pauses, markings of time when the treatment called for them. But the whole novel was to be an exhaustion of aspects, was to proceed to one culmination, to reveal once and for all, in the last sentence, or the penultimate; in the last phrase, or the one before it—the psychological significance of the whole. (Of course, you might have what is called in music your Coda.)[36]

This fictional creed implies that the novelist must pay profound attention to matters of technique and structure

---

[33] *It Was the Nightingale*, p. 254.

[34] *Joseph Conrad*, p. 191.

[35] Ford describes Moore as "the only novelist of English blood who had produced a novel that was a masterpiece at once of writing and of form." *It Was the Nightingale*, p. 35. Also, at this time, Arnold Bennett "was engaged in acquiring the immense knowledge of French tricks and devices that his work afterwards displayed." *Return to Yesterday*, p. 204.

[36] *Thus to Revisit*, p. 44. Repeated *verbatim* in *Return to Yesterday*, pp. 203-204.

before the " effect of life " is achieved. Ford took care to note, however, that the end in view was not a " machined form " but " the sheer attempt to reproduce in words life as it presents itself to the intelligent observer," whose life has a pattern, not one of " birth, apogee, and death, but a woven symbolism of its own." [37] James had metaphorically described it as " the figure in the carpet."

Drawn to metaphor himself, and proving himself more explicit than James cared to be, Ford found the closest analogies to form in the novel in the convergence of parallel lines and in the sonata. The geometric image is the later one (1938), yet is a restatement of the 1921 passage just quoted. The lines move " more and more swiftly to the inevitable logic of the end," where they converge. Again, the coda may be attached.[38] The mixed metaphor suggests that Ford was happier with the musical analogy. Shortly after the 1921 passage, he transposes what is undoubtedly an imaginary conversation with H. G. Wells, the E. N. (eminent novelist) of the following passage:

SELF. I suppose then, in the matter of Form, you arrive at the Sonata.

E. N. Yes, that's it. What *is* the Sonata?

SELF. Like this: You state your first subject (Hero or Heroine) in the key of the Tonic. You then state your second subject (Heroine or Hero) in the key of the Dominant, if the first subject is in a major— or in the key of the relative major, if the first subject is in a minor key. You repeat all that, and that finishes the first part. Then comes what is called the working out or Free Fantasia. . . .

E. N. Then there is some Freedom. . . .

[37] *Thus to Revisit*, p. 46.
[38] *The March of Literature*, p. 579.

47

SELF.   In that you mix up themes A and B, embroider on
         them in any related, or even unrelated, keys and
         tempi. You introduce foreign matter if you like. . . .

E. N.   I see. The Tertium, what is it?

SELF.   You introduce foreign matter, and generally have a
         good time. In the Restatement you restate: A em-
         phatically in his or her key, and B equally empha-
         tically, but in the tonic original key of A. That
         becomes the key of the whole Sonata: Op. 232 in E
         Flat Major! You *might* restate the Foreign Matter
         which you introduced into the Free Fantasia. . . .

E. N.   Ah!

SELF.   But that is irregular. And you may or may not
         have a Coda, a short sweet passage of reminiscence—
         the children tumbling over the Newfoundland on the
         lawn.

E. N.   Don't you mean the feeling of relief after the divorce?

SELF.   Of course, the Coda should give a feeling of relief.

E. N.   To think of you knowing all that. I thought you
         were only interested in Golf! [39]

The facetious tone of this passage might suggest that
Ford did not take the analogy too seriously. In effect, it
recapitulates his other statements of the pattern of em-
broilment, exhaustive progression, culmination, and coda.
The evidence of his own most carefully contrived works
proves his very real attempts to follow a similar pattern,
though not so rigidly as this passage suggests. In any
event, the desire to copy the form and structure of music,
and especially of the rather restrictive sonata form, set
recognizable, though ideal, limits for the impressionistic
novel. Conrad was convinced that art must aspire (in
part) " to the magic suggestiveness of music—which is the
art of arts." [40] Conrad is speaking here of " the perfect
blending of form and substance."

[39] *Thus to Revisit*, pp. 45-46.
[40] Conrad, *Prefaces to His Works*, p. 51.

Except impressionistically, it is difficult to translate analogies from music or geometry into fictional terms. However, Ford is more explicit about form when he deals specifically with the novels of Conrad and James. He always looked to them as masters of form, although he had some reservations about Conrad's later work. Conrad's earliest work, written when he was not under much pressure from literary agents, is complete. On the other hand, Ford believed, perhaps not quite fairly, that the later novels, *Nostromo, Chance, Under Western Eyes, The Secret Agent*, are " finished off with the quick, deft touches of a de Maupassant *conte* and the rapid invention of any efficient writer of short stories." The conclusion to each of these novels is not wrong but is less protracted and impressive than was warranted by the carefully " buildings-up of such an immense fabric." [41]

In his wise and perceptive book on James, which deserves more credit for being a landmark in the criticism of James's techniques than it generally receives, Ford quotes extensively from the prefaces and studies James's methods of constructing his stories. He admires James's ability to take the merest hint from life, his germ, to make it more complex and symmetrical, and to work out his stories so that every word, every action, every " apparent digression " works toward the inevitable end.[42] James maintains a sense of life by " making the digressions appear like real negligences, as they appear in the life we lead." Since James exhausts all the aspects of his " affairs " and moves his stories towards a single culmination, he attains the effect of inevitability. That is valuable

[41] *Portraits from Life,* pp. 60-61.
[42] *Henry James,* pp. 159-161. Unlike Fielding's digressions, for instance, which, Ford says, are pleasant enough in themselves but are irrelevant to his novels. *The March of Literature,* p. 590.

because it gives to his work " a feeling of destiny [. . .] a grim semblance of an implacable outside Providence." [43]

We have here a central problem of the impressionistic novelist. The form of his novels must give the effect of the formlessness and fragmentary nature of life as it meets the individual consciousness, while at the same time everything must move in a direct, carefully calculated line to the inevitable conclusion. Art has eternally sought to achieve order out of the disunity and confusion of life, but it was the Impressionists, primarily, who sought to keep the feeling of that very disunity and confusion in the forefront of their work. The reader is deceived into believing that he is experiencing life as it is, while the novelist is actually arranging and managing his tale so as to leave the reader with a view of life clearer, more organic, and more meaningful than life itself could probably ever give. The secret lies in concealing the art. Ford is right in defining impressionism as a technique which reinforced the realistic frame of mind. " Thus the real *trait-d'union* between all these authors [the modern realists from Flaubert] and modernity in general " was not their temperaments, which were all different, but " the technical one which this writer prefers to call Impressionism." [44]

One of the dangers of an extreme concern with techniques is that rules will first be formulated and then dictated. Ford's list of the rules that he and Conrad conceived seems at first glance too inflexible and inadequate for an Impressionist, but Ford is careful to mention that they " *were not unaware that there are other methods; they were not rigid in their own methods: they were sensible to the fact that compromise is at all times necessary*

[43] *Henry James*, p. 161.
[44] *The March of Literature*, p. 839.

in the execution of every work of art." [45] Ford repeatedly noted that those who have departed from the rules as established, like Shakespeare and Flaubert, have been the creators of our greatest literature.[46] Each writer must discover his own rules; the only limitation is the interest of the reader; the principal criterion for a technical rule is the degree of its success in conveying a sense of life.

Actually there are, Ford argues, as many techniques as there are writers. When Kipling writes:

There are five and forty ways
Of inditing tribal lays
And every single one of them is right . . .

he does not tell " the whole truth " because " he must have added that there is only one best way for the treatment of every given subject and only one method best suited for every given writer." [47] Hence, the greatest writers are inimitable; the quality of their work is a matter of temperament. Turgenev and Hudson are among the " beautiful geniuses " who have a talent that cannot be defined; it is " just a thing that is." Their work is " too compact, too polished " for analysis.[48] There is not much one can say about them beyond the fact that they wrote well and constructed good plots. " The longest study of Hudson or Turgenev will do no more for you than turn you into a writer of *pastiches.* Galsworthy would have been a real major writer if Mr. Edward Garnett had not forced him to read Mrs. Garnett's wonderful translation of *Fathers and Children."* [49]

[45] Ford makes this statement twice: *Joseph Conrad,* pp. 192-193 and 211. The italics are Ford's.
[46] " Techniques," p. 20.
[47] *Ibid.,* pp. 27-28.
[48] *Henry James,* pp. 9-13.
[49] " Techniques," p. 30. See also *The English Novel,* pp. 119-120.

A second, though not secondary, type of writer is the conscious craftsman, like Flaubert or James, whose temperament and technique can be more clearly defined.[50] Ford's distinction between writers like Turgenev and Hudson and those like Flaubert and James seems artificial. Actually, he draws examples of techniques from all of them, though it is true that he more often refers to Flaubert and James—and to Conrad—than he does to Turgenev and Hudson, who wrote relatively little about their craft and were perhaps less useful for illustration. Of course, Ford admired the creative practice of all these men, and especially as they adhered to the central principle of the realist-impressionist technique: the rendering rather than the relating of events in order to achieve an illusion of reality.

By " rendering," Ford means much what James meant. Rendering is the dramatic presentation of a scene to give an impression of immediacy. "Rendering is the reproduction by one art or another of the impressions made upon one by one's observations." [51] As at a play, the reader is to be carried away so that he thinks himself at the scene being depicted. Bunyan, for example, succeeds in involving the reader because he tells his story in simple language, " using such homely images that the reader, astonished and charmed to find the circumstances of his own life typified in words and glorified by print, is seized by the homely narrative and carried clean out of himself into the world of that singular and glorious tinker." [52] Ford often gives short examples of rendering. One such example, useful for its brevity, appears in *The March of*

[50] *Henry James*, pp. 13-16.
[51] *Great Trade Route* (New York: Oxford, 1937), p. 32.
[52] *The English Novel*, p. 86.

Literature. The first passage, an imaginary adaptation from *Vanity Fair*, is not impressionism; the second is.

> Disgusting as we may find it, on crossing to the window our heroine—whom the reader must acknowledge to be indeed a gallant little person—perceived Captain Crawley and the Marquis of Steyne engaged in a drunken boxing bout. . . . But such things must be when to the moral deterioration of illicit sex passion is added the infuriating spur of undue indulgence in alcoholic beverages.

> In the street the empurpled leg-of-mutton fist of a scarlet heavy dragoon impinged on the gleaming false teeth of a reeling bald headed senior. Becky screamed as a torrent of dark purple burst from the marquis' lips to dribble down his lavender silk waistcoat. That ended, as she spasmodically recognized, her life of opulence. The dragoon, an unmoving streak of scarlet, lay in the gutter, one arm extended above his unshako'd locks. (p. 841)

Ford, as he must, admits that the second paragraph is not very good impressionism, but neither is the first good Thackeray. With his characteristic exaggeration, he is illustrating a point to his technically illiterate reading audience.[53] Nevertheless, the impressionistic paragraph illustrates the invisible author, the attempt to make the reader see, the use of vivid language and the recounting of Becky's impressions, from which the reader infers what has taken place and can draw a moral, if he wishes.[54]

Ford's critical juggling brings to the fore the problem of point of view and its effect upon the form of the novel.

---

[53] See *Portraits from Life*, pp. 72-75, for a serious analysis of the opening paragraph of D. H. Lawrence's " The Odour of Chrysanthemums." See also Ford's analysis of a paragraph from Conrad's *Youth* in *Joseph Conrad*, pp. 161-164.

[54] *The March of Literature*, pp. 841-842. Ford adds that the moral is implicit in the remark that the fight ended Becky's " life of opulence."

If the author is to be invisible, some means have to be found to tell the story, to give it, as James says, focus. When James objected to Conrad's use of Marlow's consciousness as a narrative focus, Ford answered:

> [. . .] it is in that way that life really presents itself to us: not as a rattling narrative beginning at a hero's birth and progressing to his not very carefully machined yet predestined glory—but dallying backwards and forwards, now in 1890, now in 1869; in 1902—and then again in 1869— as forgotten episodes came up in the minds of simple narrators.[55] And, if you put your Affair into the mouth of such a narrator your phraseology will be the Real thing in *mots justes*, for just so long as they remain within his probable vocabulary.[56]

Thus, form is achieved less by the demands of the "Affair" a novel recounts than by the mode of the consciousnesss viewing it. The aim is psychological verisimilitude, that is, the rightness with which events are represented according to the workings of the narrative intelligence. The method applies not only to a first person narration but also to action viewed from the consciousness of one or several characters in a third person account, or to action viewed from the consciousness of the unseen author telling the story as it comes to his mind.

The narrative point of view with all its variations gave rise to the complicated time schemes of many impres-

---

[55] Ford has just related a speech of an old shepherd who employed the characteristic time-shifts in recollecting past experiences.

[56] *Thus to Revisit*, p. 55. Oddly enough, in the light of the theory Conrad and Ford evolved, the happiest product of their collaboration, *Romance*, uses a first person narrator, but, except for one lengthy expository flashback in the beginning and periodic interruptions musing about the youthful search for romance, the novel is presented in a fairly straightforward chronological manner. Conrad in *Lord Jim* (1900) had already used the rambling first person narrator to good effect, but Ford was not to exploit the technique fully until *The Good Soldier*.

sionistic novels. The time-shift was the strongest instrument these writers had found to break away from the form
and structure of the traditional, stereotyped novel. It
demanded their greatest time and effort in the working
out of their fiction. Hugh Kenner notes that "the function
of the time-shift is to do away with plot—plot in the
sense of a linear sequence of events. The 'story' is
broken up into a number of scenes, conversations, impressions, *etc.*, which function as poetic images and are freely
juxtaposed for maximum intensity."[57] And yet, to the
extent that the term "plot" means an ordering of events,
their novels are not plotless. Of course, the concept of
what constitutes an event has changed. The slightest
impression, the simplest action, like the fall of a hand
or the raising of an eyebrow or a person looking out of a
window, may be a significant and even a melodramatic
event. Milly Theale sits on a remote edge of the Swiss
Alps, then later on a London park bench; Lord Jim walks
out onto the balcony of Marlow's room; Tietjens stands
on a Belgian hillside. These are significant scenes, but
on the psychological, not the physical, level. Recollection,
then, can be an event as exciting and important as any
other. And such an event, like any other, must find its
proper place in the author's tale.

Plotting according to the impressions of the seen or
unseen narrator gives greater freedom than a method
committed to the more or less chronological unfolding of
action, for then the author can inflate or deflate the significance of thoughts, feelings, events, and arrange and
juxtapose them for the creation of specific effects. Ford
says that the "supreme function" of impressionism is to
select out of the myriad fragments of experience what is

[57] *The Poetry of Ezra Pound*, p. 268.

necessary to tell a story successfully, and then to arrange these fragments for the best effect. James is the master of this art because " he can create an impression with nothing at all."

> His characters will talk about rain, about the opera, about the moral aspects of the selling of Old Masters to the New Republic, and those conversations will convey to your mind that the quiet talkers are living in an atmosphere of horror, of bankruptcy, of passion hopeless as the Dies Irae! That is the supreme trick of art today, since that is how we really talk about the musical glasses whilst our lives crumble to pieces around us. Shakespeare did that once or twice—as when Desdemona gossips about her mother's maid called Barbara whilst she is under the very shadow of death; but there is hardly any other novelist that has done it. Our subject does it, however, all the time, and that is one reason for the impression that his books give us of vibrating reality. I think the word " vibrating " exactly expresses it; the sensation is due to the fact that the mind passes, as it does in real life, perpetually backwards and forwards between the apparent aspect of things and the essentials of life.[58]

Selection is the business of any work worthy to be called art, but Ford's emphasis is on its use to dramatize, that is to " render," a scene rather than to describe it. In practice, it amounts to a scene being rendered on a series of levels, both stated and implied. Ford might have been thinking of such a scene as that in *The Portrait of a Lady* when Isabel Archer walks into her drawing room and sees her husband sitting while her dear friend Madame Merle stands, and she realizes, as the reader does, that Osmond and her friend are lovers, though the realization is only hinted at, Isabel grasping it as " a sudden flicker of light "

[58] *Henry James*, pp. 152-153.

of " something detected " and then over. However, she
carries the impression with her in her interview which
immediately follows with Madame Merle, and she is so
sharp with her old friend that Madame Merle is led to
exclaim that Isabel is being a " little dry." The full impact
of Isabel's realization is not felt until later when she sits
before the fire all night and faces her marriage and her
life for what they have become and for what they promise
for the future.[59]

Ford called this technique the technique of " juxtaposed
situations," a discovery, as he says, of Stendhal and Jane
Austen. It is the device by which " the juxtaposition of
the composed renderings of two or more unexaggerated
actions or situations may be used to establish, like the
juxtaposition of vital word to vital word, a sort of fric-
tional current of electric life that will extraordinarily gal-
vanize the work of art. . . ." [60] It is further illustrated by
the elaborate preparation of the reader for Lady Catherine
de Bourgh in *Pride and Prejudice*. Collins praises her as a
splendid and enlightened woman, but when she appears,
she shows herself to be exactly the opposite and proves
Collins to be a patronizing snob. Miss Austen handles
these scenes without a word of direct comment. For Ford,
the advantage of this method is that it surprises the reader
with one of the little surprises that give a novel the

---

[59] *The Portait of a Lady* (New York: Modern Library, n. d.), Bk. II, pp.
164-205.

[60] *The March of Literature*, p. 804. He goes on to try two other analogies
for definition: " Let us put it more concretely by citing the algebraic truth
that $(a=b)^2$ [*sic*] equals not merely a^2+b^2 but a^2 plus an apparently unearned
increment called $2ab$ plus the expected b^2. Or let us use the still more easy
image of two men shouting in a field. While each shouts separately each can
only be heard at a distance of an eighth of a mile, whilst if both shout
simultaneously their range of hearing will be extended by a hundred-odd
yards. The point cannot be sufficiently labored, since the whole fabric of
modern art depends on it."

quality of life.[61] Though certainly not a new technique of storytelling, the device of juxtaposing situations was extended by writers like James, Conrad, and Ford, who carried it to new extremes and intensities by the juxtapositions of impressions, objects, images, and metaphors.

The synthesizing device for giving a novel the vibration of life and at the same time shaping the work into an organic form was that of *progression d'effet*: the gradual revelation of character, of the conflict to be narrated, of the meaning and significance to be perceived by the reader.[62] It offers an economical mode of rendering action and contributes to the cumulation of effect on every level of the story—the " conflicting irresolutions ending in a determination." [63] The shifts in time, the juxtaposed situations and impressions, the succession of words and images, are, so to speak, subservient to the *progression d'effet*, because by the selection and arrangement of events and by the choice of language the story progresses inevitably to its final effect. The coda may give the final illumination. Ford's favorite examples are the last sentences of " Heart of Darkness," of Maupassant's *Le Champs d'Olivier*, and of James's " The Turn of the Screw," where the word " dispossessed "—*le mot juste*—gives exactly the note desired, and " then, as it were, a lightning flash is thrown back over the whole story and all its parts fall into place in the mind. It is marvelously skillful." [64]

The examples Ford uses to explain the *progression d'effet* are all taken from long short stories or *nouvelles*. Ford seldom wrote short stories, but, like James and Conrad,

---

[61] *Ibid.*, pp. 806-808.
[62] See below, Chapter VI, where the *progression d'effet* is explained more fully.
[63] *Henry James*, p. 168.
[64] *The March of Literature*, pp. 579-580, and 711. See also *Henry James*, pp. 169-170 and *Joseph Conrad*, p. 180.

he was trying to achieve in his full-length fiction the conciseness and precision of the *conte* or *nouvelle*.[65] Despite the leisurely manner in which these writers tend to begin their novels, they are carefully constructing their *progression d'effet*, which itself shapes the structure of their stories. The novelist, if he wishes to achieve an impression of inevitability, must apply the principle of "justification."[66] He must at every turn decide what he wants to tell or withhold about his characters or the action, and exactly how he wants to do it. Ideally, every such decision is consistent with the novel's design.

A couple of cases in point are the theories Conrad and Ford worked out for the beginnings of their stories and for characterization. The technique used in beginning a story depends upon whether the story is to be long or short.

> Openings for us, as for most writers, were matters of great importance, but probably we more than most writers realised of what primary importance they are. A real short story must open with a breathless sentence; a long-short story may begin with an ' as ' or a ' since ' and some leisurely phrases. At any rate the opening paragraph of a book or story should be of the tempo of the whole performance. That is the *règle generale.* [*sic*] Moreover, the reader's attention must be gripped by that first paragraph. So our ideal novel must begin either with a dramatic scene or with a note that should suggest the whole book.

. . . .

[65] Ford is careful to distinguish between a " true short story " and a " long-short ' story." The short story is " a matter of two or three pages of minutely considered words, ending with a smack," like those of Maupassant, Chekov, and O. Henry. For the long short story, " the form is practically the same as that of the novel. Or, to avoid the implication of saying that there is only one form for the novel, it would be better to put it that the form of long-short stories may vary as much as may the form for novels." *Joseph Conrad*, p. 204.

[66] *Ibid.*

Conrad's tendency and desire made for the dramatic opening: the writer's as a rule for the more pensive approach, but we each, as a book would go on were apt to find that we must modify our openings [. . . .]

The disadvantage of the dramatic opening is that after the dramatic passage is done you have to go back to getting your characters in, a proceeding that the reader is apt to dislike. The danger with the reflective opening is that the reader is apt to miss being gripped at once by the story. Openings are therefore of necessity always affairs of compromise.[67]

A character's fate " must be inevitable, because of his character, because of his ancestry, because of past illness or on account of the gradual coming together of the thousand small circumstances by which Destiny, who is inscrutable and august, will push us into one certain predicament." [68] The traditional English novelist more often than not handled characterization as Scott does in *The Antiquary*, in which he takes forty pages to introduce setting and characters before the action begins; Ford thought this a " damning defect." [69] The danger lies in retarding the story. Ford says he and Conrad were never satisfied that they " had really and sufficiently got [their] characters in," and they usually thought it necessary to provide every character, however minor, with some sort of background. "Any policeman who arrested any character must be ' justified ' because the manner in which he effected the arrest, his mannerisms, his vocabulary and his voice, might have a permanent effect on the psychology of the prisoner." [70] Their solution, another *règle générale*,

[67] *Ibid.*, pp. 171-173.
[68] *Ibid.*, pp. 204-205.
[69] *The March of Literature*, p. 711.
[70] *Joseph Conrad*, pp. 206-207.

was that the writer must bring in the biography of his character only after the character has been introduced.[71] Actually neither seemed to worry too much about the biographies of his policemen or very minor characters. They usually described them with a deft stroke and often through the consciousness of a major character. Their major character's biography was gradually revealed, brought in here and there as needed or as recalled. In fact, they often felt a need to bring in fully the lives of characters antecedent to the action of their stories. Doing so, they realized, might retard the action, but the clever author could turn the trick to advantage by utilizing the biography as a pleasant contrasting relief to the tone of the rest of the book, for " in that way the sense of reality is procured." [72]

3

A large part of this struggle to achieve a sense of the real, a vibration of life, was the quest for a language, a style, a cadence, a word that could pass the test of " justi- fication." Since Ford was recommended to Conrad as a stylist, we would expect, as he tells us, that his main preoccupation during the collaboration was with style. His reputation as a stylist has remained in spite of the neglect he has suffered and of the complaints against his veracity. We find Conrad assuring him in a 1904 letter that Pinker, their agent, still likes Ford, even though he does not understand him. " You are for him the man who can write anything at any time—and write it well—he

[71] *Ibid.*, pp. 207-208.   [72] *Ibid.*

means in a not ordinary way. His belief in you is by no means shaken." [73] Ezra Pound, in Poem X of *Mauberley*, opposes the capitalist bankers to the more eminently worth-while stylist Ford, who " beneath the sagging roof " lives his simple, valuable life.

> The haven from sophistications and contentions
> Leaks through its thatch;
> He offers succulent cooking;
> The door has a creaking latch.[74]

By Ford's insistence on simplicity and appropriateness in the use of language in both poetry and prose, he allied himself with the Imagists and did his service in helping to clear away the elaborate literary diction of much of the writing of the " Victorian Great."

Ford's father once said that Rossetti wrote the thoughts of Dante in the language of Shakespeare. Ford replied that he should have written the thoughts of Rossetti in the language of Victoria.[75] He charges that the tendency of all poets since Prior and Gay " has been to dissociate themselves from the life and language of the day." [76] Ford's plea was always that the writer should use the language of his own day, not the fine or literary language, but the vernacular. Ford's formula for the language of poetry illuminates his divergence from Victorian poets like Swinburne, Rossetti, and Tennyson, and his revival of the Wordsworthian tradition. He writes that

---

[73] Quoted in Goldring, *Trained for Genius*, p. 125.

[74] Kenner, *The Poetry of Ezra Pound*, pp. 173-174. Kenner notes that Ford's " detailed account of the cultural state of post-war London in the first third of *It Was the Nightingale* can be made to document *Mauberley* line by line."

[75] *The March of Literature*, p. 760.

[76] *Ibid.*, p. 759.

a poem must be compounded of observation of the every-day life that surrounded us; that it must be written in exactly the same vocabulary as that which one used for one's prose; that, if it were to be in verse, it must attack some subject that needed a slightly more marmoreal treatment than is expedient for the paragraph of a novel; that, if it were to be rhymed, the rhyme must never lead to the introduction of unnecessary thought; and, lastly, that no exigency of metre must interfere with the personal cadence of the writer's mind or the pressure of the recorded emotion.[77]

The manner of verse should be " like one's intimate conversation with someone one loved very much." [78]

His formula for the manner of prose was similar:

As for me I went on working beside Conrad, trying, when his passionate and possessive material, mental and physical vicissitudes left me the leisure, to evolve for myself a vernacular of an extreme quietness that would suggest someone of some refinement talking in a low voice near the ear of someone else he liked a good deal.[79]

As Ezra Pound phrased it, the aim is to be objective and to avoid merely literary or inspired explosions:

Objectivity and again objectivity, and no expression, no hindside-beforeness, no Tennysonianness of speech—nothing, *nothing*, that you couldn't in some circumstance, in the stress of some emotion, *actually say*. Every *literaryism*, every book word fritters away a scrap of the reader's patience, a scrap of his sense of your sincerity. When one really feels and thinks, one stammers with a simple speech. It is only in the flurry, the shallow frothy excitement of

---

[77] *Thus to Revisit*, pp. 206-207.
[78] *Ibid.*, p. 213.
[79] *Portraits from Life*, p. 216.

writing, or the inebriety of a metre, that one falls into the
easy, easy—oh, how easy!—speech of books and poems that
one has read.[80]

Ford finds models of excellent vernacular prose in the
King James Version, in the English and American news-
papers of the eighteen-twenties, in Clarendon and Cobbett,
and in his contemporary W. H. Hudson. Cobbett, himself
a newspaperman, was the genius who gave the vernacular
" backbone and rigidity." When affected by what he
thought injustice, his sentences " blazed like a comet " and
were used or adopted by others whether or not they had
read the papers for which he wrote.[81] Ford had turned to
these and other writers of nonfictional English prose after
he had modified his admiration for the more intricate and
conscious literary styles of Flaubert, James, and Conrad.
He never, however, modified his faith in the methods by
which Flaubert and Conrad sought to discover exact words
and to achieve a nonliterary, nonpoetic vocabulary. Probably the major influence on Ford's theory of the " vernacular of extreme quietness " was Hudson. According
to Ford, Hudson's style is comparable only to that of
Turgenev; both have that " chief characteristic of great
writers—of writers who are great by temperament as well
as by industry or contrivance — [. . .] self-abandonment,"
whereby the whole mind goes into watching and rendering.[82]
The vernacular Ford sought meant that the writer had
to avoid words which stuck out of sentences by being
so unusual or so brilliantly apt that the reader pauses to

[80] Monroe, *A Poet's Life*, p. 267. Miss Monroe's footnote to this letter from
Pound reads: " 1937. It should be realized that Ford Madox Ford had been
hammering this point of view into me from the time I first met him (1908
or 1909) and that I owe him anything that I don't owe myself for having
saved me from the academic influences then raging in London."

[81] *The March of Literature*, p. 761.

[82] *Thus to Revisit*, p. 70.

admire them. Style is hypnosis; at its best it eludes analysis. The reader should be enticed into " thinking " that he was living what he read—or, at least, " into the conviction that he was listening to a simple and in no way brilliant narrator who was telling—not writing—a true story." [83] Simplicity is the formula: " We wanted to write," Ford says, " as simply as the grass grows." [84] Hudson, who constantly revised his writing by toning down his language, was worth emulating. Ford tells of seeing one of his manuscripts in which the sentence " The buds developed into leaves " became " The buds grew into leaves," and, finally, " They became leaves." [85]

Ford and Conrad had trouble toning down their language. Part of their difficulty was the English literary language, which they found unsuited to direct statement.[86] Ford recognized three English languages: " that of *The Edinburgh Review* which has no relation to life, that of the streets which is full of slang and daily neologisms and that third one which is fairly fluid and fairly expressive— the dialect of the drawing-room or the study, the really living language." [87] This last contained the vernacular he wished to attain in his work, and it was this level of " normal conversation " with its " polite slang " which Ford knew and with which he was able to help Conrad.[88]

Working together, Ford and Conrad spoke and read a good deal of French and were in the habit when searching for a word of finding the French one and then translating

[83] *Ibid.*, pp. 52-53. Ford notes in *The March of Literature*, p. 551, that both the blank verse of the Elizabethans and the measured verse of the French acted as hypnotics on the audience.
[84] *Thus to Revisit*, p. 52.
[85] " Techniques," p. 30.
[86] *Thus to Revisit*, pp. 52-53.
[87] " On Conrad's Vocabulary," *The Bookman*, LXVII (June, 1928), 406.
[88] *Ibid.* Or " Middle-High-English " as he terms it in *Joseph Conrad*, p. 197.

it into its nearest English equivalent.[89] Ford felt he wrote better in French than he did in English because he knew French less well. Writing in French he had to pause for words, and " it is in pausing for a word that lies the salvation of all writers." [90] Exact meanings in English elude the writer because many words have so many shades of meaning. One example of this search for *le mot juste* can suffice—one which at the same time gives some insight into the working methods of these two writers.

> In telling these stories Conrad would thus occasionally duplicate his words, trying the effect of them. Then we would debate: What is the practical, literary difference between: Penniless and Without a penny? You wish to give the effect, with the severest economy of words, that the disappearance of the *Tremolino* had ruined them, permanently, for many years. . . . Do you say then, *penniless*, or *without a penny? . . .* You say *Sans le sou*: that is fairly permanent, *Un sans le sou* is a fellow with no money in the bank, not merely temporarily penniless. But 'without a penny' almost always carries with it: 'in our pockets.' If we say then ' without a penny,' that connoting the other: ' We arrived in Marseilles without a penny in our pockets.' . . . Well, that would be rather a joke: as if at the end of a continental tour you had got back to Town with only enough just to pay your cabfare home. Then you would go to the bank. So it had better be ' penniless.' That indicates more a state than a temporary condition. . . . Or would it be better to spend a word or two more on the exposition? That would make the paragraph rather long and so dull the edge of the story. . . .
>
> It was with these endless discussions as to the exact incidence of words in the common spoken language—*not* the literary language—that Conrad's stories always came over to the writer. Sometimes the story stopped and the

[89] *Joseph Conrad*, pp. 158-164.   [90] *Ibid.*, pp. 104-105.

discussion went on all day; sometimes the discussion was shelved for a day or two. There were words that we discussed for years.[91]

For those who deplore such endless labors to acquire a style, Ford had his answer prepared. Working on the assumption that communication between man and man is man's only hope for salvation, Ford naturally demanded of writers a close and serious study of language, such as Flaubert, or he and Conrad had made. The writer who receives his inspirations like bolts of lightning from heaven, writes in the full fury of passionate emotion, and publishes without revision is very often dangerous, unless he is a Hudson or a Turgenev, for he overwrites and succumbs to slipshod habits of expression. The novelist " *must*, in order to get perspective, retire in both space and time from the model upon which he is at work. . . . Still more, he must retire in passion . . . in order to gain equilibrium." [92] Again the Wordsworthian note is sounded, as it often is in Ford's treatment of language.

The vocabulary that we shall ultimately achieve by the methods of Flaubert and Maupassant—the vocabulary achieved indeed by the Imagistes [*sic.*]—will be the vocabulary for both the prose and the verse of the future. And it will be—as today in France is the case—the vocabulary of the hatter, of the pharmaceutical chemist, and the policeman, used over counters, at street corners—and above all in schools, by the teachers. Then, indeed, we shall have a Utopia! But that day will come only when our poets have applied to language that furious earnestness which the Bollandist Fathers have used in their analyses of cases of conscience.[93]

[91] *Ibid.*, pp. 85-86.
[92] *Portraits from Life*, p. 157.
[93] *Thus to Revisit*, p. 161.

There is some reason to believe that Ford went at this task with more " furious earnestness " than Conrad always thought wise. In a friendly letter to Ford written during the collaboration, Conrad advises him:

> The value of creative work of any kind is in the *whole* of it. Till that is seen no judgment is possible. Questions of phrasing and such like—*technique*—may be discussed upon a fragmentary examination. . . . But phrasing, expression—*technique* in short—has importance only when the conception of the whole has a significance of its own apart from the details that go to make it up—If it (the conception) is imaginative, distinct and has an independent life of its own—as apart from the life of the style.[94]

Nevertheless, Ford kept at his work, developing a theory of style from the English habit of avoiding direct speech. He implies that he borrowed the idea from James, in whom, he says, was united the European international culture, with its interest in the technique of form, and the Anglo-Saxon imagination, with its habit of shrinking from direct statement and its consequent tendency to allegorize.

> Mr. James expresses matchlessly his race and its religion. These call for delicate and sympathetic deeds and gentle surmises rather than for clear actions and definite beliefs. So Mr. James first refines all action out of his work—all non-psychological action—and, little by little, sets himself to express himself purely in allegory.[95]

[94] Quoted in Goldring, *Trained for Genius*, p. 80. (Conrad's ellipsis.)

[95] *Henry James*, p. 171. Ford adds on p. 173: " Personally I should say that Mr. James' ' style ' strikes me as almost unapproachable up to the day when he concluded *The Spoils of Poynton*; it is lucid, picturesque and as forcible as it can be, considering that he writes in English. With *What Maisie Knew* it begins to become, as we should say in talking of pheasants, a little ' high.' And so it goes on until, with the Prefaces and with *A Small Boy*, it just simply soars. There is not any other word for it. . . ."

Ford felt that James may have carried his fondness for allegorical speech too far in his later novels, though he realized that James's later style comes clear when read aloud and that it " is simply colloquial " and " a matter of inflexions of the voice much more than of commas or even of italics." [96]

Ford sought a more literal translation of literate colloquial speech than James did and carried the technique much further than James and in another direction. From studying conversations he learned that people listen superficially, concentrating as they do upon their next speech, and hence there is no necessary connection between the speeches of different speakers. In the book on Conrad he gives a lengthy example of how two neighbors would carry on a conversation.[97] It is characteristically exaggerated, but for him a " carefully studied exaggeration " is perfectly within the province of art.[98] He devised the rule that no speech by one character should answer that of the one before it. Three long speeches by three characters following each other would be boring.

> But if you carefully broke up petunias, statuary, and flower-show motives and put them down in little shreds one contrasting with the other, you would arrive at something much more coloured, animated, life-like and interesting and you would convey a profoundly significant lesson as to the self-engrossment of humanity. Into that live scene you could then drop the piece of news that you wanted to convey and so you would carry the chapter a good many stages forward.[99]

[96] *Ibid.*, p. 174.
[97] Pp. 181-210, *passim.*
[98] *The Critical Attitude*, p. 38. However, the term quoted appears in *Henry James*, p. 41.
[99] *Joseph Conrad*, p. 190.

Again, the task is to convey a sense of the discontinuity of life while creating the ordered world which art communicates. The task is genuinely a poetic one, for such a close attention to the careful juxtaposition of objects, of the images and impressions they convey, and of the associations they bring to the minds of both the character portrayed and the reader, and such a concentration on the creation of rhythmic effects are traditionally more matters of concern for the poet than for the novelist. The adoption of such concerns by the novelist, echoing as they do Flaubert and preparing the way for Joyce and Virginia Woolf, demonstrate as well as anything else the shift in emphasis in the modern novel away from plotted action ordered by the sequence of chronological time to the plotted imitations of human consciousness, and from largely narrative concerns to almost completely poetic ones. Ford's work in both the theory and practice of this tradition should not be undervalued.

Because Conrad and Ford each worked hard at shaping a style to suit his own special psychological treatment of subject matter, they could not agree, Ford tells us, on questions of cadence, accentuation, and prosody in general. Ford's " view [was] that everyone has a natural cadence of his own from which in the end he cannot escape. Conrad held that a habit of good cadence could be acquired by the study of models." [100] Conrad's favorite model for cadences was Flaubert, yet Ford realized that Conrad developed those which were peculiar to himself and, particularly when he sought to be dramatic, " a cadenced paragraph of long, complicated sentences, interspersed with shorter statements, ending with a long dying fall of words and the final taptaptap of a three monosyllabled phrase." [101] Examples of such paragraphs can be

[100] *Ibid.*, p. 200.   [101] " Techniques," p. 29.

found in Conrad, but it was not the only formula for a cadenced dramatic paragraph that he used, since the various demands of the subject and the atmosphere would prevent that. Indeed, Ford probably used it more than Conrad did.[102]

Working together, they had a splendid opportunity, however, for perfecting the cadences of oral narration. As a matter of practice during the collaboration each wrote with the idea of reading aloud to the other.[103] Since both had a wide knowledge of French fiction, they would quote at length their favorite passages. Their masters in style were Flaubert and Maupassant, the former more than the latter " in about the proportion of a sensible man's whisky and soda." Often they experimented.

> We remembered long passages of Flaubert: elaborated long passages in his spirit and with his cadences and then trans-lated them into passages of English as simple as the subject under treatment would bear. We remembered short, staccato passages of Maupassant: invented short staccato passages in his spirit and then translated them into English as simple as the subject would bear.[104]

Ford tells of first writing his *Cinque Ports* in sentences of not more than ten syllables; " he found it read immensely long." [105] Conrad dallied, on Ford's suggestion, with turning his prose into blank verse.[106] What each ulti-

---

[102] Ford used this device in his first novel, *The Shifting of the Fire*, written before he knew Conrad.

[103] *Joseph Conrad*, p. 203.

[104] *Ibid.*, p. 195.

[105] *Ibid.*, pp. 198-199. Ford revised the book before publication. In a letter to William Blackwood, dated November 7, 1900, Conrad wrote of Ford's *Cinque Ports* that there seemed to him to be " a good deal of force in his quiet phrasing." Joseph Conrad, *Letters to William Blackwood and David S. Meldrum*, ed. William Blackburn (Durham, North Carolina: Duke University Press, 1958), p. 114.

[106] *Joseph Conrad*, pp. 198-199.

mately found was his own natural cadence and style. Conrad never lost his " wonderful Oriental style," a danger which Wells feared would be the result of the collaboration.[107] Ford, when he was at his best, developed his own vernacular of extreme quietness, of intimate conversation, of tiny crepitations and surprises. Neither could deny his temperament. Each in his own way sought the crystallization of art.

"Trained for genius," indoctrinated with high ideals of life and art, and bound by a demanding set of carefully formulated fictional techniques, Ford set out after the collaboration with renewed creative energy to make his own way as a novelist. His fictional theory, drawn from novelists working in the serious art novel, committed him to rendering life dispassionately, to giving the effect of the formless and fragmentary nature of life as it meets the individual consciousness, and to directing the story to its inevitable conclusion. His concern with techniques designed to achieve these aims—the point of view, the time-shift, the *progression d'effet*, the selection and juxtaposition of events and impressions, and an objective, nonliterary language—committed him to the exacting difficulties of his craft. Since Ford developed a theory of fiction before he had had extensive practice in writing novels, he first armed himelf with a method and then set out on a search for subjects which could best put it to use.

[107] *Ibid.*, p. 51.

IV

FORD'S VISION
OF HIS WORLD

1

THE THIRTY NOVELS FORD WROTE BETWEEN 1892 AND 1936 include historical romances, farces, comedies of manners, and studies of contemporary political and social life.[1] These novels, along with several of the nonfiction works which supplement them, indicate that the basic assumptions of Ford's criticism of society remained relatively consistent throughout his career. He constantly explored the causes and effects of the mechanized, commercialized civilization of his time. As artist and humanitarian, he was outraged by the intellectual and moral paralysis brought on by the acquisitive, overspecialized, fragmented society he perceived. Also something of a prophet, seeking solutions that might save mankind, he constantly modified and extended his answers for survival. Although variously

---

[1] This number does not include his three fairy tales *The Brown Owl* (London: T. Fisher Unwin, 1892), *The Feather* (London: T. Fisher Unwin, 1892), and *The Queen Who Flew* (London: Bliss, Sands and Foster, 1894).

adapted to his awareness of changing conditions, Ford's solutions were consistent in their plea for the integrity of the conscientious individual in relation to his fellows. A review of Ford's subjects and of his general criticism of society and the social solutions he offered might serve as a reasonable, if somewhat oversimplified, context in which to discuss the particular themes and techniques of his representative novels.

A survey of his novels, most of them unfamiliar to the present-day reader, will help to clarify the range and content of his subjects. There are the historical romances, which recall events and conditions of the past and succeed in giving the reader vivid impressions of life in earlier times. Medieval lore and superstitions are heavily drawn upon in *The Young Lovell* (1913), the story of a young knight seduced by a demon lover, and in *Ladies Whose Bright Eyes* (1911; revised 1935), a historical fantasy placing the fourteenth century against the twentieth. The Elizabethan spirit is captured in *The ' Half-Moon '* (1909), the tale of a young bewitched man who accompanies Henry Hudson in his search for the Northwest Passage, and in the trilogy dealing with the rise and fall of Katherine Howard in the court of Henry VIII, *The Fifth Queen* (1906), *Privy Seal* (1907), and *The Fifth Queen Crowned* (1908). *Romance* (1903), his major collaboration with Joseph Conrad, is a nineteenth-century story of a Scottish youth who is tricked into almost losing his head by a long series of circumstances and by the plots of the Irish leader of a band of Cuban pirates. *A Little Less Than Gods* (1928) narrates the complex affairs of a young British adventurer during Napoleon's Hundred Days and the terror of the restoration which followed.

Except for this last novel, Ford subtitles these histories as romances. They are all evocations of the past, usually through a central fictional character who is not a major historical figure; they all deal in some way with the dramatic exploits of honorable daring heroes we associate with historical fiction. Embroiled in their private affairs, the heroes are also usually involved with the great men and issues of the time. Except for *Romance* and *Ladies Whose Bright Eyes*, these novels cannot be said to end happily, or, at least, with any degree of complacency on the part of the hero. Katherine Howard is defeated by fighting for the lost cause of England's restoration to Catholicism; Lovell succumbs to lechery; Edward Colman in *The 'Half-Moon'* is killed by Indians on the shore of the Hudson River; George Feilding in *A Little Less Than Gods*, discovering his sweetheart is his half-sister, leaves in frustration and despair to make his fortune in America. This novel, subtitled "A Napoleonic Tale," although it has its share of disguises, duels, and narrow escapes, may not have seemed to Ford quite properly a romance since it treats of the theme of incest. In addition to the histories, two novels of the contemporary scene, *An English Girl* (1907) and *The Marsden Case* (1923), are also designated as romances, and rightly so, for they are idealized tales of a young man using his fortune to counteract business corruption and political graft and of a young brother and sister who prove their legitimacy and gain an earldom.

The Portrait (1910) and *The Panel* (1912; somewhat revised and published in America as *Ring for Nancy*, 1913) are his two farces, or "sheer comedies." They have plots of complex situations, coincidences, embarrassments. The first deals with the expensive bets of an eighteenth-century gentleman to his fellow club members that he will find, bring to London, and marry the model for a well-known portrait he has never seen; the second is concerned with the pursuit by four women of a young man who, because he has read the complete works of Henry James, is the youngest major in the British Army. These farcical comedies are not so much apart from the main lines of Ford's fiction as they might at first appear, for Ford often was attracted to the farcical, the circumstantial, and the grotesque.

The greater share of Ford's social novels deal with the contemporary scene, in one of two ways. They are either comedies of manners concerned with a small circle of participants involved in the complications of a single affair (*The Good Soldier* is the purest example), or they are panoramic novels with a relatively large cast of characters, often with representatives from various social strata, who are embroiled in affairs which illustrate a political or social commentary on the times with implications beyond manners alone (*Parade's End* is the best example). Sharing certain themes in common, these two types are essentially different in perspective, in scope, and in form.

Ford's first novel, *The Shifting of the Fire* (1892), deals with a small circle and tells a melodramatic story of a young girl who marries an old dying man for his money, so that she can later marry a young man who has lost his fortune. After endless complications, misunderstandings, and sacrifices, the plan succeeds. *The Nature of a Crime*, written with Conrad, probably sometime between 1901 and 1903, but not published until 1924, is a first person narrative, using the epistolary form, of a man who has squandered the fortune of his legal ward to allow him to forget his unconsummated love for the married woman to whom he writes the letters. *The Benefactor* (1905) is a more serious and complex handling of the sacrificial theme of *The Shifting of the Fire*. *An English Girl* (1907), though a romance, is a pallid handling of the Jamesian international theme and shows how a young American of an immense inherited fortune tries to right the wrongs of his father, who had gained the fortune, a compulsion which causes him to lose the love of his English sweetheart. *A Call: The Tale of Two Passions* (1910) is a near-farcical comedy of retribution important for its themes and for its being a preview of *The Good Soldier* (1915), Ford's subtle, complex, pitiless novel in which he fully explored the implications of tradition in a transitional society upon a few carefully selected representative characters. After *The Good Soldier* Ford had little more to say about the small group as a microcosm of society. Of the later novels, only *The Marsden Case* (1923) comfortably fits within this classification, for it deals with a relatively small group and the pursuit of a single affair. But, being a romance and a potboiler, it is not a major effort.

The novels of a broader canvas dealing more specifically with political and social criticism began with the *The Inheritors* (1901). This novel, written in collaboration with Conrad, explores the consequences of the cold-blooded, materialistic spirit of the new age through a fanciful story of the successful plot of people from the fourth dimension taking over the British government. The curious book *Mr. Apollo* (1908) probably belongs among these novels. Apollo comes to earth to observe mankind; he strikes liars dead and the selfish of heart dumb; he lives in the home of a school teacher and his wife, reminiscent of the humble home of Philemon and Baucis he had visited thousands of years earlier, and brings the doubting husband to believe in him. The novel is an indirect attack on pettiness, moral cruelty, and on man's blindness to God.

Under the pseudonym Daniel Chaucer, Ford wrote *The Simple Life Limited* (1911) and *The New Humpty-Dumpty* (1912). The first is at once a satire on a colony of " simple lifers " and a key to Ford's prewar conception of the truly simple life. Indirectly it is an attack on socialism and the inadequacies of any organized political or social utopian community. *The New Humpty-Dumpty* is a more direct attack on socialism, and the Fabians in particular, who in Ford's mind are akin to the inhuman Dimensionists. *Mr. Fleight* (1913) is a starkly realistic account—though not without fanciful overtones—of English political life, in particular, of the election to Parliament of a wealthy Jew with an inherited industrial fortune whose political career is guided by a Mr. Blood, a sardonic, brilliant, detached, and wealthy man of self-willed laziness.

Ford, tremendously affected by the war and disheartened by what he felt to be the final betrayal by the British ruling class of the cause of peace and humane government, achieved in his postwar novels a profound and penetrating analysis of the moral and material collapse of the western world, particularly of England and the United States. The fortunes of Christopher Tietjens in *Parade's End* (1924-1928) illustrate the scope and depth of that collapse within England. The last four novels that Ford wrote turn to American or Americanized protagonists. *When the Wicked Man* (1931), challenging modern business ethics, is a satirical portrait of the president of a large publishing firm, who, as he becomes in his own eyes more and more degenerate morally, gains more and more esteem from his associates and the public. *The Rash Act* (1933) and *Henry for Hugh* (1934) are companion novels which in seeking to define a commercial code of honor relate the regeneration of an impoverished, disillusioned American who for a time assumes the identity of his double, an English business tycoon with the same surname and initials who has recently committed suicide. Ultimately, the American assumes a composite personality and finds contentment in marrying the woman he loves and in

directing the English firm. *Vive Le Roy* (1936), Ford's
last novel and another tale of double identity, is a combination spy thriller and political allegory relating the
fantastic maneuverings of a Royalist faction which wishes
to establish a France of small producers loosely governed
by a benevolent paternal monarch.

In his novels Ford draws his large cast of characters
mostly from the landed gentry and the middle class. The
historical novels naturally treat of kings, emperors, nobles,
and ministers of state, although the protagonists are sometimes of lower birth, and episodes with tradesmen, common
soldiers, and hired spies are brilliantly sketched in, giving
a vivid sense of the whole life of the times. The contemporary novels just as naturally focus on the middle class,
the conglomeration of industrialists, heirs to commercial
fortunes, publishers, writers, artists, ministers, politicians,
Socialists, Communists, anarchists, and cranks. In spite of
Ford's admiration for the simple, resourceful cottager, his
fictional cottagers and working class people are " shadowy
figures," as E. V. Walter rightly calls them.[2] Mostly they
are talked about, or else they appear briefly and inci-
dentally. The most revealing portraits of people of the
lower and working classes who have more than minor
importance in the novels are those of the sentimental
shopgirl, Gilda LeRoy, and her parents (*Mr. Fleight*) and

---

[2] E. V. Walter, " The Political Sense of Ford Madox Ford," *New Republic*,
cxxxiv (March 26, 1956), 18. See Ford's *Women and Men* (Paris: Three
Mountains Press, 1923), pp. 52-58, and *England and the English* (New York:
McClure, Phillips, 1907), pp. 183-199, for his portraits of Meary Walker, the
old cottager whom he saw as a true representative of the " heart " of England.
The best example of this type in his fiction is the garrulous, dissatisfied
cottager in *Simple Life Limited* who has been displaced by the colony and
forced to live in a new house built by Lord Luscombe. Ford admits in
Great Trade Route, pp. 393-395, that he does not really " know " the wage
earner. He believes, however, that the medieval serf, who was at least like
" valuable cattle," was better off than the industrial worker of today is.

the vindictive, vicious shopkeeper's daughter, Lady Macdonald (*The New Humpty-Dumpty*).

The reflection of Ford's social consciousness seen in his characters makes clear that he was interested in the rise of commercial power over that of king, nobles, and landed gentry. He shows how the royalty and nobility in the more or less stable aristocratic societies of the Middle Ages and the Renaissance firmly held power in the face of inchoate rumblings from what was to become the commercial middle class. Several of his novels on the contemporary scene record the final struggles of this transition of power, ending in World War I. Most of his twentieth-century characters are children of their age who cover the moral spectrum from the evil to the pure in motive, but who are nonetheless products of a commercial civilization. A few among the ruling class of the landed gentry maintain the integrity of the honorable feudalistic tradition, but most have compromised with the spirit of the modern age or have retreated into idleness. Their final betrayal of all that was best in the past Ford saw in their gaining a peace without honor and in their harsh treatment of the enemy and of the discharged Tommies after the Armistice. In the novels following *Parade's End*, Ford portrays the chaotic dilemmas of men in the new age who are still mysteriously bound to the past because they find a measure of peace in the memory of it.

We see these different characters in settings which vary from humble homes to great estates, or to private clubs, offices, hotels, restaurants, and nightclubs. A good many scenes take place in cars, trains, or carriages, and out of doors, often during walks or while some one or two stand on high looking over a vast view. Ford's world is bound by the land; he never wrote a sea-story. The sea offers a beautiful view or else it is a mere passageway between countries. But there are constant comparisons drawn between city and country life. Almost all of his characters who find contentment turn to a pastoral life, for the city is the home of the new order of commercial interests, and the center of materialism, selfish interests, and moral chaos.

Unlike James, Ford tackled " down town " subjects and found in the offices and in the business minds which operate them an appropriate lesson and warning for the well-being of humanity.[3] This mind is defined by the limits of self-interest and of what will sell, whether it be products or ideas. The principal danger is an absence of conscience resulting in a Machiavellian cold-bloodedness which justi-fies any means to achieve a profitable goal. Ford does not see much difference between the pitiless methods of the Dimensionists in *The Inheritors* to gain political power and the publishers who fill the bookstalls with salacious memoirs and meretricious romances.[4] A long list of charac-ters in Ford's novels illustrate various qualities and degrees of the modern commercial spirit which pervades every area of life.[5]

This spirit was evident long before the machine, that " stupid Moloch," [6] forced man to become its servant. In effect, it began in the Middle Ages with the rise of nationalism, which slowly destroyed the feudal power of

[3] Mentioning Henry James's distaste for this subject, Ford in *Henry James,* p. 60, comments that business and what takes place downtown " is simply not worth the attention of any intelligent being. It is a matter of dirty little affairs incompetently handled by men of the lowest class of intelligence."

[4] See *Memories and Impressions,* pp. 175-196, for a full treatment of the iniquities of the contemporary press, and *The Critical Attitude,* pp. 133-143, for a diatribe against the commercialism of publishers. Ford objects to modern publishing practices in *A Panel, Mr. Fleight, The Benefactor, Mr. Apollo, The Marsden Case,* and *When the Wicked Man.*

[5] The modern spirit is one of forces, not men. It is characterized by " great organisations run by men as impersonal as the atoms of our own frames, noiseless, and to all appearances infallible." *England and the English,* p. 30.

[6] *Great Trade Route,* p. 103.

the barons. Henry VII's spy, Sir Bertram de Lyonesse, in *The Young Lovell,* is a modern man whose duty is to subdue the northern barons to the sole power of the King by whatever means his craft and intelligence can devise. By allying himself with Lovell's campaign to regain his lands, he sees his chance to weaken the power of the North by pitting one baron against another. Lovell is dissatisfied with him; " I do not like your kind," he tells Bertram, " for I have seen some of them about the courts of princes, here and elsewhere and you are the caterpillars upon the silken tree of chivalry that shall yet destroy it." [7] The same spirit pervades even the northern barons. When Lovell tries to enlist young knights in his cause, their fathers cannot see the profit of it, " for the days were past then of riding upon knight errantry, crusades, chevauchees, and other enterprises more splendid than profitable," and " all the older men of the North [. . .] knew things by hard facts rather than books of faicts and arms. These men were rather bitter, cynical, and perforce mercenary, than loyal, pious, and chivalric " (pp. 277-278). Throckmorton, in the Katherine Howard trilogy, is another such figure, who plays a dangerous and more selfish game of double spying for both Henry VIII and Thomas Cromwell.

These are somewhat romanticized characters who, although opportunists, possess courage, intelligence, and charm. With the rise of nationalism and the machine civilization most of what Ford calls the modern men degenerate into pettifogging parasites and muddlers. They are not necessarily motivated by malice aforethought, but to every benevolent business man like Everard, the producer of successful musical comedies in *The Simple Life Limited,* there seem to be at least two like the patronizing,

---

[7] *The Young Lovell* (London: Chatto and Windus, 1913), p. 224.

unctuous Horatio Gubb in the same novel, who was " a close disciple and friend of the late Mr. William Morris, a parasitic gentleman, who fattened entirely upon the associations and upon the ideas of such distinguished people as would permit him to enter their houses." [8] Gubb, having connived to establish the temporarily insane novelist Bransdon as prophet of the Simple Life colony, wants most of all to be an Oliver Cromwell, an absolute dictator for the noblest cause. When Bransdon recovers his senses, he excuses Gubb by calling him a flea, but a dangerous one. He warns the woman who is to marry Gubb: " He's cold: he's a rottenly cold prig: he'll freeze your hands off when you lay hold of him. Don't you do it, take my advice. If that man doesn't work you one way, he'll work you another, and he'll turn you into a pitiful sort of slave at the end of it " (p. 250). The Dickensian Gubb is a prototype of the literary opportunists who plague George Moffat in *The Benefactor*, of the Socialist philosopher Pett (*The New Humpty-Dumpty*), of the publishers and popular writers in several novels, of the narrator of *The Nature of a Crime*, and ultimately of the literary and political parasite Macmaster in *Parade's End*.

A similar cynical opportunism invades English political life and the consciousness of the public. Although Mr. Blood, who guides the political fortunes of Mr. Fleight, has detached himself from human affairs, he becomes a composite of two traditions: while he cynically directs Fleight's campaign by means of bribery, blackmail, purchased candidates, and deceit, the usual tools of the modern, rationalistic, materialistic spirit, he is at the same time trying to recoup the political chances of his brother, a pure model of the best of the landed Tory gentleman,

---

[8] *The Simple Life Limited* (London and New York: John Lane, 1911), p. 77.

who had had to go into retirement some years earlier after he had been, in all innocence, unwittingly involved in a divorce scandal. After Fleight just as innocently becomes embroiled in his own scandal, Blood knows that in the public eye the two scandals will cancel each other out by the time of the next election, when his brother and Fleight will be opponents. He knows that the constituents are ignorant people with transient passions who rationalize their political stupidity, as Ford says elsewhere, by assuring themselves that "you can't bloody well have everything." [9]

Although Ford in *England and the English* had admired many qualities of the Englishman—his generosity, his sentimentality, his idealism, his sportsmanship—he saw these qualities as steadily degenerating during the war and after, when England returned to a prechivalric savagery of recrimination and revenge.[10] Actually Ford never had much sympathy with the great public, in spite of their redeeming qualities. They became more and more corrupted by the spirit of the times and elected leaders " who hypnotically suggest that they and they only can fill our individual purses, our maws, our stores, our banking accounts with property that at the moment of their appeal for our suffrages belongs to the heathen stranger . . . or our fellow-countrymen." [11] Slaves to their time and following their leaders, the public submerged for a selfish opportunism the chivalric ideal of altruism, by which Ford

[9] *Provence* (London: Allen and Unwin, 1938), p. 166.

[10] In *England and the English*, pp. 239-240, Ford says that the Boer War was the last instance of English "ferocity" and describes the Englishman as sentimental and kindly. Apparently, before World War I he held some hope for humanity, although he accused the leisure class then of being socially savage and barbaric (p. 84). But in *Great Trade Route*, p. 401, he notes that the age is comparable to that of the Roman Empire in its later days, for it has "increased in ferocity and in the power of doing murder."

[11] *Great Trade Route*, p. 90.

meant a society working within prescribed limits of un-
written law and custom for the good of all.[12] By the end
of the war " prosperity broke the American tradition and
profiteering destroyed the English rich man's character." [13]
By 1937, Ford saw " humanity at almost its lowest ebb
[. . .] almost without mastery over its fate " and with
ignorant rulers who would starve if left alone in rural
solitude.[14]

What had happened was that life had become incompre-
hensible. The consequent fragmentation—in perception, in
action, in values—defines Ford's principal subject matter
and themes, particularly in novels dramatizing his own
times. He felt that the most significant and disastrous
result of the slow, steady rise of the commercial spirit had
been the loss of a view of life as a whole and a breakdown
of faith in Christianity, in the controlling generalities of
the " Victorian Great," or in any connected thought at all.
Without any belief in a grand design co-ordinating " all
Nature in one great architectonic scheme," the mind is
forced to become introspective and to deal with " little
things." [15] Contemporary life

> is a dance of midges. We know no one very well, but we
> come into contact with an infinite number of people; we
> stay nowhere very long, but we see many, many places.
> We have hardly ever time to think long thoughts, but an
> infinite number of small things are presented for our cursory
> reflections. And in all of it—in all of this gnats' dance of
> ours—there is a note of mournfulness, of resignation, of
> poetry.[16]

[12] *England and the English*, pp. 282-283.
[13] *Provence*, p. 270.
[14] *Great Trade Route*, p. 89.
[15] *Memories and Impressions*, pp. 68-69.
[16] *The Critical Attitude*, p. 186.

The "Victorian Academic Great" were valuable for their preaching of a reassuring faith in which the people could believe. However, in what Ford saw as their moral compromise with material interests, the Victorians preached the wrong lessons and inevitably betrayed the public. Their harmful platitudes and the blot of the Boer War changed " the whole tone of England " so that principles died out of politics and even " the spirit of artistry " was lost by the artists.[17] Ford directly charges that the teachings of such Victorians as Ruskin, Carlyle, Dean Stanley, Emerson, and Holman Hunt led naturally to the use of poison gas.

> So their Germanic disciples used it [poison gas] when their Day came. Inevitably! Because the dreadful thing about nineteenth-century Anglo-Saxondom was that it corrupted with its bitter comfort-plus-opulence mania not merely itself but the entire, earnest, listening world. What effect could a serious and continued reading of those fellows have had but 1914? . . . And 193 . . . .[18]

The impact of Darwin's theory and the reality of a disastrous war destroyed faith in these Victorian priests. Nevertheless, the public still craved a creed by which to live in peace with themselves but refused to consider abstract questions in any other terms than the extremes of black and white.[19] Always kindly and humanitarian, the English sought to rid their land of the unemployed and diseased, but were betrayed by their own humanity. Ford felt the ordinary man would feel pain if that goal really were achieved:

[17] *Memories and Impressions*, p. 171.
[18] *Portraits from Life*, p. 205. (First published in 1937.)
[19] *The Critical Attitude*, pp. 113-118.

Deep in his heart, deep in the hearts of all men lies the belief that we can eat our cakes and have them; that we can make omelets without breaking eggs; that in some way mysteriously, whilst august and inscrutable Destiny for a moment averts its glance, effect will dodge cause. We desire that our preachers shall give us comfort in the night by preaching through the day those comfortable doctrines; we desire that our statesmen shall find means to enrich the poor without impoverishing the rich; we desire that new standards shall be set up without damage to old traditions—or we desire as a last resort that these things, if they have to be done, should in no way be brought to our attention.[20]

This muddling dilemma characterized by humanity's refusal to be rational leads to intellectual paralysis.[21] The complexity of modern life " with so many of its inner depths, with so many of its privacies laid bare for our daily inspection—the mere number of things that we have to think about in order to remain at all in contact with our fellow-men, has sapped much of our power for sustained thought." [22]

The consequences of this paralysis are the ills and confusions of society, and Ford leaves no doubt that these have been brought about by the muddleheadedness of men who were without altruistic, selfless principles and who sought personal glory at the expense of national honor. In all his social criticism and, as we shall see, throughout his fiction, Ford likes to blame man's troubles on " inscrutable Destiny," by which he means that effect inevitably follows cause, however blind human nature may be to that fact. But destiny is a force which works through human

[20] *Ibid.*, pp. 21-22.
[21] See particularly the chapters in *The Critical Attitude* titled " On the Objection to the Critical Attitude," pp. 3-22; and " The Passing of the Great Figure," pp. 113-129.
[22] *England and the English*, p. 304.

nature, and its relentless course is determined by human motivation and action. Hence, because humanity creates its own destiny unawares, people get what they deserve. For example, nations set up protective tariffs and then go to war because they are deprived of necessary products, and yet they ask God for protection from the results of their own actions.[23] But personal relations suffer most. Ford insists not only that the greater share of humanity is merely the stuff to fill graveyards, but also that most men are selfish and cruel to each other.[24] " *Homo homini lupus*" is a favorite phrase of Ford's: "Man is to his brother man a wolf." [25]

Or, rather, Ford means that *most* men are wolves, and since they are, they betray and crucify the man of generous impulse and principle who for the good of humanity invariably wants to help them. Graham Greene notes that in Ford's writings " the little virtue that existed only attracted evil. But to Mr. Ford, a Catholic in theory though not for long in practice, this was neither surprising nor depressing: it was just what one expected." [26] This pessimistic view of human motivation, what might be called Ford's humanistic fatalism, helps to explain the impossible dilemma of modern man, who, a captive of the crass commercial spirit, is powerless against his overspecialized, fragmented existence, which lacks any single faith to sustain it. It is a dilemma, Ford warns us, that man has inevitably created for himself. Character, then, is fate, however much society rationalizes its plight by shaking its fist at destiny.

[23] *Provence*, p. 258.
[24] *The English Novel*, pp. 128-129, and *It Was the Nightingale*, p. 85, are two of the many citations in Ford's work of the statement that most men are destined only to fill graveyards.
[25] *Women and Men*, p. 21, and *The Marsden Case* (London: Duckworth, 1923), p. 165, are two of the many citations of this statement in Ford's work.
[26] "Ford Madox Ford," in *The Lost Childhood and Other Essays* (New York: Viking, 1952), p. 90.

Searching further in his analysis of contemporary life, Ford drew the conclusion that beneath England's troubles, and by extension those of the Nordic civilization, were the effects upon society of climate and food. His thoughts on where men live and what they eat, though only indirectly and by implication related to his fictional themes until his last novels, are at the center of his criticism of life throughout his nonfiction, particularly in his last extended essays, *Provence* and *Great Trade Route*. These ideas reflect Taine's theory that climate shapes character, but even more they show how a gourmet sees the world through his palate. The arid climate of the North and the diet of beef, brussel sprouts ("the source of all evil"),[27] chemically treated fruits and vegetables grown with artificial fertilizer, and cellophane-wrapped foods, in fact, all food prepared by the most scientific fashions of modern processing, adversely affect disposition and consequently action. Bad food leads to chronic indigestion which leads to arguments and wars —another evidence of "inscrutable Destiny" at work. Hence, Ford concludes, with one of those exaggerated and devastating oversimplifications of his, that the civilization north of the Great Trade Route, roughly the fortieth parallel circling the globe, has devised "massacres, football matches, *noyades*, witch-drownings, puritanisms, flayings, drawings, quarterings, Jew-baitings, Calvinisms and all the medieval and modern Nordic horrors including *autos da fé* of books, street shootings and tariffs."[28]

Responsive as Ford was to the effects of climate and food on temperament and action, he was naturally led to idealize the sunnier, more fruitful lands south of the fortieth parallel. As we might expect, the southern civiliza-

[27] *Provence*, p. 229.
[28] *Ibid.*, p. 230. See also pp. 70-71, where Ford blames the Kaiser's belligerency on his indigestible diet.

tion of the Great Trade Route, the territory from Cathay
to the Mediterranean and even as far north as the southern
plains of England (a line which Ford saw extending to the
land south of the Mason-Dixon line in the United States),
where it had not been corrupted by Nordic influences,
offered to Ford, after his self-exile from England, the only
satisfactory conditions for a serene human existence. It
was especially in Provence where he, like other artists,
found his haven. " It was the necessity for clear light, a
life of dignity and a settlement in the only territory in
the world where the tides of civilization flow for ever backwards and forwards. . . . Along the Great Trade Route
that has been the main civilizing factor of the world since
the days when the merchant was sacred." [29]

The lessons he drew from the history of the Great Trade
Route and the answers he ultimately found in Provence,
he had earlier sought in England. Prewar England had
seemed to offer a basis for salvation, as is evidenced by
Ford's stout defense of the English character in *England
and the English*, but when he felt postwar England had
betrayed the cause of honor, and when life there, for
reasons both personal and idealistic, became impossible for
him, he had to turn elsewhere for a place to live and to
dream in. The best and simplest sources we have for an
understanding of the shift in Ford's answer to the forces
of disintegration in modern society are the two editions
of *Ladies Whose Bright Eyes*.

2

In 1935 Ford published an extensive revision of *Ladies
Whose Bright Eyes*, which had originally appeared in 1911.
A glance at the thematic revisions may help to give sub-

[29] *Ibid.*, p. 232.

stance to the perhaps unduly abstract account just given
of Ford's vision of his age. The revised edition is of
interest because its criticism is essentially the same as it
was twenty-four years earlier, while the solution is significantly different.

A comedy full of sly wit and deft humor, the novel is
none the less a serious one. Mr. William Sorrell, a commercially efficient "modern" man, is a partner in his
uncle's publishing firm, although earlier he had fought with
Allenby in Palestine and had traveled over the world as
a consulting engineer. While in a coma as a result of being
in a train accident, he imagines himself near a castle on
Salisbury Plain in the fourteenth century. Still possessed
of his twentieth-century consciousness, he tries to put his
business methods to work and to capitalize upon the six
hundred years of man's progress. Accepted as a prodigious
wonder, even as a holy man, he tends at first to patronize
the medieval people for their ignorance and superstition
and for the complexities and odd niceties of their chivalric
code. But he discovers that the modern business efficiency
of which he is so proud is merely a method invented to
satisfy man's avarice and that although he knows how to
make money, he is ignorant of how to do anything useful
for himself or of value to others. He falls in love with a
Lady Dionissia, a sympathetic, patient woman, who gives
him faith and leads him to see further into the inadequacies of the twentieth century, where specialization has
made a coherent life impossible and compromise to the
popular will inevitable. His values shift so that the important things are his love for Dionissia, his learning jousting,
falconry, and husbandry, and his adoption of the chivalric
code that so carefully prescribes the behavior for a life
of honor and requires men to live by principle and, if
necessary, to die for it.

Restored to health, back in the twentieth century, and returned to busines, Sorrell, knighted during his confinement " for selling bum cyclopedias," is now head of the publishing firm and strongly dissatisfied with modern life. He seeks out the history of the story he has " lived," visits the castle on Salisbury Plain, and finds there Dionissia Morane, the first nurse to treat him after his accident, who had left the hospital before he regained consciousness. The last direct descendant of the original Dionissia, she is in love with him. She tells him that she had read Froissart and Commines aloud in his hospital room during the long hours she had spent there on duty.

Up to this point the two versions are similar. By 1935, gas bombs have replaced machine guns as the symbol of human savagery, but the social criticism is the same. Neither idealizes the Middle Ages, for Ford emphasizes the filth and squalor of life and the precarious and sometimes savage political conditions of the feudal state. In both, Sorrell is initially the proud publisher of bulky encyclopedias and racy memoirs the suburban public will buy. In both, after the collapse of his initial plans to exploit the fourteenth century in Connecticut Yankee fashion by " inventing " the railroad, telephone, and airplane, and by cornering commercial markets, he tells the Lady Dionissia that he is aware that he is slipping away from his past (i. e., the twentieth century) and is losing his sense of duty and usefulness as a successful businessman. He believes he ought to have been master of the world by then.

" But I know nothing. Don't you understand, I have been so in the habit of having all these things done for me that I am useless as the grub in the honeycomb that the bees feed. It is no use my saying that I can do nothing because I have not the materials—that is an idle excuse. We might fit out ships to go to the end of the world to get rubber; but even if we did that I do not know where rubber comes from, nor if I knew should I know from what tree rubber is procured. Nor if I had the rubber, should I know what to do with it. And it is a condemnation of a whole civilisation. There was not, of the men I knew, one who knew any of these things." [30]

Sorrell comes to learn that in the fourteenth century each man did his own work and could take pride in doing it well. A man knew where he stood, whether he was a tradesman or a knight. But the twentieth century is debased. Sorrell says, after he has returned to work:

" I've done with this show. I can't stand it[. . . .] I am not fit for work, and this work isn't fit for me. I am going. Anybody could run this show[. . . .] It isn't even a man's work, this. It doesn't need brains, courage, intelligence, or even common honesty. Nothing does here. The place is vulgar. The language is vulgar, the time is vulgar. The language we speak is vulgar. So are the thoughts we think. Everything is vulgar. Even the air! " [31]

In his disgust, the Sorrell of the original version desires only to restore the little castle, even to the garbage dump in the courtyard, and to live in a kind of medieval paradise pictured by the dream Dionissia.

" In the spring the moles come out of the woods and the little birds sing, and we walk in the gardens and take what pleasure we can. And then comes the winter, and shuts us

[30] *Ladies Whose Bright Eyes* (London: Constable, 1911), p. 257; (Philadelphia: Lippincott, 1935), p. 253.

[31] 1911 edition, p. 344. The 1935 edition, p. 345, shifts to an indirect quotation, omits a good deal, and conveys the same idea. The reference to place, time, and language has been revised to read: " The place was vulgar. And the time. And the language."

up in our castles so that it is not so pleasant; but with jongleurs and ballad-singers we pass the time as well as we may. And what is there to do? " (1911 ed., p. 256; 1935 ed., p. 252)

The more practical Nurse Dionissia persuades him to have the castle modernized and to return to the publishing business, for he can still make an honorable job of it. She reminds him that one century is as good or as bad as another, and when he reminds her that any fool could be a successful publisher, " she just answered that in that case it was the business of a person who wanted to stand out from the ruck, to do it not only successfully, but well " (1911 ed., p. 357). Hence, he vows " to do something for literature "; he will give up encyclopedias and salacious memoirs to publish poetry.

The novel ends in a conversation between Sorrell and Dionissia. When he asks her if he will make her happy, she replies:

" We set out together, and we take our chances of what we find in each other. Happiness is a sort of thing you can't put in a bank and draw upon. We've got to find it from day to day as if we were houseless wanderers upon the roads."

She got down from the window and set her two hands on his shoulders.

" It was the same then; it's the same now," she continued. " Don't you see? These are things we can't take precautions about. We have our glorious moments and, even if our lives go to pieces, if disasters come, and ruin, and death, we shall have had our glorious moment, and that's all there is in life, and that's all there ever was." (1911 ed., p. 361)

She has him repeat after her that it is a beautiful world and as beautiful as it ever was. The last sentences are a harbinger of pastoral bliss. " From the distance there came the wailing sound of sheep bells over the sunny grass. The sheep were beginning to feed again " (1911 ed., p. 263).

When some six years after he had finished the Tietjens saga Ford set out to revise a novel written over twenty years earlier, he sought not only to make it different but to make it better. The novel in each of its versions is a piece of special pleading that presents both an analysis or record of his age and a prospectus for its regeneration. The charges against a mechanistic society are so general that they apply in 1935 as well as they had in 1911, but Ford came to see that Sorrell's concession to culture in his decision to publish poetry was hardly adequate to reform society or even to allow his protagonist " to stand out from the ruck." In 1911 Ford could suggest only an ineffectual reversion to medievalism and fails to convince us that Sorrell can publish poetry either successfully or well without the support of the suburban public. Ths resolution is consistent with Ford's hopes for the kingdom of letters he had proclaimed in his *English Review* editorials, but as his concerns widened and deepened, through war and the trials of his life and art, his thinking shifted its emphasis to larger social problems and from England to all western civilization. He came to see that poetry and the arts are still essential for the reformation of society, but that they are no longer by themselves the only means of redemption. In 1911 Sorrell was not ready to confront the twentieth century because Ford was not.

In the final pages of the 1935 edition, once Sorrell and Dionissia meet, they talk in elliptical half phrases, and almost everything definitely stated before is left out.[32] Their love is taken for granted; they talk about " new

[32] 1935 edition, pp. 348-351. Unless noted otherwise, the following quotations are taken from these pages.

beginnings " and the similarity of their " mental processes," and then pledge themselves to face the future
together.

Dionissia still plays the wise counselor. When Sorrell
suggests they might recapture that earlier life, she reminds
him that they need to find some place which offers a new
beginning: " Beginning all over again. Inspired of course
with faith." He remembers his promise to himself to
return to a valley in the Russian Caucasus, where he had
prospected for the Russian Imperial Government in 1913.
" ' If you saw a little castle then,' she said, ' it would be
a ruin now. . . . But of course *they're* beginning.' " She
agrees to the hardships he mentions: " ' Stamps . . .
Crushers, you know. . . . For ore. Worked by water
power. In the bottom of a valley. You're snowed in all
winter. . . .' " In the earlier version no structural importance was given to the fact of Sorrell's having been an
engineer, unless his knowledge would have helped in
restoring the castle. In the revision, by putting to use
his skill in a modern profession and in a society attempting
a modern experiment he avoids what is essentially the
compromise with commercial interests that the prewar
Sorrell had made. In Sorrell's and Dionissia's consciousness the fourteenth century still co-exists with the present
as though behind a curtain, by what Sorrell calls " a new
factor in psychics," but a new awareness is evident in the
later version. In addition to happiness, faith is necessary.

" It's getting back to a beginning of everything that matters
[Dionissia tells Sorrell]. It doesn't matter where or even
when. Then you can go forward with courage. That's
what's the matter with to-day and here. We go forward into
doubt because there's nothing but doubts into which to go
forward. Faith is a thing you cannot borrow. Not even the

Jew Goldenhand from whom they used to borrow can lend you that. It comes from your surroundings. From hard, unatrophied things and minds."

Dionissia echoes here the postwar Sorrell's complaint that modern civilization is " atrophied." " That was what they knighted you for, these days. Because you sold things that were atrophied. Atrophied knowledge, atrophied faith, atrophied courage! " (1935 ed., p. 345). Dionissia tells him that at first she also had thought they could restore the castle and " only dress in homespuns. . . . That sort of physical and moral deflatism." After the doctors had given up hope for his life, she realized her day-dreaming had been wrong.

> " I should have been thinking into tomorrow. Not six hun-
> dred years ago. So I came to this village. Have always had
> a room here. Then I heard you had recovered . . . I am
> going back to-morrow. That is why I came here to-day.
> He exclaimed:
> " You are never going back."
> She looked at him for a long time.
> " Then you must never go back either," she said at last.
> She added: " What we have to do is to go forward—don't
> they say: over the graves? "

Thus the novel ends. And without talk of " glorious moments " which act as a barrier against " disasters," " ruin," and " death." Any simple reversion to the past is denied. Instead of an escape, the 1935 edition offers a confrontation. Its more clearly perceived, more convincing pleas for a strong sense of personal responsibility, for skill in the crafts of one's livelihood, and for purpose and method in the art of life, though perhaps inadequate as solutions to the complexities of our increasingly urban civilization, have nevertheless appealed to a number of people who seek to discover a new sense of personal identity in an impersonal society.

From the conditions of his own life and times, Ford in effect seemed to discover not only his subject matter (first fully evident in *The Good Soldier* and *Parade's End*), but also a less superficial and factitious basis for survival. The betrayal of the British government to the cause of peace by not pursuing the Germans to Berlin (which led Mark Tietjens to his vow never to speak another word), the growing inclination of mankind to place its enemies up against a wall (a steady refrain in *Provence* and *Great Trade Route*), and the ever increasing horrors of the commercial, mechanized society (bitterly satirized in *When the Wicked Man*) were proof that a faith in the spirit such as had mobilized the Middle Ages—and even the eighteenth century—had been irretrievably lost.

> There have been stolen away from us, unperceived, Faith and Courage; the belief in a sustaining Redeemer, in a sustaining anything; the Stage is gone, the Cinema is going, the belief in the Arts, in Altruism, in the Law of Supply and Demand, in Science, in the Destiny of our Races. . . . In the machine itself.[33]

Indeed, Ford had come to believe that " courage," " endurance," " the pioneering spirit," and " thrift " were " virtue-vices " that led only to acquisition and hence to wars. Ironically he suggests that " the only thing that could save us is degeneracy. We must become lazy, shiftless, languid, disloyal, cowardly, unadventurous, undisciplined." He then adds:

> Our virtue-vices are all devoted to training us for acquisition. . . . Self-help they used to call it in Victoria's spacious

---

[33] *Provence,* p. 261.

days. It was considered virtuous then to rob—deprive—
your fellows. And all our training, all our idealism, since
then has been devoted to making us more deft at robbing
our fellows. For do not forget that every penny you make
by your honesty, endurance, courage, cleanliness, technical
instruction has been taken from a starving child. . . . It
might have saved a child from starvation. . . . But you
have it. There were last year 270,000 starving children
roaming one country in bands.[34]

The only virtue left is charity, not the kind which is
administered by organizations, but rather that which is
shown by the nonacquisitive individual who can live
beside his neighbor without friction.[35]

Ford's apparent fascination with the Russian Communist experiment in the revised *Ladies Whose Bright
Eyes* is misleading if we accept it as a total commitment
or as his answer for civilization. Although from his early
association with his " anarchist " Rossetti cousins and
Kropotkin, and with his interest in such schemes as
Marwood's worker's compensation insurance, Ford leaned
toward idealistic leftist thinking, he seemed always to
distrust organizations which championed such ideas. He
had a special dislike for the Fabians, whom he saw as a
" Socialist Tammany Hall " which " proposed to reform
society by means of statistics, and [whose] publications
were so dull that no one not spurred on by a sort of sadic
lust to destroy his fellow men could possibly have read
them." [36] He feared that as the socialist ideal was put into
practice it would become more ruthless: there would be a

---

[34] *Great Trade Route*, p. 400. On pp. 232-233 of *Henry for Hugh* (Philadelphia and London: Lippincott, 1934) Ford mentions seeing a newspaper
article about 270,000 American children wandering homeless over the United
States.

[35] *Great Trade Route*, pp. 400-401. See also pp. 29-30.

[36] *Portraits from Life*, p. 119.

time when production would fail to meet the demand of the huge populations to come and when the mentally and physically diseased and all the weak would logically have to be led to starvation or the gas chamber. In an early novel, *The Simple Life Limited*, Ford shows how ideal communities and socialism are corruptible by materialism, impersonalism, and inhumanity. Horatio Gubb and the militant Socialist Miss Stobhall, who preaches total subjection to the state, best illustrate these shortcomings. In the last novels, the Communists are not treated sympathetically.

In *Provence*, written in 1935, Ford tells us he writes as an " observer of life," not as a politician, and that he cares little whether the Communists or the Fascists eventually win. But because it put its faith in machines, he never trusted the USSR.[37]

> [. . .] if Lenin had preferred to establish agricultural rather than industrial communities I should have been wholeheartedly in favour of them. The curses of humanity are not property but the sense of property, not war but the ill-nature and ignorance that lead to wars. Both these evils would have been swept away by Christianity[. . . .]
>
> You cannot, however, have vast organizations without faith—and Christianity as a faith died a few days after the 4th of August, 1914.[38]

The Church's defense of war had doomed Christian faith, and nothing in Ford's time had appeared to replace it.[39] What had happened was the horror of the Fascist slaughter

---

[37] *Great Trade Route*, p. 205.

[38] *Provence*, p. 304. On p. 67 of *Great Trade Route*, Ford notes that Stalin finally had to realize the importance of the small producer and allow every man working on a communal farm two acres and a house of his own.

[39] *Provence*, pp. 305-306. On pp. 110-111 of *Great Trade Route*, he charges that Christianity died " under the attacks of contagious indifferentism."

in Abyssinia and tyranny in Communist Russia.[40] Actually, Ford did care who won. But he expected political communities to copy the various churches that could live in relative peace together, or the governments of Monaco, France, Switzerland, and Italy, that until recently had lived peacefully next to each other for generations.[41]

Certainly Ford was attracted to many of the basic premises of the idealized Communist philosophy, but Sorrell's decision to seek new beginnings in the Caucasus is less a seal of approval for Russian Communism than it is an expression of Ford's even more idealistic and less rational solution.

In his terms, it was what was " logical " in the socialistic systems or in any political system that was dangerous.[42] Science had given a method to an acquisitive society with the result that any social or political system working " logically " and " scientifically " toward particular ideal goals ultimately and inevitably became relentless and inhumane. The cruel, cold logic of the Dimensionists, the pursuit of material success and power by such men as Horatio Gubb and Macmaster, the corrupt electioneering of Mr. Fleight, are all manifestations of the modern scien-

[40] " ' Tyranny is a necessity to them [the Communists] because according to the dictates of their theory of government men must be adapted to their machine not their machine to the tastes and desires of men. Lenin [. . .] was a very admirable tyrant—but still a tyrant, his machine lopping off heads, arms, feet, where they would not conform or could not conform to the perfect sphere of his governmental theories. . . . It is an ideal that, like another . . .' " *Vive Le Roy* (Philadelphia: Lippincott, 1936), pp. 68-69. The hero of the novel, a scientist named Walter Leroy, originally has Communist leanings " because the whole world seemed in an atrocious muddle. The Russian Republic presented the spectacle of the only government that knew where it was going or how to get what it wanted in quiet. He desired to see a world fitted for bacteriologists " (p. 16). Ford, however, gives the victory neither to the Communists nor the Fascists but to the royalist faction championing the small producer.

[41] *Great Trade Route*, pp. 395-399.

[42] *The Critical Attitude*, pp. 18-19.

tific frame of mind. The logical extremes of scientism in politics are best illustrated in *Mr. Fleight* during one of Mr. Blood's cynical briefings of the relatively innocent candidate.

" Now I'm going to tell you the absolute truth about Society as it is, and the life we lead. The society we live in is an extraordinarily cruel and disordered machine. It is like a quantity of huge metal discs whirling around and running the one upon the other. In this society your business is not to love the classes below you or to sympathise with them, or to seek to help them; your business is to seek to crush and to extract the last drop of blood from their mangled bodies, the last drop of sweat from their dripping brows. That is the meaning of the word democracy as we understand it to-day. It is better, because it is more scientifically honest to look at the matter in that way. You must regard yourself as a member of the governing classes just as you regard yourself as a Jew. You are as distinct from them as you are from the Gentile race. They are the material to be exploited; you are the exploiter. There is no other way of looking at it.[43]

Ford is obviously saying that in the politics of his day the end justifies any means, but Machiavelli, for one, had preached this logical doctrine long before the age of science. Ford's objection is to action without principle, a course which many men of his day rationalized by citing the evolutionary theory of the survival of the fittest. If Ford had little faith in the instructions of politics, or commerce, or the church for man's salvation, he had even less faith in pure science.

Science has done more than anything—more than the Churches themselves—to break the faith in its imperial

[43] *Mr. Fleight* (London: Howard Latimer, 1913), p. 249.

destinies, of humanity. . . . For a generation before 1914 we were deafened by assertions of the benign services that Science would render to humanity . . . and then when came the day of humanity on its trial, just as the Albigenses saw that the first use to which Christianity was put was their extermination, so the first use of Science in the mass was to put an end to infinite millions of human lives.

. . . .

Science at once evolves the principles of eugenics, preserves the lives of infinite millions of the mentally and physically defective and enables millions of men to move about the world carrying cans of explosives and bacteria and other cans containing inferior, scientifically preserved foods, and so to destroy other millions of their fellows. In the meantime, with those same preserved, pasteurized, refrigerated, chemicalized and *ersatz* foods it lowers the vital and intellectual forces of whole continents and at the same time throws into hopeless confusion the markets of the universe. . . .[44]

It is no wonder, then, that, denying the values the society of his day offered, Ford turned to the south of the Great Trade Route, to Provence and Paris, to the artist's havens, for the basis of his utopian way of life. His is an aesthetic vision, a natural recourse of the artistic temperament against the horrors of society. " I don't want our civilization to pull through," he writes in *Provence*. " I want a civilization of small men each labouring two small plots—his own ground and his own soul. Nothing else will serve my turn " (pp. 124-125).

He visualizes a collection of small communities, small nations, small churches. There will be no national patriotism, no sense of property, or, only enough for the small plots one will own in his little community. If he is unhappy, the small producer can move to a more congenial

[44] *Provence*, pp. 314-315.

place (p. 319). Great cities will be saved as cultural centers, along with the seaports and university towns. The administrators of the world will be centered in the ugly cities of Washington, D. C., and Geneva, where they will work only half-time at the most routine duties and chafe to get away.[45] Industrial workers will work only a day and a half a week, the rest of their time being spent on their square of land or entertaining themselves in the museums, theaters, libraries, and night clubs of the cities.[46] Each country will produce only what is best fitted to its climate and people, and the goods will circulate freely around the world, "preferably by barter"; such free trade would abolish wars " since no country could dispense with the products of any other country," and civilizations instead of bombs would be exchanged.[47] Those " venial pimps and prostitutes," the professional politicians, will have to be exterminated by the " moderate people who read or write books, visit picture galleries, listen to concerts, weave things on handlooms, make chairs by hand . . . and work on our land." They will " come out of the gas-filled cellars and start again on the weary task of rebuilding our civilisations . . . we who have never yet seen any civilisation at all." [48]

Actually what he wants is an aristocracy of compatible interests, a kind of adaptation of medieval Provence to present conditions. If he could have his way, each small principality would copy the way of life of the troubadours before their civilization was invaded by the northerners in the thirteenth century. The populace would divide itself into the local aristocracy and protectors on one side, and the farmers and providers on the other, " the knights being without discipline, the rural thinkers without prejudices

---

[45] *Great Trade Route*, pp. 311-312.   [47] *Provence*, pp. 362-363.
[46] *Ibid.*, pp. 175-177.   [48] *Great Trade Route*, p. 305.

as without puritanism." [49] But with both the leaders and workers at their jobs part-time, everyone would have time to be a small producer in congenial communities. Industry and politics would be relegated to secondary importance. Individuality and self-sufficiency would be proclaimed. Life would be reduced to its simplest and best terms, for the small producer

> is the man who with a certain knowledge of various crafts can set his hand to most of the kinds of work that go to the maintenance of humble existences. He can mend or make a rough chest of drawers; he will make shift to sole a shoe or make a passable pair of sandals; he will contrive or repair hurdles, platters, scythe handles, styes, shingle roofs, harrows. But above all he can produce and teach his family to produce good food according to the seasons. . . . In sufficiency to keep his household supplied independent of the flux of currencies and the tides of world supplies—and to have a surplus for his neighbours. He is the insurance premium of his race. In short a Man.[50]

Ford's charge of faith to the small producers of the world is simply " that you must love your neighbour better than yourself and that, all men being born free and equal, every man's neighbour—and in particular niggers and the Mediterranean races—is as good as oneself . . . and better." [51]

This idea of the small producer, derived from William Morris, from Ford's knowledge of Provence and medieval history, from his own not very successful experiments in

---

[49] *Provence*, p. 129.
[50] *Great Trade Route*, p. 170.
[51] *Provence*, p. 320. The sentence before this one reads: " The Boston tea-party led to the declaration that all men—except niggers, Jews and Catholics —are born free and equal and that everyman is as good as his neighbours— and better."

truck farming, and perhaps a little from Tolstoy, is one which represents his search for a coherent, faithful, honorable life amid the confusion of his day. In effect, by thinking in terms of small independent social units, he discovered one way in which to give meaning to the fragmented and atrophied conditions of contemporary life.

The different resolutions of the two Sorrells define, in terms of Ford's fiction, the basis of a workable solution within existing society. The Sorrell of 1935 is not any less idealistic than the Sorrell of 1911; yet he is able to walk over the graves of the past in order to discover a "new beginning" in a job demanding craft and skills and in a land which at that time seemed to hold the only promise of perfection for the future. Both versions illustrate that Ford was less capable of devising solutions than of perceiving the iniquities in the society of his day. The two texts also illustrate Ford's shift from a Pre-Raphaelite medievalism to a commitment to the future inspired by a faith in the power of honor and integrity to effect reform in a commercial, mechanized civilization. His suggestion for a reversion to the simple life is probably unrealistic and far too oversimplified, but it would seem that the humane virtues he championed have relevance in any age. Although he gave us some directions, his failure was in not discovering a way in which these virtues could flourish in the modern world. It is a failure we may allow the idealist.

V

THE EARLY NOVELS

1

STELLA BOWEN, LIKE VIOLET HUNT BEFORE HER, CAME TO know that Ford's passion for literature subsumed everything else. " I don't think," Miss Bowen wrote, " his personal relationships were important at all, they always loomed very large in his own view, but they were not intrinsically important." [1] On the other hand, she perceived that he had the aesthetic detachment which enabled him to understand the secrets of human emotions.

" When I got to know him better, I found that every known human quality could be found flourishing in Ford's makeup, except a respect for logic. His attitude to science was very simple. He just did not believe a word of it. But he could show you two sides simultaneously of any human affair, and the double picture made the subject come alive, and stand out in a third-dimensional way that was very exciting. What he did not know about the depths and

[1] *Drawn From Life* (London: Collins, 1941), p. 165. Violet Hunt had earlier charged that Ford had a " lack of sympathetic imagination," and that he had an " habitual disregard of the mentality of others." *The Flurried Years*, pp. 67 and 155.

weaknesses of human nature was not worth knowing. The hidden places of the heart were his especial domain, and when he chose he could put the screw upon your sense of pity or of fear with devastating sureness." [2]

Adept in analyzing the conditions of society and in revealing the disparities between worthy and unworthy motives, Ford seldom in his early work, except in the Katherine Howard novels and intermittently elsewhere, chose to seek out the mysteries and depth of the heart. He was perfectly aware that most of his earlier novels were potboilers designed to please, or to preach, or to create impressionistic atmospheres. It was not until he had completed his long apprenticeship in both life and letters that at the age of forty he could successfully call upon his real powers of craftsmanship and psychological insight.

A spokesman for the English aristocracy, to which he did not belong except temperamentally, Ford had a strong sense of class and of its importance within the British tradition. Perhaps by being a semi-outsider, only part English, he could see more clearly than they the plight of the decadent ruling class—the inheritors of the feudal aristocracy. In his early novels of the contemporary scene (twelve of the nineteen he wrote before *The Good Soldier*) he worked at finding plots and methods to dramatize his analysis of the emotional havoc wrought by the slow crumbling of the ruling class tradition. Many forms and customs survived, but the spirit which gave birth to them had died. He perceived that the effects of commercialism and the fragmentation of society profoundly affected human relationships. It is his concern for the complexities and subtleties of personal relations that is at the heart of

[2] Bowen, *Drawn from Life*, p. 62.

his work. The emotions and conscience of his principal characters are constantly in conflict with the inner lives of others, and all struggle or come face to face with the vestigial standards of training and behavior which govern manners and repress any public expression of emotion.

Of the early novels, *A Call*, an ironic comedy of retribution, best illustrates the conditions and effects of this struggle and frustration. Robert Grimshaw, the protagonist, is a half-Greek, half-English man of wealth whose self-appointed mission is to make out of his best friend— the good, phlegmatic, and totally harmless Dudley Leicester—a responsible manager of his estates, an M. P., and eventually a lesser cabinet minister. He realizes the stalwart, completely British Pauline Lucas is the woman Dudley needs to spur him on, and though he is in love with her himself, he feels that he can marry her to Dudley without suffering the consequences.

" Englishmen haven't any sense of responsibility [Grimshaw says in justifying his attempt to remake Dudley]. Perhaps it's bad for them to have it aroused in them. They can work; they can fight; they can do things; but it's for themselves alone. They're individualists. But there is a class that's got the sense of duty to the whole. They've got a rudimentary sense of it—a tradition, at least, if not a sense. And Leicester comes of that class. But the tradition's dying out. I suppose it was never native to them. It was forced on them because *someone* had to do the public work and it was worth their while. But now that's changing, it isn't worth while. So no doubt Dudley hadn't got it in his blood. . . . And yet I don't know," he said, " he's shaped so well. I would have sworn he had it in him to do it with careful nursing. And Pauline had it in her—the sense of the whole, of the clan, the class, the county and all the rest of it." [3]

[3] *A Call* (London: Chatto and Windus, 1910), p. 179.

Dudley, thoroughly trained in the manner befitting his class, has a mortal fear of gossip, of original ideas, and of the power and sanctity of women. He represents the frightful self-consciousness and inertia which has consumed the traditional governing class. He wants only to satisfy his simple needs. " To him a man was a man, a woman a woman; the leader in a newspaper was a series of convincing facts, of satisfying views, and of final ideals " (p. 46). He had never done anything, except to have a flirtation with Etta Stackpole—now Lady Hudson—and to break with her because she flirted with servants and flaunted the rules of her class. A hypochrondriac afraid of his own shadow, Dudley's most glaring weakness is a blindness to the feelings of others.

> The minute jealousies, the very deep hatreds, and the strong passions that swelled in his particular world of deep idleness, of high feeling, and of want of occupation—in this world where, since no man had need of anything to do, there were so many things to feel—Dudley Leicester perceived absolutely nothing, no complexities, no mixed relationships. (p. 46)

One evening Dudley is forced to escort Etta Stackpole home. While there, he answers the telephone, and the caller recognizes his voice. He panics, fears that all of London, even his valet, will hear of it, and later when he believes Pauline knows the truth, he collapses into speechlessness. Living up to the implicit contract of her arranged marriage, Pauline ascribes his silence to the flu and deep thought, maintains their usual schedule of rides, calls, and visitors, and does nothing to jeopardize his chances for election to parliament. But she reaches the breaking point. In the interview with Grimshaw in which they agree to ask for help from Katya Lascarides, a successful nurse of mental patients who had earlier broken her engagement to Grimshaw because he refused a common-law marriage,[4] Pauline allows herself her one emotional outbreak: " You do not love Katya Lascarides: you are as cold to her as a stone. You love me, and you have ruined all our lives. But it doesn't end, it goes on. We fly as far asunder as the poles, and it goes on for good " (p. 275). Pauline realizes that her not making an outcry or scandal about Dudley is true to her day and class.

" But look at all the difference it's made in our personal relations! Look at the misery of it all! That's it. We can make a day and a class and rules for them, but we can't keep any of the rules except the gross ones like not making scandals."

. . . .

" We haven't learned wisdom: we've only learned how to behave. We cannot avoid tragedies. [. . .]

" Tragedies! Yes, in our day and in our class we don't allow ourselves easygoing things like daggers and poison bowls. It's all more difficult. It's all more difficult because it goes on and goes on. We think we've made it easier because we've slackened the old ties. You're in and out of the house all day long, and I can go around with you everywhere. But just because we have slackened old ties, just because marriage is a weaker thing than it used to be—in our day and in our class "—she repeated the words with deep bitterness and looked unflinchingly into his eyes—" we've strengthened so immensely the other kind of ties. If you'd been married to Miss Lascarides you'd probably not have been faithful to her. As it is, just because your honour's involved you find yourself tied to her as no monk ever was by his vow." (pp. 272-274)

---

[4] When Katya had discovered her parents had never married (her mother had come from a Greek harem and no Greek priest had been available in London at that time), she had refused to marry Grimshaw, for she idolized her mother and wished to imitate her in every way.

Grimshaw finally admits to making the call; he had seen Dudley and Etta together and had suspected the worst. His English training had given away before his passions:

> When he had practically forced Dudley Leicester upon Pauline, he really had believed that you can marry a woman you love to your best friend without enduring all the tortures of jealousy. This sort of marriage of convenience that it was, was, he knew, the sort of thing that in their sort of life was frequent and successful enough, and having been trained in the English code of manners never to express any emotion at all, he had forgotten that he possesed emotions. Now he was up against it. (p. 282)

When Grimshaw realizes the pain and horror resulting from his interference, he cries out that all he wants is the " the peace of God " (p. 260). Subscribing to the maxim, taught him by his mother, " Do what you want and take what you get for it," it takes a Greek Orthodox priest to remind him to add: "And God in His mercy pardon the ill we do " (p. 216). Although he succeeds with the help of Pauline in establishing Dudley, he fails to find the " peace of God " and is forced by weariness and loneliness to submit to Katya, who has meant to have him from the first. Katya's sister tells Grimshaw that Katya has the " determination of a tiger; she has been play-acting from the first, and she has meant to have you since you were in your cradles together. But she's meant to have you humbled and submissive, and tied utterly hand and foot " (pp. 260-261). She also tells him that if he had insisted, Katya would have married him long ago. Now Katya, realizing Pauline and Grimshaw love each other, agrees as an added precaution to marry him. The retribution for his folly and meddling is complete.

This frustration and waste of passion, this dogged maintaining of the smoothly ordered habits of behavior in the face of disaster, and this paralysis of action and speech out of fear of the consequences, all illustrated in *A Call*, define the basis of the collapse of personal relations of the upper ruling classes that Ford saw taking place in the early twentieth century. Manners have become so refined that " it is the height of good manners to have no manners at all." [5] Because the typical Englishman is a man of emotions who " reasons very little," he takes refuge in optimism and " hides from himself the fact that there are in the world greed, poverty, hunger, lust or evil passions, simply because he knows that if he comes to think of them at all they will move him beyond bearing." [6] Even so, one has political, social, and moral views, but they are not to be aired publicly for fear of giving offense to one's neighbor. Life in the best society is a game of " delicacy," the rules of which must be followed.[7] Wise Mr. Blood in *Mr. Fleight* tells Augusta MacPhail:

" You know, Augusta, what you'll have to do is to get an encyclopaedia and go through it carefully, marking out how you may talk about the things that it contains. Thus, in general company you mustn't ever talk about marriage and its problems except in terms of the servants. And you mustn't ever talk about the servants except in terms of the lower classes. And you mustn't ever talk about the lower classes because they're the poor. And you mustn't ever talk about the poor except in terms of the Bazaar at St. Mark's, Kilburn. And you must be very careful about St. Mark's, because St. Mark's has something to do with God, and God you must never mention at all." (pp. 291-292)

[5] *England and the English*, p. 83.
[6] *Ibid.*, pp. 334-335.
[7] *Ibid.*, pp. 336-337.

" We've all got too polite, you see," Mr. Blood had said earlier, " and too kindly and too friendly ever to look anything in the face " (p. 254). The person who is capable of feeling or deep passion is immediately and irrevocably in a frustrating and devastating conflict with the " game," with decorum, and with the preconceived and resolute opinions of the people who count. Another dictum is that private lives must be kept truly private; public exposure not only kills self-respect, it also damages the foundations of established society.

Most of Ford's protagonists are people of feeling who are dedicated to the preservation of established society, or, at least, of the best of it. Robert Grimshaw's desire, for example, is a noble wish to maintain the ruling class traditions through Dudley Leicester, that pale, frightened remnant of the chivalric ideal, but Grimshaw is ignorant of the secrets of the human heart, including his own, and of the terrible toll of meddling with the passions of others. Ford uses many sides of his imaginative lenses in order to discover and disclose in both the past and the present and through a variety of temperaments and actions, or " affairs " as he preferred to call them, the conditions of existence he saw centered in those dilemmas of the individual conscience battling against itself and against society. He discovered the true focus for his picture of life in the trials of the gentleman of honor. His early novels, within the limits of the affairs they represent, generally explore various facets of the theme of honor. From Clement Hollebone in *The Shifting of the Fire* to Sergius Macdonald in *The New Humpty-Dumpty*, several protagonists, different as they are, become progressively more complex and significant workings of what are to become the Ashburnham and Tietjens figures. Here also in the early novels, somewhat pale and remote but yet clear, are the prototypes of Sylvia Tietjens, Leonora Ashburnham, and Valentine Wannop.

The early novels, like those that follow them, offer various portraits of the chivalric ideal. Usually the gentlemen who possess the soul of honor are contrasted with those who do not and with those who fall somewhere between the two extremes. Morton Dauwen Zabel has recognized that Ford was

> never essentially self-deceived. He knew in his own life the risks, ignominy, and treacheries of his period. Whenever he drew on his two soundest resources—his instinct of honor, his generous sense of justice—he wrote out of a saving reserve of character. He could locate and trace the problem of honor in history—the Katherine Howard trilogy or *Ladies Whose Bright Eyes*—and find an original means to define it there. He could define it even better in his own age—in *The Good Soldier* and the Tietjens series.[8]

What sort of a man is Ford's gentleman of honor? Endowed with integrity, compassion, and altruistic desires, he possesses an almost instinctive sense of responsibility to his class, his party, his nation. At the expense of personal misfortune and vilification he stoutly maintains his ideals while his disciplined conscience controls his moral decisions. He is benevolent and so unselfish for personal gain or commendation that he will give his fortune, his house, or the shirt off his back to those he deems worthy. He is self-effacing in public. Because his greatest fear is having to bare his private life or thoughts to the public view, he tries never to make any show of his real emotions or to state his real views on controversial matters. He is a determined but not stodgy defender of the fine

---

[8] "Ford Madox Ford: Yesterday and After," p. 260.

traditions of his class, his party, and his nation, for he realizes they give him the assurance of knowing where he stands when moral decisions face him. He usually devotes his energy to maintaining what has been or is valuable, or beautiful, or kind. His ideal is to discover the art of life, which has been vulgarized by mechanization, opportunism, and the celebration of personal glory. He is generally languid in manner but thoroughly knowledgeable about the matters of his estate or profession; he is just and is confident that heaven on earth is possible. Most significant of all, he bears no malice and never wittingly injures the heart of another. Lady Aldington tells the jealous, vindictive Mr. Pett about Count Macdonald:

> " Count Macdonald never thought an unworthy thought and never did an unworthy action. He is what you and I aren't, and what almost no one is to-day—he is chivalrous! And it is chivalry that I am looking for in the world, and that I should like to reintroduce into the world. I don't know that my affairs will prosper in the hands of this gentleman, but I know that he will never do anything that is against my heart. That is what I should like you to understand. And I really do think that if Count Macdonald puts his mind and his whole soul into any adventure, that adventure will prosper. I think he will never prosper himself, and that is because he is quixotic. But it is a great thing to have in any sort of enterprise a man with a quixotic spirit, if only because it prevents your doing injustices that will set many people against whatever your undertaking may be. [. . .] it is well that you should know that what I think of Count Macdonald is that his ' strength is as the strength of ten because his heart is pure.' " [9]

[9] *The New Humpty-Dumpty* (London and New York: John Lane, 1912), pp. 319-320.

Towards women, in particular, even to those who most injure him, the gentleman of honor shows an almost finicky deference; he is usually willing to make any sacrifice for any woman, because womankind is to be respected and honored at all costs, for women symbolize, if they do not all embody, the ideals of purity, of strength of character, and of devotion which give balance to men's lives and the power for them to see things through.

He is innocent of evil, or, if aware of it, refuses to believe that virtue will not eventually win. When moral anarchy or evil confront him, as they inevitably do, he is hurt and abashed but determined to fight back without hate. He is vulnerable before the forces of petty selfishness, professional hatred, and sexual jealousy. Sooner or later he discovers " the difficulty which sanctifies." [10] He is doomed to some kind of martyrdom by an almost willful drive toward disappointment or failure or destruction. Refusing the world's ways, his goal is not happiness, but serenity; not success, but perfection. In the world as it is, this quixotic child is an outcast and an enemy, if only because he reminds others less conscientious and noble than he that he possesses the virtues they lack. Their envy victimizes him.

Naturally, this type of character evolved in the course of Ford's writings. He seems to have begun with a type and to have ended by the time of *Parade's End* with a symbol. Ford's first published novel, *The Shifting of the Fire* (1892), an almost entirely amateurish work, as one would expect from the pen of a nineteen-year-old, explores the theme of guilt and sacrifice, but only superficially. Clement Hollebone, the hero, is a confused, innocent young man who loves an equally confused, innocent young girl.

---

[10] The quoted phrase is from *The Nature of a Crime* (London: Duckworth, 1924), p. 90.

Each sacrifices needlessly for the other; each misunderstands the other until the story is happily resolved. Unlike George Moffat in *The Benefactor*, Hollebone offers to sacrifice his moral sense for the sake of love when he decides to conceal his conviction, which later proves false, that the heroine had murdered her aged husband whom she had married for his money. In *Romance*, John Kemp, drawn from a long line of romantic heroes, allows his sense of honor to complicate and endanger his life and that of the girl he loves by his gentlemanly refusal to kill his enemies O'Brien and Manuel-del-Populo when he has the opportunities to do so. Everything he does out of the best of motives conspires against him, but he is saved at the last moment by the convenient arrival of friends who clear him of the charges of treason and piracy.

The Benefactor (1905), the second novel written entirely by Ford and the first after his collaboration with Conrad, presents the fullest early portrait of the gentleman of honor. The middle-aged benefactor, George Moffat, is a highly respected poet and writer of small but choice volumes. He is the soul of honor, generosity, and courtesy. He devotes endless hours, stolen from his writing, both to the mad Reverend Brede, in the hope of curing him of a psychotic fixation that he killed his wife, and to his young literary protégés, who ungratefully turn against him once they no longer need him. He is the first protagonist in Ford's gallery whose fatal weakness is his goodness. He is vilified, perjured, bankrupted. Everything he does he does out of the best of motives, and everything turns out badly. Moffat wants particularly to conceal his love for Clara Brede, but he is forced to declare it to her in order to assuage her pain and anger for his not telling her he is bankrupt, has sold his home, and is leaving the country. After Brede collapses into total madness and is hospitalized, Moffat agrees to go away with Clara, but later, feeling guilty for the tragic muddles he has brought about and stricken with an oversensitive concern for the proprieties, he refuses. His marriage to a woman who has left him because she could not bear his senseless generosities does not deter him so much as the realization that such things as running off with a girl whose father you have just put in an asylum are simply not done. Clara, as unlucky as Moffat in achieving what she sets out to do, is destined to be nursemaid, first to her mother and then to her father, and to have life pass her by. She sees her last chance for happiness fade and cries out: " Self-sacrifice. . . . Doesn't that ever end? " They are both sacrificial victims " to that tremendous ghost "—the memory of the man they had loved and brought to a living death.[11] They are equally victims of a graceless society and, one must admit, of their own conscientious meddling. It is a measure of Ford's cynicism that those who live for others or for a noble cause (in Moffat's case the continuation of the kingdom of letters) are doomed to failure.

Ford's handling of the international theme in *An English Girl* is suggestive of James, but it nonetheless reflects his growing concern with a specialized subject matter.[12] Don Kelleg, though thoroughly American in his confidence in the future and in his energetic quest for new, idealistic worlds, is an extension of the earlier protagonists into a savior of mankind. He is ambitious to do nothing less than to combat American political corruption by using his millions to counterbalance those other millions yearly spent in graft.[13] To do this he sacrifices the woman he

---

[11] *The Benefactor* (London: Brown, Langham, 1905), pp. 347 and 349.

[12] The book cover and title page of the first edition (London: Methuen, 1907) reads *An English Girl*. However, on page one and on all of the following even-numbered pages, the title is written as *The English Girl*.

[13] Jimmy Kasker-Ryves in *The Shifting of the Fire* is similar to Kelleg in

loves, who keeps her allegiance to her British tradition and established standards.

While working on *The Benefactor* and *An English Girl*, Ford was writing his Katherine Howard trilogy (1906-1908). A saint and a savior, Katherine Howard is perhaps the first major character in Ford's fiction for whom the reader can feel a wholly deep sympathy and compassion. She lacks that excess of quixoticism which opens Moffat and Kelleg to the charge of being ridiculous.[14] Katherine is a splendidly realized portrait of a woman of spirit who fights nobly for a lost but distinguished cause.

Her single purpose is to restore Catholicism to England. She is opposed by all of the ministers of state and Church and ultimately by King Henry himself. She alienates them all, except Henry, because she is a woman of conscience, of transcendent passion for her cause, a woman who will not use immoral or selfish means to achieve her generous and moral ends. She is a fifteenth-century Christopher Tietjens; like him she is civilized, in emotions as well as deeds; she is naive about the evil of the world and the men in it; she is motivated by an overwrought sense of duty; and like Tietjens she is brought to her ruin by the worldly, selfish connivings of others. Unlike Throckmorton, the vacillating spy, she fails to understand that to win in the world one has to use the tools the world offers. She is the Christian gentlewoman fighting for the order and serenity of the past. In a very real sense, she is incapable of wholeheartedly loving any man. She is indulgently fond of her drunken cousin and suitor Culpepper,

---

that he is also determined to right the wrongs of his wealthy industrialist father. For a revealing treatment of the influence of James in *An English Girl* and of Don Kelleg as an early prototype of Tietjens, see Richard W. Lid, "Tietjens in Disguise," *The Kenyon Review*, XXII (Spring, 1960), 265-276.

[14] That the impression of ridicule is slyly intentional on Ford's part makes little difference in the final effect of these earlier novels.

and she has a sincere affection for Henry, but her real love is the Church and the salvation she sees in its restitution.

Sergius Macdonald in *The New Humpty-Dumpty* is a somewhat different case. His cause is more remote, more nebulous, and he is capable of love. Educated to the English code of schoolboy honor, which he takes seriously, he searches out causes which he feels offer opportunities to put the code into action: anarchism, socialism, and finally the New Toryism of the defected Fabian Mr. Pett, who reverses the Fabian formula (as Ford saw it) by proposing that the lower classes should be brought up to the standards of the best of the upper classes. Years earlier Macdonald had turned over his fortune to Pett, who subsequently had become the intellectual leader of the New Toryism but had remained the essential shopkeeper he was in his pettiness (hence his name) and malicious jealousy. Macdonald's immediate adventure is to engineer the restoration of the somewhat shabby though benevolent monarchy of Galizia, a Mediterranean country recently taken over by an impoverished, unimaginative, mostly corrupt republican council. Macdonald is less interested in Galizia than he is in regaining for the world a little of the lost humanity and charm of the past which a benevolent monarchy by its very nature seems to possess.[15] Like Ford's other gentlemen of honor, he is beset by the selfish envy and cruelty of others, but his principal antagonist is the mentality of the British shopkeeping class. Pett had emulated the natural chivalric virtues he saw in Macdonald and in Lady Aldington and had projected them into a social philosophy. But in a fit of jealousy over

---

[15] " It wasn't the mere setting up again in a ridiculous little republic of a ridiculous little monarchy; it was a question of proving to the world that certain things were good, and that there was enough to go round." (p. 123)

Lady Aldington's refusal of his advances and over her growing affection for Macdonald he says to a couple of Galizians that Macdonald should be murdered; they, like the assassins of Thomas á Becket, take the wish for a command, and another martyr is added to the English roster.[16]

But Macdonald's greatest trial is his wife. A daughter of a London shopkeeper and an ardent Socialist, the Countess is the first thorough and ravenous bitch in Ford's fiction.[17] She is driven by a wanton and reckless sexual anger against the almost inhuman virtues of her husband. Like Katya Lascarides, she wants her man body and soul; he must have no other consuming attachments, either physical or idealogical. After Macdonald leaves her, she persecutes him mercilessly trying to get him back. " If I don't get him," she says, " I'll ruin him body and soul. [. . .] I've got ways to do it. And then when he's beggared he'll come back to me " (p. 215). She finally drives him to divorce. Being the only one of Ford's men of honor to divorce his wife, Macdonald is used by Ford to criticize the inhumanity of the British divorce laws, which require evidence of adultery before a decree is granted.[18] The Countess' final desperate action is to appear in Galizia on the day of the successful revolution armed with vitriol and a pistol. She first meets Pett, who has repented of

[16] Ford uses the reference to Becket on p. 340.

[17] Katya Lascarides in *A Call* and the heroines of the farces *The Portrait* and *The Panel* are designing women who use all of the female guiles and subterfuges to capture their men, but they are more or less stereotyped figures of romantic comedies of pursuit. The Lady Blanche in *Ladies Whose Bright Eyes* is more viciously cunning and savage, but she resembles more a fairy tale witch, for her motivation is primarily sexless. The White Lady in *The Young Lovell* and Anne Jeal in *The 'Half-Moon'* are in fact witches, drawn respectively from medieval legend and the superstitious tales of the seventeenth century.

[18] Macdonald, being a Russian citizen, actually gets an ukase from the Czar dissolving the marriage.

his calumnies and realizes now that Macdonald is a better man than he or the Countess. He tells her:

> " That's what you are, a product of tradespeople. The difference between you and gentlefolk like Macdonald—Good God!—the difference between both you and me and him is that we haven't got a spark of generosity in us. We've both conspired to injure that fine gentleman mortally. I'm ready to say that I'm Judas. But I'm ready to say too that all you've ever thought of in your life is the forty pieces of silver, of your own dirty personal vanity. We aren't either of us fit to loosen the shoe latchets of Sergius Mihailovitch. That's how the world has always been. That is how it will always be. If you manage to get your vitriol on to him, he'll still be fifty thousand fathoms above the heads of you and me. We're the lower classes, that's what we are, because we haven't got in the whole of our compositions a spark of generosity." (p. 427)

When the news of Macdonald's assassination is brought to them, the Countess cries for joy as Pett falls into a moaning fit of remorse.

The Countess Macdonald is in part a symbolic vehicle for Ford's criticism of the inhumanity and savagery he found in the lower shopkeeping classes and among Socialists. She is a symbol not only of her class but also of the predatory sexual drive for the total submission of the male, especially of the superior male whose self-sufficiency and rigid devotion to an ideal is galling. She is in effect a synthesis of the social and sexual lawlessness destroying the traditional humanities, and she is Ford's first literary representation of his awareness of the importance of sexual possessiveness in determining the destinies of public and private life. The Countess uses unlimited means to project her sexual hunger: lies, slander, meddling —all frantic and irrational but deliberately designed to destroy the male's worthy image of himself. Macdonald brings himself to expect anything from her, but remains baffled by her immorality. There is nothing by which he can measure her actions; " she seemed to be perpetually breaking out in a new place " (p. 304). Not a very convincing character because her malignity is too black and unrelieved and because her motives are too simple, the Countess is nevertheless the most interesting, deeply felt, and fully drawn precursor of Sylvia Tietjens.

Ford's ideal woman, at the opposite extreme, is an embodiment of sexual wisdom and tact. This early model of Valentine Wannop is intelligent and possesses a steady and unselfish devotion to the heart and spirit of the man she loves. She is capable of supporting his idealism, his vagaries, his scruples, and of distinguishing between his public and private lives. She will support his cause and protect him from his enemies, but she will never endanger his public reputation or violate his integrity. Willing to defy convention for the sake of his love, she is often doomed to suffer. Of the early women of this type, only Dionissia in *Ladies Whose Bright Eyes* is happy at the end of the book, but she marries the " reformed " Sorrell, who, though an honorable man, was not to the manor born. Clara Brede, who is prepared to live with a married man, has to give in to the moral claims of Moffat's more sensitive conscience. The stupid and unnecessary death of Macdonald on the day of their marriage destroys Lady Aldington's chances for happiness.

A third type of woman begins to emerge, best represented in the early novels by Pauline Leicester in *A Call*. An efficient manager of the proprieties, a custodian of the outward, superficial appearances, she defends the illusion before the world of a smoothly ordered, contented upper class home. Lady Aldington before her divorce had taken to managing the affairs of her listless husband; Margaret in *The Young Lovell* energetically labored to regain the usurped lands of her betrothed lover. But these women merely suggest and do not define the type which is to be fully realized and explored in the relentless Leonora Ashburnham of *The Good Soldier*, who herself has certain affinities with Sylvia Tietjens.

Ford's traditional opposition in his medieval legends between the witch and the fair lady is carried over to his contemporary stories in the contrasting temperaments of the predatory and the compassionate, or ideal, woman.[19] It is not until the hero is bound by engagement or marriage to the predatory woman that he meets the fair lady and desires her. The struggle to rid himself of the one to gain the other precipitates a crisis within his conscience which parallels and complements his struggle against moral decadence, selfishness, and inhumanity. The women, like the contemporary issues surrounding the hero, take sides, so to speak, and in doing so signify the limits of the hero's conflicts. The issues, like the women, are simplified and slightly exaggerated in the manner of medieval lore, but the crisis is less in terms of good against evil than it is in terms of the worthy against the unworthy.

2

After examining his early novels and the books which supplement them, how else can we see Ford except as an

[19] Examples of the witch and the fair lady in the early novels are Anne Jeal and Magdalena Koop in *The ' Half-Moon '*; The White Lady and the Lady Margaret in *The Young Lovell*; Lady Blanche and Dionissia in *Ladies Whose Bright Eyes*; Katya Lascarides and Pauline Leicester in *A Call*; Countess Macdonald and Lady Aldington in *The New Humpty-Dumpty*. A remotely similar contrast is apparent between Kate Hallbyne and Edith Ryland in *The Shifting of the Fire*, although Kate is more mercenary than predatory.

incurable romanticist and idealist who has pledged himself to a rigorous realistic method? His fairy tales, historical romances, fantasies, and adaptations of old legends attest to the strong romantic strain in his nature. In spite of his distaste for the preaching of his Victorian forebears, he had a sermon, a gospel, to preach, which in its antagonism to the Philistines was a familiar one indeed. He often turned to irony, satire, parable, and allegory. The steadfast and heightened conscience of his gentleman of honor, the martyr-savior, is pitted against some dragon of society—socialism, or corrupt politics, or selfish opportunism, or moral anarchy. Committed to the aesthetic prescriptions of the French Realists, of Turgenev, James, and Conrad, Ford sought to convey his message in ways similar to theirs by seducing the reader through sheer literary skill into an emotional and moral involvement without the direct intrusion of the preaching author.

In his curious first novel, *The Shifting of the Fire*, he goes in all directions at once. Essentially it is a sentimental melodrama of guilt and sacrifice developing the theme that love needs sacrifice and adversity before it is genuine. Throughout there are feeble attempts to counteract the sentimental excesses. At one point, after an interview between the hero and the heroine's *confidante*, some ravens sitting in a nearby tree comment ironically on the odd morality of the *confidante's* notions about betrayal and honor. There are so many chatty, patronizing, authorial intrusions and apologies about the innocence of young girls, and the rapacity of old men falling in love with them, and the like, that the reader soon is aware the book is also a satire on the Victorian novel, an impression which is later verified by some direct references.[20] Also

---

[20] " Now, as a nineteenth century author is bound to know everything, from the management of the stops of an organ to the slaying of a pig, there is little

a social comedy remarking upon the trials of innocence in an unseeing, unsympathetic society, the novel is a confusion of models and tones. The young author fails in trying to handle the essentially serious themes of sacrificial love and guilt within a threefold context of ironic social comedy, melodrama, and literary satire. He merely succeeds in belittling everything—his characters, their story, the theme. Perhaps the novel's most telling weakness is the faltering attempt of youth to write detachedly of youth by seeing the action as though through the disillusioned and sentimental eyes of a man of experience, who is the sometimes unseen, but too often seen, narrator.

Ford probably realized after his amateur confusions in *The Shifting of the Fire* that he needed some control over his romantic and idealistic excesses. Writing every day of his life, publishing two or three books almost every year, constantly strained by personal worries, often in need of immediate funds, Ford wrote hurriedly, sometimes without conviction, and too often without attention to the details of his craft. Even so, he continuously sought out and ultimately found the control he needed in the elaborate, individualized technique characteristic of his later novels. For, if Graham Greene is right, a true artist recognizes his inadequacies and in trying to overcome them creates a technique.[21] The difference between Ford's first novel and *The Benefactor*, written after the collaboration with Conrad, is that between lawlessness and discipline, between trying everything and trying only what he can do best. Showing remarkable restraint, *The Benefactor* seems to have been inspired by Turgenev's *A House of Gentle-*

wonder that the young Mr. Ryves, in his capacity as author, had an intimate acquaintance with the remedies best in an emergency for a slight attack of apoplexy." *The Shifting of the Fire* (London: Unwin, 1892), p. 215.

[21] " Dark Backward: A Footnote," *London Mercury*, xxxii (October, 1935), 562.

folk. Ford admired this above all of Turgenev's novels for its " rendering of pain rendered hopeless, of desire intense but self-frustrated on account of ethical scruples, of self-immolation, of eternal regret." [22] Ford, on one level, in *The Benefactor,* is trying to achieve these very effects: he is writing a tale of an impossible passionate attachment between an older married man and a young girl, but because he focuses on the man of honor he places the final renunciation with the man instead of the girl. Although lacking the enlightening subtlety of Turgenev, and weakened by an overcontrived series of coincidences in an attempt to give an impression of inevitability, *The Benefactor* is economically constructed and artfully written. In its sensitiveness to moral and social distinctions and in its close attention to the nuances of dialogue, it suggests James as much as it does Turgenev. Perhaps only in its visual impressionism does it show Conrad's influence.

The search for *le mot juste,* the proper cadence, a new form, which consumed the attentions of Conrad and Ford, resulted during their collaboration in a political allegory (mostly by Ford), a historical romance (originally Ford's story), and an ironic tale of a comic deception (also mostly by Ford). Perhaps Ford more than Conrad took the opportunity to experiment with ways to catch fleeting impressions. According to Ford's own testimony, it was Conrad who added the detailed observations which gave substance to their prose and to the overvague, romanticized expression of fine shades Ford sought to express.[23] Later, Ford, working on his own in various romantic

---

[22] *Thus to Revisit,* p. 99. Ford is also thinking here of *Under Western Eyes:* " But whereas, in the work of the ' beautiful genius ' of Russia, the passion is the thing that wrecks the lives of both Lisa and Lavretsky, in the work of our very great poet the lives are wrecked by the concrete material surroundings. . . ."

[23] See the "Appendix " to *The Nature of a Crime,* pp. 106-107.

genres, in contemporary comedies of manners, and in novels analyzing politics and society, developed a variety of techniques to render his gospel and to contain his vision of life.

Using similar techniques in all the types of his early fiction, Ford experimented with presenting his stories in impressionistic renderings through dramatic presentation of key scenes. He found early the value of authorial detachment, perhaps inspired by his admiration for Turgenev and James. Graham Greene rightly charges that " Mr. Ford is unable to write narrative; he is conscious of his inability to write, as it were, along the line of time." [24] Greene sees Ford's adoption of the time-shift as the ultimate answer to his inadequacies in writing narrative, but before Ford perfected that complex device he capitalized upon his ability to handle scenes and the transitions between them with a minimum of interference from the meddling author. The simplest and best way he found for treating scenes was to plunge the reader into the middle and to record in *mots justes* and careful cadences and by properly selected details the atmosphere of the scene as filtered through the consciousness of one or several characters or of the observant author-narrator. The time-shift, of course, can evolve naturally from the rendering of a consciousness, but Ford's first attempts were merely to find ways to give verisimilitude to the affairs he was recounting. Usually he avoided the single point of view by using more than one center of consciousness and often by having one view contradict the others or penetrate more deeply. At his best, he achieved a heightened sense of reality which could give credibility to the struggles of his somewhat over-idealized characters.

[24] " Dark Backward," p. 564.

The Katherine Howard trilogy is probably Ford's first totally successful attempt to fuse a romantic, idealized character with a realistic method. Because in this novel (the three are in effect a single novel) he showed his mastery of scene, it is a good one from which to take an example of Ford's early scenic technique. No one scene demonstrates every device at Ford's command, but the first one in *The Fifth Queen Crowned*, the third of the series, is illustrative.[25]

King Henry is discussing with Archbishop Cranmer and later with the Archbishop's spy Lascelles the writing of his letter of contrition to Rome, which he has promised Katherine Howard, now his Queen, to send. This is Henry's scene, but like every scene in the trilogy it points to or embellishes the story of Katherine Howard. Henry is torn between his new-found happiness in his love for Katherine and the sting to his vanity of having to write such a letter, although he is aware he is getting old and needs to "redd up" his house. He begins by taunting the Archbishop with the fact that if the Pope accepts the petition, the Archbishop will be a heretic and no longer the King's servant. Henry then notes the shabbiness of the proud Archbishop's quarters in the basement of Pontrefact Castle where the court is now staying. After more of Henry's mocking of Cranmer for putting on a crucifix and hair shirt and acquiring monkish ways to court the favor of the new Catholic Queen, Lascelles, the "blonde fox," enters and upon Henry's order kneels down at a low desk to copy the letter Henry will dictate. Henry begins by reciting his titles and using high-flown language, then changes to simple, humble phrases confessing his sin of pride. But he gives up in indecision and brooding discom-

---

[25] *The Fifth Queen Crowned* (London: Nash, 1908), pp. 1-13. All references are from these pages unless otherwise noted.

fort and leaves, saying he will send " a letter much more good from the upper rooms." Lascelles realizes the Queen will write the letter.

The scene is divided into three envelopes of action, each set off by extra spacing between paragraphs. The first begins with an unfinished statement by Cranmer taken from the middle of the scene. The action is taken up from there until page five, the conclusion of the first envelope, when Ford mentions that Henry had entered Cranmer's chambers saying, " Make you ready to write a letter tơ Rome." The second section begins by picking up dialogue suspended before the end of the first, introduces Lascelles, and ends with Henry leaving. The third, less than half a page long, shows Cranmer and Lascelles reacting to their realization of the Queen's power. " Then their eyes met. The one glance, panic-stricken, seeing no issue, hopeless and without resource, met the other— crafty, alert, fox-like, with a dance in it." Note the preciosity of the syntax and the word " dance," le mot juste with its slight and perhaps slyly intentional suggestion of triteness. The scene has successfully dramatized Henry's indecisiveness, which is going to lead him to postpone the letter time and again, and Lascelles' latent treachery, prefiguring his crafty lying and spying which will help bring Katherine to her doom.

Except for two or three glimpses into Henry's thoughts and one retrospective glance into Cranmer's consciousness, most of the action is seen from the outside as though by a sensitive observer, the unseen narrator, who draws the reader's attention to the facial expressions, the glances, the hands of the actors. Especially the hands. With studied artfulness, the narrator, like a roving camera, focuses upon the hands, upon Henry's swollen fingers nervously tapping the table or his hand striking it or pulling at his collar.

And upon Cranmer's opening his thin hands " as if he were letting something fall to the ground," fingering his crucifix, or at the end, as Henry leaves, suddenly stretching out, " with a timid pitifulness, his white hands." The dialogue is vivid, and because this is a scene where long speeches are unnecessary, Ford does not use the device he often employed of rendering lengthy speeches by both direct and indirect quotation.[26] The effect of the whole scene is almost cinematic in its close-ups of telling movements and details, and in its rendering of dialogue. The method is dramatic, the impression primarily visual.

There is the quality of music, too, in the careful varied cadences, from Cranmer's first incomplete statement, " The Bishop of Rome—," introducing the topic of the whole chapter, through Henry's shifts between sardonic humor, anger, pride, despair, and frustration, to the last view (also as though seen through a film camera), of Henry at the end of the second envelope: " He pulled the heavy door to with such a vast force that the latch came again out of the hasp, and the door, falling slowly back and quivering as if with passion, showed them his huge legs mounting the little staircase." The final envelope is both a coda of the whole chapter and a presentiment of the future. The main actor has left the stage; the two who remain give the scene another ironic dimension by their implied commentary on what has taken place and by the subtle suggestion of their evil intent. The last two sen-

[26] Ford uses this device periodically in the trilogy; for example: " ' I am, in short, no stoic,' he [Udall] said, ' the stoics being ancient curmudgeons that were low-stomached.' Now, he continued, the Old Faith he loved well, but not over well; the Protestants he called busy knaves, but the New Learning he loved beyond life. Cromwell thwacked the Old Faith; he loved him not for that. Cromwell upheld in a sort the Protestants; he little loved him for that. ' But the New Learning he loveth, and, oh fair sharer of my dream o'nights, Cromwell holdeth the strings of the money-bags.' " *Privy Seal* (London: Alston Rivers, 1907), p. 44.

tences, a short cadence followed by a long one, add the final tap. " The glances transfused and mingled. Lascelles remained upon his knees as if, stretching out his right knee behind him, he were taking a long rest." The long, langorous cadence, as well as the picture formed, perfectly describe Lascelles, the cunning fox who is to be Katherine's craftiest antagonist.

The novel is a progression of such skillfully contrived scenes, each one in itself dramatizing contrasts in characters and motivations, emphasizing shades and shadows, showing the effects of one character upon another (by action and speech, not exposition), and visualizing highly selected details which create a full picture. And each chapter somehow contrasts or comments on the one preceding it until the colorful, almost sensational, tapestry is complete. The novel is constructed upon a series of oppositions: of low against high life, of comic against serious; of intrigue against intrigue, of character against character, and ultimately of Katherine against everyone. By the contrarieties in representation and story Ford gives us remarkably rich impressions of the times and of the issues involved. At the same time, by his rigorous method of selection and arrangement, the effect is one of surprising simplicity and clarity. Conrad was moved to write to Galsworthy that " Ford's last *Fifth Queen* novel is amazing. The whole cycle is a noble conception—the swan song of Historical Romance—and frankly I am glad to have heard it." [27] Ford himself later noted that his early novels before *The Good Soldier* were mere *pastiches*, or *tours des force*, or fakes " more or less genuine in inspiration and workmanship." [28] This seems a remarkably astute observa-

---

[27] In a letter dated February 20, 1908. G. Jean-Aubry, *The Life and Letters of Joseph Conrad* (Garden City, N.Y.: Doubleday, 1927), II, 67.

[28] *Joseph Conrad*, pp. 175-176. In *The March of Literature*, p. 666, he charges that historical novels are usually " atmospheres more or less specious."

tion, for the trilogy, however brilliant, is a mere *pastiche*. At the same time, in its attention to the scenic art it is the most carefully wrought of the early works.

Almost always the tools of his craft are perfectly under Ford's control. He shows here that if he wishes, he can do anything he wants to with a scene, that he is a master at creating atmospheres and at arranging them in a complex, though here fairly close, chronological sequence. Probably the novel is too elaborately done for some tastes. There are inadequacies. The low comedy scenes of Margot Poins and her brother, of Udall and the Widow Amnot, though deftly visualized and excellent in themselves, acquire an importance they do not fully warrant. It is possible to become surfeited with the profusion of sensual impressions or to become annoyed with the indirect, drawn out, slow revelation of scenes, somewhat overembellished in order to complete the rhythmical pattern or to intensify every shade of the intended impression. Nevertheless, it is technically the best work Ford produced before he wrote *The Good Soldier*, though it is not necessarily his most interesting and provocative one. He achieves a moving portrait of a figure who is both a savior and martyr and does it according to the theoretical requirements of his technique, here inspired mostly by Conrad's charge to the writer to make us hear, feel, and see. He manages to subdue the more obvious allegory of such novels as *An English Girl* and *Mr. Apollo*, written during the same period, or of his later *The New Humpty-Dumpty*. The novel's finest success in realistic technique is that Ford is not directly apparent at all; Ford as narrator has managed to achieve a kind of double distance, by never blocking the view between the reader and his characters.

3

Techniques used to create individual scenes are reflected in formal techniques Ford employed throughout a novel. Characteristically, the novels are divided into parts; usually each part, whether titled or not, completes one segment of the action and prepares for the following one.[29] As the divisions or envelopes are to the scene, so are the parts of the novel to the novel as a whole. And as the complete novel is an exhaustion of an affair, so is each part an exhaustion of one stage of that affair. This observation is best illustrated in the early novels by the employment of the time-shift only within scenes or sections of the novels. Cross references between sections are kept to a minimum necessary for clear narrative.

In the light of his later novels and of his account of the collaboration, Ford's handling of time in his early novels seems conservative, although he often on a small scale and for special purposes dislocates time. One of his favorite devices is to plunge into the midst of a scene, advance it a bit, work back to the beginning, and then return where he left off, as in the scene from *The Fifth Queen Crowned* outlined above. The same scene also illustrates his practice of beginning with an unexplained remark or quotation, then interrupting it or continuing the scene until he later returns and explains it. A variation of this jumbling is sometimes used when a substantial length of

---

[29] Several early novels have titled sections, which are either mere guides to the action, as in *The 'Half-Moon'* ("Out of Rye Royal," "Going Abroad," "Towards the Poles," "The 'Half-Moon'") or are metaphorical glosses on the action, as in *The Benefactor*, where the titles sustain the metaphor of the hero as a jeweller ("The Jeweller and His Stones," "The Golden Circle," "The Blackening Pearls," "The Bankrupt Jeweller"). Customarily the sections end ironically or set the stage for an ironic turnabout.

time has passed between chapters or parts; he will begin a new scene, announce the time that has passed, interrupt it to recapitulate important intervening action in complete scenes or by a narrative summary, and then return to the point where he left us.[30] Occasionally, as in the story of Lovell, who has been bewitched for three months, he will use messengers to bring the hero up to date. Sometimes Ford works carefully toward a climactic scene, interrupts just before it is to start in order to present concurrent action, and then renders it.[31]

The values of the time-shift and of representing action

---

[30] This method was first used in *The Benefactor*. Mr. Richard W. Lid in his unpublished dissertation on Ford's handling of the time-shift (University of Michigan, August, 1958) proves that it was in this novel that Ford first employed the time-shift contained within an envelope. It covers pages 187 to 219, starting with Moffat and Clara Brede walking along the beach and then returning to present in scenes the events of the intervening three months since the marriage of Dora Brede and Thwaite, and ending by picking up the scene and the dialogue where it had been interrupted.

By the time of *Mr. Fleight* (1913) the method is extended, there being a major flashback within each of the three parts, and each flashback being preceded by a jump ahead to an important stage in the fortunes of Mr. Fleight. A variation of this is used in *The New Humpty-Dumpty*, in which Part III ends with the financial arrangements for the counter-revolution with the world's greatest financier Hodges P. Mordaunt (J. P. Morgan?), and Part IV begins with Macdonald and Lady Aldington on a yacht in the harbor of the Galizian capital. The rest of this part recapitulates the action from the end of Part III up to a crucial point shortly before the departure for Galizia. Part V begins again on the boat in the harbor, finishes rendering the events until the time of departure, and then returns to the harbor and begins the sequence of final scenes.

[31] *The Young Lovell* offers another good example. After Lovell returns from his first period of enchantment by the White Lady, everything points to his meeting with the Princess Rohtraut of Croy, his grandmother, who will help him retake his lands. The Princess is holding court at the bishop's palace in Durham where there is talk of Lovell's disappearance and rumored bewitchment; then Lovell's voice is heard on the stairs as the chapter ends. The next chapter is an interview between the Bishop of Durham and Lovell's friend, the monk Francis, wherein the Bishop agrees to pardon Lovell of the charge of sorcery. The next chapter then shows Lovell appearing before the Princess in his own suit of armor, which had been sold by the usurpers. There is a flashback of eight pages to explain how he came by it before the scene with the Princess actually begins.

primarily by scenes and gatherings of scenes into segments or parts of the story seem to have become more apparent to Ford as he continued to write. These narrative methods are means to arouse interest, to achieve compactness and surprise, and to establish, usually with an ironic intention, contrasts in actions, settings, characters, and motivations. The primary time-shift device in the early novels is the flashback, which is peculiarly appropriate to plots of discovery or revelation, as writers of the detective story have realized. Its use places the emphasis on why and how things happen rather than on the events themselves, on "moral tensions," as Joseph Warren Beach says, rather than on suspense.[32] Dealing almost invariably as he does with plots which are designed to reveal the plights of the gentleman of honor, or conversely of the moral delinquent, such as Etchingham Granger in *The Inheritors*, or Grimshaw in *A Call*, Ford required methods which would subordinate action to motivation and stress the conflicts of motivation set against motivation.[33] The best way he found to do this was to make artful rearrangements in the chronology of his fictional affairs.

In *Mr. Fleight*, for example, Ford contrives his tale to reveal the not altogether admirable encroachment of the monied Jew into British politics, which the tired feudalists, like Fleight's mentor, Mr. Blood, had almost abandoned.[34]

---

[32] *The Twentieth Century Novel* (New York: Appleton-Century-Crofts, 1932), p. 129.

[33] This is true, except for the farces, where the emphasis is on action, usually of the revelation of withheld information.

[34] Ford saw the Jew as a foreign influence in British politics and life and as a power behind the commercial interests which were destroying the old order. Reginald Blood says to Augusta Macphail in *Mr. Fleight*: " The appearance of the Jew in our society means that the Jew is an unrivalled soldier of fortune. He isn't part of our country; he hasn't got our morality, but he's extraordinarily able as a ruler. So our side [the Tories] takes him up and uses him. It doesn't matter to him which side he's on, because he can't begin

Ford also wishes to illustrate that when the usual nefarious political practices do not ruin a candidate, scandal can. The novel is divided into three parts, and each includes a major flashback detailing the events of Fleight's relationship to the shopgirl Gilda Leroy who involves him in a personal scandal which nearly precipitates his failure. Each flashback performs the useful function of marking a critical event in the scandal and of establishing the probability that Fleight's campaign will fail. But the logical structure of the plot collapses at the end, for it is only by a kind of *deus ex machina*, the death of Fleight's opponent on election day morning, that he wins the election. The flashbacks, along with clever handling of concurrent action, also help to intensify contrasting areas of the political scene and to juxtapose the personalities of the three women with whom Fleight is involved: the simple Gilda; his avaricious Cockney mistress who poses as a baroness; and the determined, ambitious, masculine, mostly German woman who marries him with the sole determination to make him the lesser cabinet minister he feels he should be. The novel offers a varied, interesting picture of English political and literary life at the beginning of the century.[35] Edgar Jepson thought that it

to understand our problems or our ethics or our morality or our way of looking at things." (p. 213)

[35] The picture ranges all the way from the omniscient Mr. Blood's superior cynicism to Fleight's political innocence. Placed between these and off-setting them are brief portraits of such types as the idealistic generalizer (the Chancellor of the Exchequer), the "new democrat," who is a mere parrot of second-hand ideas which bolster his middle class ego (a post-office clerk), a Dickensian poor man of leisure who wants only to be left alone by do-gooders in the government (Mr. Leroy), a political parasite (Mr. Garstein, who sells the candidacy to Fleight), some scatterbrained Soho intellectuals, and the true chivalric gentleman of the traditional ruling gentry (Reginald Blood). The novel also manages to include satirical sections on the Bohemian intellectuals of Soho, on shopgirl mentality (represented by Gilda Leroy), and on contemporary legal and judicial procedures.

and *The New Humpty-Dumpty* were " the best presenta-
tions of polite and cultured London at the end of the
Edwardian Age." [36]

From the time of *The Benefactor*, Ford maintained—
though not consistently—the detachment of the omniscient narrator. At least in his narrative manner he maintained this detachment, although as is apparent to any of
his readers, his novels are often burdened with digressions
which hinder the advance of the story while they offer
him a kind of podium from which to develop his ideas.
But at their best even the digressions are rendered rather
than stated. The point to make here is that Ford as
author-narrator almost from the first assumes a definite
character of his own which he imposes on his stories.
When he is careful, Ford renders his narrative in scenes
and by expository summaries, both more often than not
through the eyes of one or more of his characters, but
sometimes through those of the author-narrator or the
objective reporter. And yet Ford's personality is evident
everywhere. By the actions of his characters, by the
motivations he ascribes to them, often by the extreme skill
and brilliance—or sheer carelessness—of his craftsmanship,
the reader's thoughts are constantly being directed toward
the storyteller and his view of the affair. The narrator is
essentially a sentimentalist imbued with both a godlike
contempt and regret for his creations. Like the ravens in
The Shifting of the Fire, he sits above and to the side
of his characters, never failing to comment on the tragi-
comic ironies or the pathos inherent in their predicaments.
Ford once chastized Galsworthy for not having for his
characters " enough contempt, enough of the *saeva indignatio* " and for not heeding Turgenev's lesson to be sym-

---

[36] Jepson, *Memoirs of an Edwardian*, p. 134.

pathetic and yet "infinitely above" his characters. One character is not much better than another, one is "just as futile, just as human, deserve[s] spitting on just as much" as another. "Yes, spit at them sometimes . . ." Ford concludes. "Put more shadow into it; there *is* more shadow. One's fellow creatures are despicable as well as pathetic. . . ." [37]

Ford himself in his novels seems to say that although it is sad and sometimes maddening that man is a wolf to his fellow man and that most people are "merely the stuff to fill graveyards," there does appear to be some hope that "all humanity, if you could understand them, if you could get at them in the right way," are at least as chivalrous as the gentleman of honor.[38] But it is apparent Ford feels both *saeva indignatio* and regret even for his chivalric protagonists. One can seldom say that he totally admires them. Men like George Moffat, Don Kelleg, Count Macdonald are often so out of tune with their times, are sometimes so close to being stubborn fools and guileless meddlers, that one wonders if Ford does not see his own message as fool's talk. It is not quite this, of course, for Ford's irony is patterned after that of Cervantes, and his composite hero is a twentieth-century Don Quixote.

In *Mr. Fleight*, to return to a fairly typical example, Ford as narrator assumes the interested detachment of one who knows these people well and who has been an observant spectator of the whole affair. A few scenes or parts of scenes are seen through the eyes of a single character, but mostly they are reported with occasional omniscient glimpses into a consciousness by a storyteller who is

[37] H. V. Marrot, *The Life and Letters of John Galsworthy* (London: Heinemann, 1935), p. 123.
[38] *The New Humpty-Dumpty*, pp. 303-304.

intimate with the past, the customary opinions, and the gossip about his characters.[39] The biographies of major and near-major characters, the " getting in " of which so concerned Ford, are managed either through dialogue (as with Fleight's background), or by interrupting the story for a few pages after the character has been introduced (as with Augusta Macphail, who is to become Mrs. Fleight, or as with Parment, the Chancellor of the Exchequer), somewhat in the manner of Turgenev, who in *A House of Gentlefolk*, for example, gives one chapter to Liza's biography and several to Lavretsky's. These biographical intrusions state characteristic thoughts and attitudes of the characters, but again more often than not resemble insights of a perceptive close friend. Satirical passages are handled either dramatically or by an ironically tinged narrative summary reminiscent of Dickens.[40] Occasionally the author-narrator makes comments like a cynical Olympian who in his world view can give a more proper ironic perspective to human affairs. The attack on Fleight by the neighborhood youths is reported (" They had given him no particular explanation. They just hit him while they shouted. They struck him in the face with their fists."). But an explanation follows:

There was nothing personal about that cleansing of their neighbourhood: they none of them had any admiration for Miss Leroy, who appeared to them a mean-spirited sort of

[39] See, for instance, the second paragraph of the first chapter of *Mr. Fleight*, p. 1. Mr. Blood is sitting in the What Not Club. " It was not a good club; its membership conveyed no social prestige. Mr. Blood took no active part in the affairs of the world. That he was a nonsensical Radical amused his friends, since he was a large landowner; that he had a violent character gave him a certain distinctness. He was said to have strangled a groom at Newport, Rhode Island, where, presumably, grooms are cheap."

[40] See especially Ford's treatment of the trial of the youths who had attacked Fleight (pp. 262-266), or the publication party (pp. 281-287).

young female. They had, in short, just done their manly
duties, acting like lynchers of the United States, the fo-
menters of pogroms in Russia, or like the Wehmgericht of
mediaeval Germany, which acted in the dark when the
public authorities did not perform their functions. And they
knew that they had as worthily upheld the traditions of
their neighbourhood as could have been done by Spitalfields,
Bethnal Green, Islington, or the vicinity of the Caledonian
Market. It was an act of justice of which they boasted for
many weeks afterwards in that neighbourhood.[41]

The brash intrusions of *The Shifting of the Fire* have been
brought under control. Ford's ideal narrator who tells his
story with apparently artless ramblings, digressions, and
side comments from the comfort of his armchair is already
beginning to take form, but it is not until after the extensive experiment with the first person narrator of *The Good
Soldier* that Ford himself as omniscient narrator thoroughly exploits this method.

4

Perhaps because he had not yet found a coherent
method which would give an aesthetic point of reference
for the renderings of his " affairs," the author-narrator of
the early novels often blunders. In several novels the
action is slowed or suspended by digressions which are
relevant to themes but which deploy the reader's interest.
They often allow Ford to ride a hobby horse, as in *The
Panel*, that curious farce which is both a satire and an
imitation of James, and in which he includes a long digres-

---

[41] *Mr. Fleight*, p. 150.

sion on booksellers, whom he sees as conspiring against true artists like James by booming only what will sell.[42] He registers here the same complaints he has elsewhere, notably in *The Critical Attitude* (pp. 133-143). In *Mr. Fleight* the amusing, ridiculous dinner speeches of the Soho intellectuals at the Enamel Club have only a tenuous relation to the plot; the same charge can be brought against several other novels, especially those like *Mr. Fleight*, which attempt a panoramic picture of some social or political area of contemporary life.

There are several other distractions and irritations to the reader. There are, for example, the numerous and today mostly obscure references to personalities of Ford's day. Joseph Chamberlain, Balfour, J. P. Morgan, and several others less well known are projected. Mr. and Mrs. Pett in *The New Humpty-Dumpty* might very well have been remotely modeled on Sidney and Beatrice Webb, although Pett is a renegade Fabian who holds Fordian ideas. More serious is the extensive use of coincidence, especially of the coincidence which resolves a plotting difficulty. Appropriate enough to fairy tales, medieval legends, or farces, which thrive on coincidence, the chance meetings, convenient arrivals of good or bad fortune (in *The Benefactor, The New Humpty-Dumpty*, and *Mr. Fleight* in particular), and the sudden appearances of characters to complicate or solve issues are often in the contemporary novels strains upon the reader's credulity.

" F. M. Ford wasted 40 novels, as I see it," Ezra Pound once wrote to W. H. P. Rouse, " excellent parts merely buried in writing done at his second best." [43] There are certainly surprising lapses in style, in taste, in the narra-

---

[42] (London: Constable, 1912), pp. 263-281.
[43] *Letters: 1907-1941*, ed. D. D. Paige (New York: Harcourt Brace, 1950), p. 297. Letter is dated October 30, 1937.

tive procedure. In *The Simple Life Limited,* the incestuous, though unconsummated, marriage of Hamnet and Ophelia is less shocking than it is ridiculous, especially when Hamnet reveals in the final paragraph that he had known from the first he was Ophelia's half-brother; he had married her to "get away from those sickening, slack conditions." [44] But more serious are the times the narrator breaks down altogether. The most startling example of this is in *The Young Lovell,* which shows every evidence of having been written hurriedly under great pressure.

The novel manages to move deftly between the enchanted world of the White Lady and that of the worldly concerns of greed, spying, politics, feudal manners, and the modes of chivalry. But the novel often loses its balance and focus by extended expository scenes, and especially by one long slow scene interrupting the aroused suspense, which takes so long to gain its effect that the perspective of the whole book is lost. [45] Twice Ford uses the shabby narrative device of chatting with the reader and showing his hand. At one point he intrudes by announcing, "Now let us turn for a moment to what passed in the house of The Princess Rohtraut. . . ." Later, as Lovell, after a considerable jump in the narrative, stands upon the ramparts of his tower, apparently near success in the struggle to regain his lands, Ford lists a number of people who helped him get there and then writes, "Let us consider them in that order." Fifty pages later, Lovell is again on his tower and the battle ready to begin. In the early part of the story a witch tells Lovell that Magister Stone will be his master, but after Stone does some necessary plotting

[44] *The Simple Life Limited,* p. 389. Although this Ophelia does not go mad, the allusion to Hamlet and Ophelia is intentional.

[45] *The Young Lovell,* pp. 184-204. This is the scene between the Bishop of Durham and the monk Francis. See above, p. 136, footnote 31.

for the usurpers, he passes out of the story and the threat
is never realized. At one point the weather is beautiful,
the fields lush and green; not so much later we are told
the land is suffering from a drought, a drought Ford needs
in order to prepare for the storm of the final scene when
Lovell is carried away in a water spout by the White
Lady. In the jumblings of time Ford loses a month. And
yet the novel has brilliantly conceived scenes catching the
nostalgic echoes of medieval romance; especially notable
is the first scene where Lovell endures the lonely prayer
vigil on the eve of his knighting sorely tried by evil visions
and in the hour of the false dawn submits to the beautiful
but lecherous White Lady. The novel is a somewhat
extreme example of an impression many readers besides
Pound have had about much of Ford's work: it is excel-
lently wrought in many scenes, which succeed in catching
the intended atmospheres of both romance and reality,
but it fails as a coherent work of art by virtue of its narrative faults, which point to weaknesses in Ford's creative,
shaping imagination.

The techniques of the early novels, even of the best
ones like the Katherine Howard trilogy, and *Ladies Whose
Bright Eyes* (1911 edition), and perhaps *The Benefactor*,
are not altogether successful in embodying and rendering
Ford's themes. Conversely, and probably more to the
point, the themes do not always warrant the techniques
lavished upon them. Ford is not always able to meet the
challenges of his themes or subject matter. He deals
extensively with the surfaces of social and psychological
experience—with the trivia of manners, with the somewhat
oversimplified motives of characters who represent personal and social virtues and vices and who, working at
cross-purposes, precipitate complex and sometimes ridiculous, harrowing personal relationships. But there is not,

as in the best work of Conrad or of James, a very strong sense of life being lived. There are the surfaces of appearance and the analysis of the paradoxical realities beneath them, but there is no profundity, no great depth of inner spiritual and psychological suffering or commitment. Ford's characters often seem to move in a realm slightly above if not completely out of the world in which we live. Perhaps this results from his somewhat specialized subject matter, or from his avoiding character analysis in the manner of traditional novelists and his failure to delve beyond conscious thoughts, or from the types of characters he favors. No complete world is realized—one comparable to that in *Nostromo*, say, or in *The Spoils of Poynton*, both favorite novels of his. Ford's emphasis is on the human muddlement, and although his better characters are felt and seen with some conviction, their world is attenuated not beyond belief or endurance but often beyond the faith that we are observing an altogether real world. He was later to give a depth and a significance to his surfaces by careful rearrangements of time in order to place one motivation, one " fact," against another, so that what results is not merely a series of contrasting characters and actions which illustrate social themes, but also artful juxtapositions which render desperate human situations. Not until *A Call* and *The New Humpty-Dumpty* did he approach at all seriously the study of the sexual passions in determining human affairs.[46] *A Call* is

----

[46] It is possible that Ford's relationship with Violet Hunt and the scandal and recriminations which accompanied it might have inspired insights into the subtleties and cruelties of sexual passion. Except for the witch Anne Jeal in *The 'Half-Moon'* (1909), as I noted above, there is no parallel in the earlier novels to either Katya Lascarides or Countess Macdonald. Violet Hunt's *The Flurried Years* lends some credence to the speculation that Ford used her as a partial model for his predatory, possessive females. See below, p. 276, footnote 6.

subtitled " The Tale of Two Passions "; the epigraph to
The New Humpty-Dumpty reads:

> " There be summer queens and dukes of a day,
> But the heart of another is a dark forest." [47]

The key for *The Good Soldier* and *Parade's End* has
literally been found.

One might speculate further that in his early novels
Ford had not yet found the catastrophes he needed to
objectify and give meaning to his vision. Demon lovers
and witches (*The Young Lovell* and *The ' Half-Moon '*) ,
a god appearing on earth (*Mr. Apollo*), socialism (*The
New Humpty-Dumpty*) , political corruption (*An English
Girl* and *Mr. Fleight*) , a telephone call to a frightened,
innocent social fool (*A Call*) , a train accident and delusive
memory-transference (*Ladies Whose Bright Eyes*) , insanity and mental collapse (important in *The Shifting of
the Fire, The Benefactor, The Simple Life Limited,* and
A Call) , and the loss of Catholic power (the Fifth Queen
trilogy) are the catastrophes created by Ford's imagination. He handles them with various degrees of success,
but it seems it was not until World War I and his own
physical and emotional involvement in it that he found
his most dramatic and effective symbol of the collapse of
social virtues. *The Good Soldier*, written before the war,
is in itself the representation of a cataclysm culminating
in the collapse of personal relations. It is Ford's ultimate
picture of the plight of contemporary upper class society,
the catastrophe being centered in the release of passions
from the boundaries of convention.

---

[47] The phrase "Another person's heart, you know, is a dark forest " appears
in the W. R. S. Ralston translation of Turgenev's *Liza* (London: Dent, 1914),
p. 84.

VI

THE GOOD SOLDIER

*" If then the parts are managed so regularly, that the
beauty of the whole be kept entire, and that the variety
become not a perplexed and confused mass of accidents,
you will find it infinitely pleasing to be led in a labyrinth
of design, where you see some of your way before you, yet
discern not the end till you arrive at it."* John Dryden:
An Essay of Dramatic Poesy

1

" THE GOOD SOLDIER " IS UNIQUE AMONG FORD'S NOVELS
written before the war because its complex technique
almost perfectly mirrors the complexity of its subject.
It was on the 17th of December 1913, he tells us, that
he " sat down to show what I could do." He wanted to
put in a novel all that he knew about writing. It was to
be his literary swan song, his " great auk's egg." [1] But

[1] " Dedicatory Letter to Stella Ford," *The Good Soldier* (New York:
Vintage Books, 1957), pp. xviii-xix. All page references are to this volume.

Violet Hunt writes that she rescued the manuscript from a " dustbin at the bottom of the orchard," mended it together, and sent it to her publisher. Ford knew, she says, when his interest faded in his books, for he would hurry up after he reached that point and, when finished, would have the urge to tear them up. " He never did start a game, a book, or even a love-affair, that he did not lose interest in before he came to *finis*." [2] Although there are lapses in the narrative technique, *The Good Soldier* does not show evidence of haste. Ford worked on it for at least a year and a half and rightly came to regard it as his best book.

The story, he says, is a true one. " I had it from Edward Ashburnham himself and I could not write it till all the others were dead." He carried it in his mind for ten years, " thinking about it from time to time." [3] The germ was apparently planted sometime before 1907. In *The Spirit of the People*, published in that year, Ford tells of staying one summer at the home of a married couple, prototypes of English " good people."

There was also living in the house a young girl, the ward of the husband, and between him and her—in another of those singularly expressive phrases—an attachment had grown up. P— had not merely never " spoken to " his ward; but his ward, I fancy, had spoken to Mrs. P—. At any rate, the situation had grown impossible, and it was arranged that Miss W— should take a trip around the world in company with some friends who were making that excursion. It was all done with the nicest tranquility. Miss W—'s luggage had been sent on in advance; P— was to drive her to the station himself in the dogcart. The only betrayal of any kind of suspicion that things were not of their ordinary

[2] Violet Hunt, *The Flurried Years*, p. 244.
[3] " Dedicatory Letter," p. xx.

train was that the night before parting P— had said to me: "I wish you'd drive to the station with us to-morrow morning." He was, in short, afraid of a " scene." [4]

P—, " playing the game to the bitter end," did not even say goodbye to Miss W—, and after the train had left, he went to pick up a parcel and drove away, forgetting Ford, who could not help admiring the amazing performance.

> It may have been desirable, in the face of the eternal verities —the verities that bind and gather all nations and all creeds —that the parting should have been complete and decently arranged. But a silence so utter: a so demonstrative lack of tenderness, seems to me to be a manifestation of a national characteristic that is almost appalling.[5]

This event was to become a key scene in *The Good Soldier* and to inspire one of its more central themes.

Since Ford approached the telling of the Ashburnham affair as a challenge to his skill, the problem was somehow " to get in," as James might say, the secrets, the nuances, the subtle difficulties, the intricacies of passion inherent in the affair. The simple but illustrative episode of Mr. P— and Miss W— evolved through the courses of Ford's imagination into a tale of intricate personal relationships which called upon every technical device at Ford's command to render. Actually, he added difficulties to those already there.

The novel is presented to us in the form of the memoirs of a foolish man who reveals the story of the unfaithfulness of his wife with two men, one the protagonist and his closest acquaintance, nothing of which he discovers or

---

[4] " The Spirit of the People," Part III of *England and the English*, p. 338. *The Spirit of the People* was published as a separate volume by Alston Rivers (London) in the same year.

[5] *England and the English*, p. 339.

suspects until after his wife and friend are dead. More specifically, it deals with John Dowell, the narrator, a wealthy, leisured landowner from Philadelphia, who meets a Florence Hurlbird at a Browning tea, soon becomes engaged to her, although discouraged by her aunts, and in 1901 elopes with her to Europe, where they continue to live. On the passage over, Florence feigns heart trouble and forces Dowell to become her permanent nurse. In Paris, unknown to Dowell, she renews a love affair with her first lover, a worthless fellow who had accompanied her and her uncle, himself supposedly a heart patient, on a trip around the world a year or so earlier.[6] In Nauheim in 1904 the Dowells meet Captain and Mrs. Edward Ashburnham, upper class British landowners, recently returned from India. Florence soon becomes Ashburnham's mistress, a fact of which his wife, Leonora, is aware, but Dowell is not. This knowledge profoundly shocks Leonora because she thought that she had finally reached the point where Ashburnham after several affairs, one financially disastrous, would return to her and their fortunes would be recouped. Taking charge of his estate duties and finances after his first affair, her splendid business sense and a series of cold-blooded calculations and investments had brought them back to their former financial security, all without a stain upon their reputations. But, motivated as she was by both a passionate love and hatred for Ashburnham, she had failed to prevent later love affairs, one perhaps platonic, the other resulting in blackmail, with two officers' wives in India, where they had gone to save money. From there to Nauheim they had

---

[6] Mr. Hurlbird's practice of carrying numerous crates of California oranges around the world to give away as the fancy struck him Ford borrowed from his own novel *An English Girl*, where another aging American, a Mr. Huston, also travels on board ships with a carload of oranges to give to people in out-of-the-way places.

brought Mrs. Maidan, a genuine heart case, who soon dies
of a heart attack after she overhears Ashburnham tell
Florence that she is " a poor little rat " whose passage to
Nauheim had been paid by Leonora.

Leonora, frustrated by the knowledge of her husband's
new affair, and fearful he will bolt with Florence, insists,
however, that neither Ashburnham nor Florence tell
Dowell the truth, so Dowell remains in ignorance while
Florence, now with a fierce control over Ashburnham,
continues to be his mistress and at the same time tells
Leonora that she has been trying to convince Ashburnham
to go back to her. Over a period of years the two women
between them bring Ashburnham close to his moral ruin.
In 1913, Florence, discovering that Ashburnham has fallen
in love with his ward, a young innocent named Nancy,
and faced by her husband's discovery of her first affair,
commits suicide. Dowell, believing she has died of a bad
heart, finds that he, too, all unconsciously up to this time,
is in love with Nancy. He goes back to America to settle
Florence's and her uncle's estates with the idea in mind
of returning to marry Nancy. The Ashburnhams and the
girl return to England. Ashburnham, realizing Nancy is
the real love of his life, takes to drinking heavily; Leonora
is frantic because she realizes his love for Nancy is killing
him; Nancy begins to understand that the marriage of
her foster parents is unhappy. In desperation, morally
debilitated, Leonora goes to Nancy, pleading with her to
give herself to Ashburnham. Nancy refuses until Leonora
tells her of all his past affairs, even agrees to divorce.
Nancy appears at Ashburnham's bedside one night, but
he recoils in horror and sends her away.

Dowell is sent for from America, but soon after his
arrival he hears that Nancy is being sent to her father in
India, an action he is not able to prevent. The night before

she is to leave, Ashburnham tells him of his love for Nancy and of the impossible position he is in. After she leaves, Ashburnham declares she no longer matters to him, but upon receiving a flippant telegram from her, he commits suicide. After his funeral Leonora reveals everything to Dowell. She soon marries a respectable neighbor. Dowell goes to India to retrieve Nancy, insane since she read of Ashburnham's death, and takes her back to Ashburnham's estate, which he has bought. He lives there bemoaning his loneliness, emulating Ashburnham, nursing Nancy, writing his memoirs.

More than any novel of Ford's written before it, *The Good Soldier* penetrates the social, moral, and psychological tensions working beneath the restraints of refinement imposed by the conventional behavior of the best people. This novel, in showing how social convention and communication allow for no public show of private emotion, is similar to *A Call*, but it penetrates more deeply and pessimistically the social dilemma of the leisured class. The protagonist and several characters in *A Call* are members of London society " ' going fanti,' running amuck through the laws of public opinion," as Ford had earlier described their life in *England and the English*. " In the body politic they do not ' count,' " Ford had also written in that lengthy essay, which serves for him almost as a writer's notebook:

> they are a shade more hopeless than the very poor, they will run their course towards ruin, physical decay, or towards that period of life when ginger being no longer hot in a mouth that has lost all savours, they will become aged devotees and perhaps make for edification.[7]

[7] *England and the English*, pp. 84-85.

The Ashburnhams are not members of London society but of the landed gentry who, when not at their estates, spend their time on the Continent, in India, or traveling. They have diligently maintained in public the traditional controls over behavior, the pride, the reserve, "the saving touch of insolence that seems to be necessary." [8] It might have been better if they had gone "fanti," for "the extraordinarily safe castle" they seem to be has crumbled from within, being destroyed by the release of the invading passions. "It was a most amazing business," Dowell says at one point, "and I think that it would have been better in the eyes of God if they had all attempted to gouge out each other's eyes with carving knives. But they were 'good people'" (p. 249). The gentry compose a class who do "count" in the body politic, or, rather, they had "counted" before they had given over their sense of responsibility to a mere show of respectability to lead "normal, virtuous and slightly deceitful" lives.

The social restraints are paralyzing; eventually the tensions demand release. And when tensions are released, emotions go out of control and moral barriers collapse. The Ashburnhams and the Dowells are both victims and agents in a moral wasteland created by the release of sexual passions against the fortress of social manners, the calm respectable citadel. These people are forced to face the discovery that their lives lack any center of moral belief or action. Deceit, subterfuge, jealousy, and pimping are the chaotic devices to which they have to resort in order to keep up appearances. The consequences are loneliness, insanity, suicide.

Relentless in her pursuit of conformity, Leonora will do

---

[8] *The Good Soldier*, p. 9. Hereafter, page numbers will be enclosed in parentheses following lengthy or significant references or quotations from *The Good Soldier*.

almost anything to possess her husband body and soul and
to bring her marriage within the limits set by her narrow
Irish Catholicism. Her view is that life is " a perpetual
sex-battle between husbands who desire to be unfaithful
to their wives, and wives who desire to recapture their
husbands in the end " (p. 186). Willing to allow men
their " rutting seasons," she expects that they eventually
will settle down in the arms of their patient wives.
Leonora is so instructed by the Mother Superior to whom
she turns after Ashburnham's disastrous affair with the
Spanish dancer. She is told: " Men are like that. By the
blessing of God it will all come right in the end " (p. 186).
She cannot wait; with a masculine determination she
manages her husband's estate and love affairs, and hence
destroys what she most wants to have and moves toward
her own mental and moral collapse. In her final frustration
and despair she forces Nancy on Ashburnham, an action
which is a true measure of her misunderstanding of his
sense of moral honor. She breaks away from the restraints
of her religion, and, as Dowell writes, acts " along the lines
of her instinctive desires " (p. 203). But these are not
simple, for her ambivalent emotions have reached a crisis.
Love, hate, pity, respect for Ashburnham tear her apart.
While she desperately hopes this is his last affair, she
knows it is a true passion, and though she is certain Ashburnham will not touch Nancy, she is aware that she has
lost him for good (p. 203). When the innocent, idealistic
girl assures her that she and Ashburnham are soul mates,
Leonora reveals Ashburnham's infidelities and extrava-
gances, and both women, acting along the lines " of the
sex instinct that makes women be intolerably cruel to
the beloved person " (p. 245), force Ashburnham into a
frightful moral crisis.

    Florence had earlier done her part in destroying Ashburnham, but without even the excuse of Leonora's sincere passions, for Florence is an absolute materialist for whom emotions and sex are weapons needed to acquire the luxury and prestige of being the wife of a British landed gentleman. Essentially she is sexless, a condition Ford, oddly enough, saw all Americans as trying to attain.[9] Dowell himself is the sexless American male, incapable of passion. Since his sudden realization that he is in love with Nancy is merely a partial release of frustrated emotion, he is actually more in love with love than with her.[10] Blind to the feelings of others and lacking clear or useful moral yardsticks, he seeks recourse in self-pity and in emulation of the tortured Ashburnham.

Although foolish and sentimental through several adulterous affairs, Ashburnham is the only one able to meet a real moral test. He is the victim of the three women who surround him and of sheer bad luck. The Rodney Bayhams can keep a mistress quietly in Portsmouth and manage their estates economically, but Ashburnham must

[9] *Women and Men*, p. 29. Ford writes here: "In America where they have not begun to think about life but merely exhaust themselves in uplifting search after the dollar, the men are entirely emasculated. Poor America! Like the young puppy it has all its troubles before it." In *The Good Soldier*, p. 86, Florence's uncle in his "full-blooded lecture" to the newly married Dowell "concluded, as they always do, poor, dear old things, with the aspiration that all American women should one day be sexless— though that is not the way they put it. . . ." Perhaps Ford's view is not so odd after all, for Henry Adams saw that "American art, like the American language and American education, was as far as possible sexless" and that "society regarded this victory over sex as its greatest triumph." *The Education of Henry Adams* (Boston: Houghton Mifflin, 1918) p. 385 (in "The Dynamo and the Virgin").

[10] Dowell describes his "passion" in terms of giving Nancy "a good time" and of wanting to marry her as someone wants to go to Carcassonne; he visualizes himself as a "convent" to which Nancy will come to "make her vows" (pp. 121-122). Dowell is merely releasing his emotions toward the one most available and desirable, for he made clear at the first that though he "loved" Leonora, he "never had the beginnings of a trace of what is called the sex instinct towards her" (p. 32).

pick a prudish nursemaid, a mercenary courtesan, a woman
with a blackmailing husband, a coldly ambitious woman,
and finally his own ward, who has been brought up almost
as a daughter. He is equally a victim of his own generous
emotions and of his sentimental view of life, inspired by
traditional schoolboy and military aphorisms of British
honor and by sentimental fiction, where true love, once
found, is eternal. Dowell, studying Ashburnham, comes
to realize that the male passion is for tenderness, understanding, someone to talk to, and for identity with the
woman loved, and that ultimately " for every man there
comes at last a time of life when the woman who then
sets her seal upon his imagination has set her seal for
good " (p. 115). This Nancy does and without a word
from Ashburnham. In one of those unconscious outbursts
which occur frequently in the novel, he lets slip to Leonora
that he will be satisfied if Nancy still loves him when she
is five thousand miles away. When he is brought to doubt
that she does, and when Leonora threatens to take over
his bank account again after he has paid £200 to save a
gardener's daughter from charges of killing her child, he
has no resources or reasons left for living. His refusal of
Nancy is a victory for the generous emotions over the
selfish ones; his suicide is a victory for the moral anarchy
of individual passions over the collective passions directed
toward the order and well-being of the body politic. He
is the last of a tradition. His later counterpart, Tietjens,
is at least left in possession of his true love, but Tietjens
is blessed by the gods, has tested himself in a war, and
has a greater resilience to misfortune than Ashburnham
does.

And yet the victory and the defeat are not so simple
as I suggest. As Dowell reminds us, Ashburnham, by
insisting that Nancy be sent away, acts conventionally:

". . . . it was in tune with the tradition of Edward's house. I dare say it worked out for the greatest good of the body politic " (p. 238) . Leonora could have managed the girl's departure earlier and thus taken " the decent line," but since the return to Branshaw House " poor Leonora was incapable of taking any line whatever," acting irrationally as she shifted between pity and loathing for her husband (p. 204) . The decent line is the conventional one, but, ironically, convention will not allow for passion. Leonora ultimately sacrifices the conventional line to indulge the contrarieties of her passions; Ashburnham sacrifices his passion to the conventional line. The conventional line which determines social behavior, or appearance, is thus a reality, and as much a reality as the private passions that tend to destroy that line, unless those passions are controlled or sacrificed.

Ford exploits the ironies inherent in the psychological conflicts between the passions and the conventional line. *The Good Soldier* is literally his study of the heart of darkness encased within the calm surfaces of leisured upper-class manners. One of its principal themes is the " dark forest which is the heart of another." Florence, her uncle, Ashburnham, and Maisie Maidan supposedly suffer from bad hearts, but Maisie is the only one to die of a heart attack. Mr. Hurlbird goes through life thinking he has heart trouble, but he dies of bronchitis. Florence, using the ailment as a tactic in her campaign to achieve a European establishment, is essentially heartless. Ashburnham's heart is Leonora's deception, giving them a reason to stay in Nauheim several months a year, where living is relatively inexpensive. But he does suffer from an excess of heart, of too much sympathetic concern for others. The cold Leonora, once her heart shows itself, is torn between love and hatred. Ford fully explores the

motivations of the heart. " I know nothing—nothing in
the world—of the hearts of men," Dowell says early in
the first chapter (p. 7). And it is true; even after everything has been revealed to him and he has written the
record of the affair, the secrets of the heart are still a
darkness. Passion, generosity, deceit, disease, chivalry,
innocence, sterility, craven sensuality—all are part of the
undecipherable language of the heart.

Passion *versus* paralysis is the keynote of the struggle.
The Ashburnhams are sexual innocents whose marriage
had been arranged by their parents. Leonora, then only
eighteen, " had been handed over to him, like some patient
mediaeval virgin " (p. 140). Until a couple of years later,
neither knew how babies are produced (p. 147). Leonora
was a Catholic born into a small, impoverished, land-
owning family. Her convent had shielded her from
thoughts of sex and had never bothered to explain the
realities of adultery and sexual jealousies, and her family
had shown her the necessity of maintaining a niggardly
economy and respectability. Nancy comes out of the
same convent and we are to see in the latter part of the
book her suffering the shock of sexual discovery. Ashburnham, though equally innocent, is an Anglican of the
feudal aristocracy with wealth, though not great wealth,
and with an idealized conception of woman's character
and function. He and Leonora are fatefully mismated.
It is to be expected that Ashburnham, finding her cold,
would turn to mysterious women with a past, or motherly
women, or even to a flighty but dazzling woman like
Florence; and it is to be expected that Leonora, finding
him extravagant and sanguine, would seek to recoup his
fortunes and direct his love affairs. But through it all,
except for her rantings against his extravagance after the
discovery of each new infidelity, they never talk of inti-

mate matters and barely converse at all. Outside of expressions of remorse, Ashburnham remains silent, ignorant of how much she really knows. Their sexual life is paralyzed; their bedroom doors are always locked to each other, but Leonora blames their childlessness on the will of God (p. 147). Actually, of the foursome, Florence is the only sexual initiate before marriage, but her union with Dowell is never consummated. She acquires her " heart " the first day of their honeymoon voyage to Europe, forcing Dowell to become the " sedulous nurse " from the very beginning. Although Florence talks incessantly, she and Dowell also seldom speak to each other. Occasionally she throws him a coquettish glance to baffle him (pp. 22, 23).

What should have happened to these people? In the depth of his bitterness against Florence, Dowell relates a recurrent dream of his, a " vision of judgment " (pp. 70-71). Three figures stand, suspended in air, upon an immense plain, which is the " hand of God." Ashburnham and Nancy are embracing; Florence stands alone; Dowell feels the urge to help her, though he hates her " with the hatred of the adder." Leonora does not appear, but he imagines that she " will burn, clear and serene, a northern light and one of the archangels of God." He, himself, perhaps, will be given an elevator to run. This vision is not only a key to Dowell's self-deprecatory, almost masochistic temperament, but also the clearest clue to the ideal truth of the matter: Ashburnham should have been allowed Nancy, Florence should be alone, Dowell should seek to comfort her, and Leonora should be a devoted angelic manager. The vision belittles the human struggle for social, moral, and psychological equanimity by its denial of the realization of human hopes. Dowell laments near the finish of his memoirs that no one got what he wanted.

" It is a queer and fantastic world. Why can't people have what they want? The things were all there to content everybody; yet everybody has the wrong thing. Perhaps you can make head or tail of it; it is beyond me " (p. 237). The reader is likely to feel at this point (Dowell has just declared himself in his unconscious desires as a faint follower of Ashburnham) that they are five ignorant fools hounded by bad luck but almost deserving what they get. But upon reflection one realizes there are still too many darknesses, a fact which Dowell constantly emphasizes by his questions. One illuminating fact does become evident, however. The world has been taken over by the emotionally and morally incompetent who relentlessly pursue respectability and conformity without the saving graces of honor and sympathy. Ford does not want to suggest a remedy but only to paint a picture, to leave a record. But it is clear that he is saying here what he has said often elsewhere: the best of England's past has been lost or, rather, has been driven out by a strident individualism governed by expediency rather than principle.

2

The Good Soldier is to Ford's fiction what *Madame Bovary* is to Flaubert's. It is Ford's record of wasted lives torn between dreams and what the world offers in their place. His upper class " good people " are as thoroughly dissected as Flaubert's middle class. Both novelists utilize limited centers of consciousness which must without faltering give us the intended impression of life or, at least, lead us to it. Both relentlessly pursue the horrors of their subjects; both retain a measure of affection for their protagonists. One significant difference is that while Flaubert's irony tends to dissipate into anger at life itself, as James perceived, Ford's leaves us in a mood of grim humor, bemused and suspended between pity, shock, and despair.[11] Ford, unlike Flaubert, is writing comedy, although, like Flaubert, he sees the tragedy in the lives of the devoutly conventional. Ford's single reflector is not the main character, while Emma, Flaubert's primary reflector, is. Ford, as storyteller, places himself at one further remove from both his protagonist and his reader than Flaubert did and manages to achieve levels and shades of irony not open to Flaubert.

Considering the Ashburnham affair, with Dowell relegated to his proper minor role, the story is close to being a domestic tragedy relating the disintegration of two upper class families, one British, one American. To the extent that society is indicted, the story is a social tragedy, a catastrophe resulting from the inherent weaknesses and inhumanity of a debilitated society. Ultimately the domestic tragedy is illustrative of the social tragedy. The characters are not, however, merely types who serve to point up society's shortcomings; they are rather highly particularized individuals who because of environmental conditioning, certain strokes of bad luck, and the nature of their own temperaments are brought to their inevitable end.

Even though the Ashburnham affair evokes tragic implications, we are never allowed to react to the story with the

---

[11] I am thinking here of James's statement that Flaubert " is sustained only by the rage and the habit of effort; the mere *love* of letters, let alone the love of life, appears at an early age to have deserted him. Certain passages in his correspondence make us even wonder if it be not hate that sustains him most." " Gustave Flaubert " in *The Art of Fiction and Other Essays*, p. 125. See also Alfred Kazin, " The Anger of Flaubert," *New Yorker*, xxx (September 11, 1954), 134-139.

emotions usually accompanying a tragedy of the classical type. Ford's technique of telling the story through the opaque eyes of a naive, bewildered, myopic, fatalistic American who slowly and painfully reveals the horrors to which until recently he had been an unseeing witness moves the story into the realm of the comic and ironic. The irony of allowing Dowell to tell the story he seems least qualified to tell must have suggested to Ford the value of such a narrator to make us see and feel the ironies inherent in the story. As Mark Schorer says: " Irony, which makes no absolute commitments and can thus enjoy the advantage of many ambiguities of meaning and endless complexities of situation, is at the same time an evaluative mood, and, in a master, a sharp one." [12] The intricacies of the manner, the narrative point of view, the time-shifts, the language, of which I shall treat shortly, heighten the sense of the ridiculous and the grotesque and permit the fullest ironic exploitation of the situation. The reader is never to be satisfied with a simple interpretation or a single emotion. Ashburnham has several of the endearing qualities of Ford's gentleman of honor, but even his sacrifice of Nancy, which would ennoble him in a less distorted account, as James for instance might write, is largely vitiated by our view of him as a man who muddles through life, who seeks self-indulgent solace from several adulterous attachments, and whose sentimental innocence prevents him from telling his wife of his affairs for fear of sullying the virginity of her thoughts. And yet Ashburnham is the most worthwhile character in the whole novel. One wishes for him better luck than he has. Surprisingly enough, the reader's final view of him approaches Dowell's, although it is certainly difficult to see him as one of " the ancient Greek damned " (p. 252) .

[12] "An Interpretation," p. xiii.

The novel eludes precise classification. In one sense it is a satire because it does, at least by implication, hold up to ridicule prevailing vices and follies, but unlike satire it does not have as its end the improvement of humanity or its institutions. There is literally at the end no hope of improvement, for Ashburnham and what he represents are dead. The emphasis is not so much upon depicting the amusing or ridiculous behavior of stereotyped characters, as in the comedy of manners, as it is upon seeking out the innermost emotions and motives of highly particularized people trying to live in a conventional world, which they ultimately illuminate and condemn by virtue of being the kind of people they are. So considered, the novel is closer in type to high comedy. It deals, first of all, with upper class life, but, more tellingly, it treats of its subject with a remarkable authorial detachment, evoking thoughtful if somewhat despairing laughter and a sense of tragic undertones, while constantly demanding the intellectual attention of the reader. "The world," Horace Walpole says in his famous adage, "is a comedy to those that think, a tragedy to those who feel." In this novel the characters feel more than they think; Ford thinks (primarily in his carefully worked out, intellectualized methods) as much as he feels. The result is an ironic view of life, of a world in which appearances hide a frightful reality and in which reality has too many faces.[13]

Electing to tell the story through Dowell's eyes, Ford chose about the weakest of all possible vessels. Perhaps he thought he could do what James felt to be impossible, or what Flaubert had tried and failed to do in *Madame*

---

[13] For a defense of *The Good Soldier* as a tragedy around whose tragic core Ford "placed a context of comic irony," which served for his commentary, see John A. Meixner, "The Saddest Story," *The Kenyon Review*, XXII (Spring, 1960), 234-264.

Bovary. Ford was certainly familiar with James's 1914 essay on Flaubert in which the master claimed *Madame Bovary* to be " really too small an affair." With both Emma and Frederic Moreau of *Sentimental Education* (whom James calls an " abject human specimen ") Flaubert

> wished in each case to make a picture of experience— middling experience, it is true—and of the world close to him; but if he imagined nothing better for his purpose than such a heroine and such a hero, both such limited reflectors and registers, we are forced to believe it to have been by a defect of his mind.[14]

The prospect of a sentimentalist so easily duped and with such limited resources of perception telling the whole story would have appalled James, but Ford's choice of his central consciousness was derived from his realization that using a morally complacent narrator with several short-comings of insight was the best means of revealing the moral chaos of the affair he had in mind. Because Ford is not handling " middling experience," or attempting to give a simple view, he needs the advantages which his indirect, fragmentary, ironic method can give.

Percy Lubbock, in *The Craft of Fiction*, one of the most fruitful books written on the modern novel, also feels that Emma is too mean a figure to sustain the reader's interest. Her being so indicates to Lubbock that the situation out of which Flaubert made the novel was " pictorial " rather than " dramatic."

> But for a picture, where the interest depends only on what she *is*—that is quite different. . . . she can make a perfect impression of life, though she cannot create much of a story.

[14] James, " Gustave Flaubert," p. 135.

Let Emma and her plight, therefore, appear as a picture; let her be shown in the act of living her life, entangled as it is with her past and her present; that is how the final fact at the heart of Flaubert's subject will be best displayed.[15]

Ford himself felt that Flaubert failed in *Madame Bovary* because he became too attached to his heroine, hence came too close to the reader.[16] Ford chose, therefore, the first person point of view, in spite of its difficulties, in order to achieve a detachment and an immediacy not possible in an omniscient account.

Dowell is used to help clarify the action he narrates but in a special and indirect way. Ford does not even utilize Flaubert's practice in *Madame Bovary* of moving away from the central consciousness for a while to the outer world of such people as Homais, Binet, or L'Heureux, or to the inner consciousness of Charles, itself extremely limited, at the beginning and end of the novel. Ford, rather, has Dowell force himself on us with all the irritating ways of an egotistic, sentimental, overtalkative gossip. Dowell startles us into attention, causing us to protest and to seek the balance of other interpretations. Our sense of superiority to him excites us to discover the truth. Because Ford makes Dowell initially more foolish and more easily seen through than Emma, it is as though he had thought of the artistically exciting difficulties of writing *Madame Bovary* from the point of view of Charles.

Lubbock writes that " Emma's rudimentary idea of them [the facts of life about her] is entirely inadequate; she has not a vestige of the humour and irony that is needed to give them shape " (p. 86). Ford, as we shall see, achieves both humor and irony by such means as the

---

[15] (New York: Peter Smith, 1947), p. 83.
[16] *The English Novel*, p. 135.

time-shift, a careful ordering of the action for *progression d'effet*, and imagery. In addition, he makes his narrator disarmingly honest and capable of reporting action. Dowell records rather faithfully the physical details of places, speeches, and actions. By his being so thorough we get a truer picture than perhaps would be available from someone who felt he had things to hide, as, for example, Leonora would have. As a leisured American of good family living on the Continent, he is acutely sensitive to the customs and behavior of upper class society in the capitals and watering spots. Although no scene is fully reported or dramatized without the intervening comments or thoughts of Dowell, the novel none the less achieves the intensity of drama because the consciousness of the narrator is so limited, so full of self-justifications and distorted half-truths, and because the points of view of others are diligently reported. The implications of what it all means are left almost totally up to the reader.

It is in this way that *The Good Soldier* is dramatic in method. Elsewhere in *The Craft of Fiction*, Lubbock, after contrasting the use of the first person in *David Copperfield* and *Harry Richmond*, concludes:

> It comes to this, that the picture which Harry Richmond gives of his career has a function essentially dramatic; it has a part to perform in the story, a part it must undertake as a whole, over and above its pictorial charge. It must do something as well as be, it must create even while it is created. (p. 135)

We are constantly occupied with Harry's " consciousness, its gradual enlargement and enrichment. . . . Pictorial, therefore, in form, dramatic in function—such was the story that Meredith elected to tell in the first person " (p. 137) . But because Richmond is the main character, because we cannot " get behind his description and judge for ourselves," and because his consciousness is not dramatized, Lubbock feels Meredith chose the wrong narrative point of view (pp. 139-140). But Ford, by telling the story through a minor character inadequate in perception and judgment, chooses the best and most economical means to achieve a multiple view of the affair and to present his picture in dramatic terms. In effect Dowell's consciousness is dramatized. He tells us everything we need to know; his reportings, his analyses are themselves dramatic events. His view, as Mark Schorer realizes, is not always the wrong one; it is " merely *a* view." [17]

Elliott B. Gose, Jr. is right when he says that our evaluation of the excellence of *The Good Soldier* " depends on our reaction to the novel, and this in turn rests on our reaction to Dowell." He sets Dreiser's view that Dowell is merely Ford's mouthpiece against Schorer's description of the narrator as a " weak and passionless self-deceiver." He himself takes a middle position, seeing Dowell " as an essentially honest if not very passionate person whose attitude toward the characters and events with which he deals is in constant evolution as the novel progresses." He adds that " we will find that the two [Dowell and Ford] make essentially the same evaluation of life." [18] Dreiser's view is inadequate, Gose's seems to me to contain an error of emphasis, Schorer's to be more nearly the best reading. For Dowell is used both to make *and* render Ford's evaluation of the affair and, through it, of life. It is true that Dowell is not totally blind, for he is capable of insights, and some are Ford's, but he is at the same time (another certainly intentional irony) a living illustration of those

[17] "An Interpretation," p. vii.
[18] " The Strange Irregular Rhythm: An Analysis of *The Good Soldier*," *PMLA*, LXXII (June, 1957), 494-495.

insights. Given Dowell's innocence, his insights are hind-sights, but hindsights are not always useless. With all of his pitiful self-glorification in identifying himself with Ashburnham as one of " the passionate, of the headstrong, and the too-truthful " (p. 253), with all of his self-indulgent bitterness, he none the less is competent to present Ford's analysis of society, of the anomalies of the good people in the present commercial age, although he cannot discover the reaches of the human heart or the secrets of human motivation. But neither can the others. Together, all their views point to Ford's conviction that humanity works at cross purposes with itself, that the heart is infinitely complex, and that it is not for one to know the heart of another, or even his own.

Such ignorance of the heart, as he says in *Women and Men*, leads a woman to say when a man irritates her: " What can you expect? He is a man." And when a woman irritates a man, he can only say, " What can you expect? She is a woman." The truth, Ford adds here, is that " actually since God made us all and the world is a trying place we are most of us poor people trying to make the best of a bad job " (p. 43). The muddle is caused by conflicts of the male and female point of view; the " abstract male " a woman chooses will be determined by the qualities ascribed to her father by her mother, and the male will have been brought up to believe in the inferiority of women (pp. 37-43). Quite literally, only unutterable confusion can result when such ideals face realities. All the characters in *The Good Soldier* are limited by the boundaries of their passions and insights—all differing, each shifting, but never coalescing. When these people are set against each other, the battle lines are drawn.

Using Dowell as the chronicler of the affair is one of the

central ironies in *The Good Soldier*. To register his moral
protest and yet to disappear, Ford needs a narrator who
lacks strict moral preconceptions, who is, in fact, without
narrow moral blinders which might prevent him from
seeing or representing the view in contexts other than his
own. During the act of reminiscence, collecting memories,
making continuous, tentative, shifting judgments and
analyses, Dowell comes to see that there was no excuse
for what Florence did, that Leonora was wrong in what
she did to reclaim Edward, and that Edward could not
help what he did. Except possibly for Florence, he can see
why they did what they did. But what should Leonora
have done? At one point he says she should have let
Ashburnham become a gentlemanly bum married to a
drunken barmaid who would cause scenes in public (p.
61). In another place he says Leonora should have shared
Edward with Florence "until the time came for jerking
that poor cuckoo out of the nest" (p. 193). He admits
he would have pimped for Florence with Jimmy (as he
probably later would have with Ashburnham) if he had
known and had been convinced it was a true passion, for
true passion transcends moral restrictions (p. 91).[19]

[19] The reference reads as follows: "As God is my Judge, I do not believe
that I would have separated those two if I had known that they really and
passionately loved each other. I do not know where the public morality of
the case comes in, and, of course, no man really knows what he would have
done in any given case. But I truly believe that I would have united them,
observing ways and means as decent as I could. I believe that I should have
given them money to live upon and that I should have consoled myself
somehow. At that date I might have found some young thing, like Maisie
Maidan, or the poor girl, and I might have had some peace."

Gose is wrong in assuming that the term "those two" in this passage
refers to Florence and Ashburnham. "The Strange Irregular Rhythm,"
(p. 500); in fact it refers to Jimmy and occurs within the six pages (87-
92) dealing with her affair with him. In light of Dowell's earlier remark
(p. 85) that "an overmastering passion is a good excuse for feelings. You
cannot help them" and of several other hints, it seems likely he might have
"united" Florence and Ashburnham also. That he might do it with less

His fond *if's* and *should's* establish Dowell's moral confusions at the same time that they point to the only conditions for passion possible in contemporary life. For Dowell appears to be Ford's representative not only of the contemporary American but also of one predominant contemporary point of view, which can best be described as a moral relativism approaching inertia.[20] He is a creature of fragments who lacks a view of life as a whole and who finds solace in both self-effacement and self-glorification and in a kind of self-indulgent loneliness. As an American from one of the first English Philadelphia families, he has ancestral longings for the feudal life, hence the appeal of Ashburnham, but as a leisured American who does nothing, not even manage his own affairs, he lacks the ballast of tradition and the duties it imposes, a ballast which Ashburnham possesses until even that is stolen from him. It seems that it is only out of Dowell's inertia and the detachment which it gives him, even in

grace is suggested by his remark that if Leonora had admitted she was jealous of Florence, he would have " turned upon Florence with the maddest kind of rage " (p. 67).

[20] Ford, of course, was not such an extreme moral relativist. He desired, as he implies by the qualities of his honorable protagonists, a humane but nevertheless prescribed code of behavior. Gose thinks that Dowell's " diffidence in trying to evaluate the events he has witnessed is not the sign so much of his stupidity as of a lack of ready-made solutions to the problems of our time. Because both narrator and author accept the human condition of change and uncertainty, neither will pass final judgment." " The Strange Irregular Rhythm," p. 509.

This is true, but it seems to me that this is a condition Ford *sees* but does not necessarily approve of. Gose also quotes Ford's statement that the duty of the novelist " is to draw an unbiassed picture of the world we live in." On this level, I see *The Good Soldier* as a bitter moral protest against a time without any code at all. It may be Ford's " unbiassed picture of the world we live in," but in the back of his mind may have been a hope of inspiring a reformulation of faith and order. Being a long-range rather than an immediate hope, it reiterates Ford's echoing of Flaubert's belief that if more people had read *Sentimental Education*, and read it correctly, the " *débâcle* " of the 1848 revolution would have been prevented. *Memories and Impressions*, pp. 202-204; *The Critical Attitude*, pp. 29-30.

the midst of his pain and distorted self-analysis, that he is able to see as much and to paint as accurate a picture as he does. On the other hand, he cannot be the true representative of the Ashburnham tradition, nor is he, except in the most amorphous way, identifiable with Ashburnham; he is perhaps the last ironic heir of that tradition, a symbol of the directionless, sentimental, self-centered despair that has taken over.

Along with Leonora, Florence and Nancy, Dowell has lost the simplicity and clarity of moral purpose characteristic of the Ashburnham tradition. They are all representatives of the age of doubt about which Dionissia speaks in *Ladies Whose Bright Eyes* (1935 edition), and they have failed to reclaim the faith necessary to achieve an honorable contentment. In fact, among them, in destroying Ashburnham, they have destroyed the generous sentiments, the only basis of that renewal of faith. They suffer "broken, tumultuous, agonized, and unromantic lives, periods punctuated by screams, by imbecilities, by deaths, by agonies" (p. 238), a characteristic exaggeration by Dowell of the view of life Ford ascribed to James: "a series of [. . .] meaningless episodes beneath a shadow of doom." [21] It is a declaration of the wasteland of the elders of Eliot's and Hemingway's lost generation.

There are three apparent breakdowns in the narrative point of view, but only one materially affects the total impression. Ford has the difficult problem of getting into Nancy's consciousness so that we can see her Catholic innocence faced with the shock of her first realization of the facts of divorce and of the unhappiness of the Ashburnhams, with her agonized discovery of love, and, finally, with her awareness that she is in love with Ashburnham and he with her. Almost every instance of a revelation of

[21] *Henry James*, p. 155.

her consciousness breaks the narrative illusion. We are told that one night she drank a wine glass full of whisky and then " dragged her tall height up to her room and lay in the dark," where " she gave way to the thought that she was in Edward's arms, that he was kissing her on the face " (p. 225). It seems incredible that Nancy would ever tell this to Leonora in their long, agonized talks together. It does not seem likely either that she would tell Leonora that she saw her as becoming " pinched, shriveled, blue with cold, shivering, suppliant," or as a " hungry dog, trying to spring up at a lamb that she was carrying " (pp. 228-229). It is equally difficult to conceive of these omniscient intrusions as coming only from Dowell's imaginative reconstruction of what must have happened, unless we consider them as his sentimental elaborations.[22] The intrusions are too important: Ford needs to explore Nancy's consciousness in order to give point and depth to the *progression d'effet* which will culminate in her offering herself to Ashburnham and in her eventual madness. But even though our credulity is threatened, Ford manages in almost every instance to sustain our suspension of disbelief by the skill with which he engages our attention and renders Nancy's involvement in the final crisis.

[22] The other two apparent violations of the point of view must also be seen as Dowell's fanciful reconstruction of what might have happened. He tells us during the scene when Leonora boxes Maisie Maidan's ears that Maisie had gone to Ashburnham's room, after he had left, to return a case of scissors. "She could not see why she should not, though she felt a certain remorse at the thought that she had kissed the pillows of his bed. That was the way it took her" (p. 66). How does Dowell know this? Maisie writes in her last note to Leonora: "You never talked to me about me and Edward, but I trusted you" (p. 73). It is not the kind of thing Maisie would tell Leonora anyway. Later, on page 245, Dowell reports Ashburnham's thoughts on Nancy's telegram ("He thought she only pretended to hate him in order to save her face and he thought that her quite atrocious telegram from Brindisi was only another attempt to do that . . ."), but as he reports the arrival of the telegram and Ashburnham's quietly removing the penknife from his pocket, there is no time for any such statement from Ashburnham.

3

By his manner of telling the story and through his characteristic interpretations and impressions, beyond which we are able to see other points of view, the character of Dowell contributes significantly to the structure and form of the whole novel. " I don't know," he says at the beginning of the second chapter,

> how it is best to put this thing down—whether it would be better to try and tell the story from the beginning, as if it were a story; or whether to tell it from this distance of time, as it reached me from the lips of Leonora or from those of Edward himself.
>
> So I shall just imagine myself for a fortnight or so at one side of the fireplace of a country cottage, with a sympathetic soul opposite me. And I shall go on talking, in a low voice while the sea sounds in the distance and overhead the great black flood of wind polishes the bright stars. From time to time we shall get up and go to the door and look out at the great moon and say: " Why, it is nearly as bright as in Provence! " And then we shall come back to the fireside, with just the touch of a sigh because we are not in that Provence where even the saddest stories are gay. (pp. 12-13)

The rambles through conscious memory, telling events as they come to mind, recalling earlier impressions, adding present ones, repeating certain scenes and seeing them somewhat differently each time, occasionally breaking down under the strain of recalling painful moments, intermittently posing questions he cannot answer and then offering them to the reader to ponder, are not only artful devices to claim the close attention of the reader's thoughts and feelings but also tools to mold the pattern of the novel.

The discursive, associative patterns of memory create the *rationale* of the pattern, for the rambling is only apparent; the succession of events and impressions is under remarkable control, as is the language which recreates them.

The control Ford places upon his tale is that dictated by *progression d'effet*. Difficult to define precisely, it involves the employment of all devices in order to gain verisimilitude and a sense of inevitability; all the conflicts and forces released by the author must ultimately coalesce, not so much by resolutions of heretofore unrevealed actions at the climax as by the accumulation of the reader's emotional responses and of his moral and intellectual evaluations.[23] The focus is on the effect to be aroused cumulatively from combined effects throughout the novel. The result is a complex of information discovered, attitudes aroused, and implications drawn, the " conflicting irresolutions ending in a determination." [24] The irresolutions in *The Good Soldier* are not fully resolved, a result perhaps of what Hugh Kenner calls Ford's " impasse of sympathy for all sides." In effect, he thinks, Ford projected his own bewilderment through Dowell; " a suspension of judgment that looks like technique . . . is in fact bewilderment." [25] And yet Ford's comment seems clear enough, the irresolutions themselves being part of the fabric of the theme. Not all of the

---

[23] Robert F. Haugh in *Joseph Conrad: Discovery in Design* (Norman: University of Oklahoma Press, 1957), p. 7, defines *progression d'effet* as follows: " The term, employed by Conrad and Hueffer in their conversations on the art of fiction, embraces growth, movement, heightening of all elements of the story: conflict and stress if it is a dramatic story; intensity and magnitude of image if it is a poetic story; complexity of patterns; balance and symmetry; evocations in style used for mood and functional atmosphere." Haugh analyzes the *progression d'effet* in several of Conrad's novels.

[24] *Henry James*, p. 168.

[25] " Conrad and Ford " in *Gnomon* (New York: McDowell, Oblensky, 1958), p. 169.

questions Dowell or Ford asks are answered, but then they cannot be in an age of doubt and faithlessness.

So many conflicts and forces are released that *The Good Soldier* appears to be nothing but a series of shocks, outbursts, and breakdowns. We are literally thrown into the middle of the affair and have to face the same discontinuities, confusions, and demands upon our powers of judgment that we muddle through in everyday life. But Ford knew that a novel, if it is to make any claims to being a work of art, must discover, must clarify, the truth of the selected instances from life that it chooses to represent.

The device of memoirs written by a rambling narrator is a ruse. With its dislocations of time and its free movement between reporting, evaluating, and questioning, it is a method to conceal art. The method is psychologically justified in its acceptance of the mind's time, *le temps humain* (in addition to the sun's) as a phenomenon of reality. The mind characteristically jumbles, with evidence of an associative pattern, memory and expectation of the future in its awareness of the present.[26] Naturally, Ford treated time as an aesthetic, rather than as a philosophical, principle, and more and more in his work he sees the time-shift as an artificial structural device in the ordering of his " affairs " to achieve a sense of the immediate present, to offer opportunities for the juxtaposition of actions, moods, temperaments, meanings, and metaphors, and to develop the *progression d'effet*. The time-shift, Hugh Kenner tells us, is less a method to achieve reality than it is a method to achieve a poetically

---

[26] See Chapter 1 of Hans Meyerhoff's *Time in Literature* (Berkeley and Los Angeles: University of California Press, 1955), pp. 1-10, for a discussion of the distinction between psychological and clock time. This distinction serves Meyerhoff as a foundation for his lengthy treatment of literary time within a general philosophical and social framework.

constructed impression of reality.[27] By de-emphasizing suspenseful plot, the method forces the unusual involvement of the reader, tearing him away from his assumptions and preconceptions about the significance and order of human events and leading him to a new awareness of complexities and of patterns not heretofore suspected. Albert Guerard, identifying *Lord Jim* as Conrad's " first great impressionist novel," places it as the first novel of this century in a new form: " a form bent on involving the reader in a psycho-moral drama which has no easy solution, and bent on engaging his sensibilities more strenuously and more uncomfortably than ever before." He notes that, as with the detective story, the reader becomes a kind of collaborator with the author and mentions Ford's statement that the aim of impressionism is to experience life as the sensitive observer does.

> The digressive method does indeed convey the " feel " of life. But the impressionist aim is to achieve a fuller truth than realism can, if necessary by " cheating; " and to create in the reader an intricate play of emotion and a rich conflict of sympathy and judgment, a provisional bafflement in the face of experience which turns out to be more complicated than we ever would have dreamed.[28]

In *The Good Soldier* structure is achieved by both short and long *progressions d'effet*, themselves shaped by what the narrator's dislocations in the sequence of action disclose and imply at every step of the way. Bewilderment is transformed into revelation. The novel leads us from the appearances to the realities, although the appearances

---

[27] *The Poetry of Ezra Pound*, pp. 268-269.
[28] *Conrad the Novelist* (Cambridge, Massachusetts: Harvard University Press, 1958), pp. 126-127. Guerard adds that " the culminating triumph of Conradian impressionism is *Absalom! Absalom!* "

also have their realities; [29] from paralyzed silence on intimate matters to extended, frenzied talks: Florence with
Leonora, Leonora with Ashburnham and Nancy, Leonora
and Ashburnham with Dowell, and Dowell through his
memoirs to us; from Leonora's moral certainties to her
reckless abandonment of them; from Ashburnham's unre-
strained passions to his regeneration through sacrifice of
his love for Nancy to his traditional sense of honor; from
Dowell's ignorance to his baffled knowledge and partial
insights. What Ford wants to achieve is an imaginatively
documented record of his age, for, as he says, " the greatest
service that any novelist can render to the Republic [. . .]
is to draw an unbiassed picture of the world we live in." [30]

Every chapter, every paragraph, almost every word is
artfully contrived to create the desired impressions and
to infuse them with meaning. Because the intricacy of
the manner as much as the limitations of space prevent
any thorough treatment of how Ford succeeds in squeezing
everything out of this affair and in putting his fictional
theory fully into practice for the first time, I will try to
suggest only the principal lines of the pattern.

The first chapter deftly sketches some of the main
figures and shadings in the picture that is to be drawn
for us. The impression is strong but not clear. " This is
the saddest story I have ever heard," Dowell begins, and
with the exact *mot juste*, for " sad " has several shades of
meaning, most of which are exploited only by implication.
Originally an Anglo-Saxon word meaning " satisfied " or
" sated," its current meanings range among " being down-
cast, gloomy, melancholy," or " affected with grief or
sorrow," which are various intensities of the same feeling.
It also refers to somber or dull colors and sometimes play-

---

[29] Schorer, "An Interpretation," p. vii.
[30] *Henry James*, p. 46.

fully to something shocking or wicked. The word has ironic potentialities Ford does not let pass. In Dowell's mouth it is a sentimental understatement; in the context of the novel it is both that and an outright lie, for it is sad to see the comfortable assurances of the past slip away, but outrageous to suffer in the vacuum that their disappearance has left.

One paradox follows another. The Dowells knew the Ashburnhams " as well as it was possible to know anybody, and yet, in another sense, we knew nothing at all about them." Dowell intends " to puzzle out " the affair, but until recently he " had never sounded the depths of an English heart," for he had known only " the shallows " (p. 3). Thoughts of the physical heart are evoked, and Dowell leaves us with the false impression that Florence had died of a bad heart and strongly intimates that Ashburnham had also. An apparent cohesiveness is established between the Ashburnhams and the Dowells by the fact that they are all " ' quite good people,' " descended from the best families; there is even the coincidence of Florence's ancestors having come from Fordingbridge and the estate now owned by Ashburnham.

But the illusion of their coherence is immediately brought into doubt by a series of paradoxical metaphors centering on decay and permanence. Dowell justifies writing his memoirs because he is like one who has " witnessed the sack of a city or the falling to pieces of a people " and is inspired to leave a record for the future and to purge his mind. The collapse of his " little four-square coterie " he likens to the death of a mouse from cancer, a process which is the same as " the whole sack of Rome by the Goths " (p. 5). These four did seem " an extraordinarily safe cattle " or like " one of those tall ships with the white sails upon a blue sea, one of those things

179

that seem the proudest and the safest of all the beautiful and safe things that God has permitted the mind of men to frame " (p. 6). He likens his tranquil life before the shock of discovery to " stepping a minuet " (p. 6). Because it is a refined, genteel dance with carefully prescribed steps, bows, and curtsies, it serves as a symbol of the manners of public behavior that gave to Dowell, and to them all, a sense of assurance and stability. Dowell is enamored of these surfaces and clings to the dream of their reality, for he tells us that " the mob may sack Versailles, the Trianon may fall," society may collapse, but the dance goes on. " You can't kill a minuet de la cour " (p. 6). Not fully assured, he sentimentally asks, as he is to do several times, if there is not " any heaven where old beautiful dances, old beautiful intimacies prolong themselves " (p. 6).

The question jolts him into another reality. Their life was not a minuet but " a prison full of screaming hysterics " (p. 7). But no, it was " true ": the sunshine, the music, the sounds of fountains, and the fact that they were four people with the same tastes and desires (a fatuous half-truth). He tries to settle this contradiction with a rationalized compromise by asking that if he possessed " a goodly apple that is rotten at the core " and did not recognize the rottenness until after nine years, did he not still possess a goodly apple? (p. 7). It appears merely " a little odd " to him that he never knew " that the physical rotteness of at least two pillars of our foursquare house never presented itself to my mind as a menace to its security " (p. 7). He knows nothing, except perhaps " the life of the hearth and of the smoking-room."

Even the assurances that the hearth and the smoking-room seem to offer are enigmas, and since Dowell's impressions are not stabilized, he never allows the reader's to be.

The rest of the chapter slowly moves around to posing questions of personal motives and morals. He offers partial portraits of Florence, Leonora, and Edward. He dismisses Florence lightly by exclaiming his bafflement at her finding the time to know and do so much, since he was her constant " sedulous, strained nurse " (p. 8). The Ashburnhams seemed a model couple, the very best combination of county family, wealth, and the perfect manner, but they never spoke to each other in private. Leonora was " the real thing," but when she explained her failure to carry through her only attempt at an affair with another man by admitting " she wasn't playing the game," Dowell cannot decide whether this was " the remark of a harlot, or is it what every decent woman, county family or not county family, thinks at the bottom of her heart? " (p. 9).

Similar diametrically opposed questions are asked with relation to Ashburnham. Dowell assures us Edward was not a brute, which gives the reader the first indication he *may* be. The " excellent magistrate, a first-rate soldier, one of the best landlords " (p. 11), Ashburnham seemed pure for he never in the smoking-rooms told " gross stories " or even listened to them. He was one to trust your wife with. "And I trusted mine—and it was madness " (p. 11).

Characteristically Dowell turns to himself for comparison, the first hint of his final identification with Ashburnham. He vouches for his own clean thoughts and chastity. But if chastity of speech is the sign of the libertine, what is he? "Am I no better than a eunuch or is the proper man—the man with the right to existence—a raging stallion forever neighing after his neighbour's womenkind? " (p. 12).[31] Again, he does not know; there

[31] In *England and the English*, p. 84, Ford describes the "barbaric" actions of the members of London society, of their "'going fanti'": "It

are no guides to either "the morals of sex" or to "the more subtle morality of all other personal contacts, associations, and activities[.] Or are we meant to act on impulse alone? It is all a darkness." In these areas there are no intelligible limitations like those for the minuet.

The first chapter previews the methods of the whole novel. It establishes that the primary concern will be to reveal precisely what has happened and to penetrate the significance of the events which have led the narrator to call it "the saddest story."[32] Dowell's practice is to shift between statements of fact and judgment, between what he felt at the time and what he feels at the particular moment of writing. Usually he moves from the general to the particular, as in the first chapter where he first generalizes on the impact of the whole affair and then moves to the particular dilemmas posed to him by Florence and by Leonora and Edward Ashburnham. More often than not specific events are recalled in the midst of certain observations and recollections, as in Part II, which moves from his cynical reflections on Florence and the recounting of their courtship and marriage and her affairs to *his* observation of events on the night of her suicide.[33] Most characteristic of Dowell's manner is his habit of juxtaposing understatement with overstatement and valuable insights with fatuous self-important interpretations, of

---

may not go further than putting our feet on the dining table, than pouring champagne cup upon our host's head, or, as an amiable bishop put it the other day, 'neighing after our neighbours' wives' [. . . .]"

[32] Bruce Harkness notes that *The Good Soldier* is partly a "plot of penetration." He adds that "we do not move from a state of misconception, in which we at first think the foursome to be ideal, but from a state of incomplete and hazy knowledge, to a state of full knowledge about their relationships." "The Handling of Time in the Novels of Joseph Conrad" (Unpublished Ph. D. dissertation, Department of English, The University of Chicago, 1950), p. 192.

[33] "What had actually happened" is explained shortly after as Dowell got it from Ashburnham and as he was able to piece it together (pp. 109-113).

shifting between disparagement and aggrandizement of himself and others, and of changing moods and evaluations.

One of the consequences of the narrative method by which Dowell juxtaposes past and present views is that a scene asks more questions than it answers and is often misleading. According to the nature of memoirs, much of the novel is related by a narrative summary interspersed with glimpses of scenes and snatches of dialogue. Although several of the key scenes are carefully prepared for, most of them are not fully developed once we get to them; we are offered only the critical dialogue which completes the revelations already hinted at, as are the scenes of Nancy's offering herself to Ashburnham, and his suicide.[34] We are usually introduced to a new view of earlier references and to allusions which will be developed later. The resulting confusion is only apparent; the meaning slowly unfolds.

Any one of the key scenes could illustrate how Ford manages his several techniques and through them reveals his themes. The reader is first impressed with the observation that Ford has added new dimensions to his scenes since his best ones in the Katherine Howard trilogy. In general, the scenes are now less elaborately prolonged, are more indirectly approached, are more often interrupted, and are more likely to refract a variety of points of view, which may shift and often contradict each other. There is still the camera eye ranging over the scene picking out details for pictorial and ironic purposes, and there is still the conscious control of varying rhythms. But these have been intensified until we are offered a

---

[34] Nancy's offering herself to Ashburnham is partly prepared for by returning two or three times to the scene of the night when Leonora goes to Nancy's room. In order to achieve the fullest ironic impact, the scene of Ashburnham's suicide is deliberately withheld until the last page.

total, sometimes almost suffocating, sensory and emotional interplay, suggesting an intentional borrowing of musical techniques, especially of those from a virtuoso piece of variations on a theme.[35]

For example, in rendering the action at the castle at M—, Ford uses his favorite device of a scene as a framework or envelope enclosing other actions, bits of information, and revelations which will clarify and complicate our view, add ironic overtones, and comment on every level of the novel's meaning. The scene starts casually as Dowell in his disarming way says he will use it as an illustration of his notion that it is difficult to get beneath the surface of the prescribed rules and rituals of " the good people." The ostensible purpose is actually to reveal to us that Florence is making her claim for Ashburnham, and that it is a fact of which Leonora is aware but Dowell is ignorant, although he senses a crisis. The whole scene is splendidly evocative in its quickening cadences, as the foursome moves steadily up to the room containing the copy of Luther's Protest, where Florence indirectly declares her intentions and places one finger on Ashburnham's wrist; and in its gradually lengthening cadences as Leonora grabs Dowell's wrist, rushes him outside, and in the face of his innocence checks her panic and assumes her public pose. At this point the scene is interrupted by twenty-one pages of digressions, the principal ones revealing something of

---

[35] See Guerard, *Conrad the Novelist*, p. 127 and Edward Crankshaw, *Joseph Conrad* (London: Lane, 1936), pp. 130-131. Crankshaw takes a good deal of space to develop the relationship of music to the structure of Conrad's fiction. " In all Conrad's work every incident, every character, every sentence almost, is made to do at least double duty, and that is the beauty of the fugue." He cites *Chance* as a novel where " this faculty of compression " is most evident. " This kind of thing in prose fiction is, with ' cutting ' in the cinema, the only thing strictly analogous to musical counterpoint in all art. And of all music the contrapuntal is the highest, since it permits of the simultaneous expression of numerous shades of meaning."

Ashburnham's infidelities and reporting the earlier scene, witnessed by Florence, of Leonora's striking Maisie Maidan. The scene returns to the lawn of the castle, where Leonora accepts Dowell's apology for Florence's behavior as he sees it. Ashburnham and Florence appear, the foursome leaves for Nauheim, the scene is over.

But with its enclosed revelations it reverberates everywhere. First of all, it illuminates the brilliantly comic hotel dinner scene rendered earlier. The digression explains that Leonora and Florence had entered the dining room arm in arm because Florence had seen Leonora striking Maisie and had understood Leonora's reason for doing it, information that throws further light on Florence's sense of triumph in announcing her campaign to capture Ashburnham. Maisie's story itself serves as one of the overlapping frameworks for the castle scene. She is not introduced until early in Dowell's digression, where he tells us that Leonora had paid her way to Nauheim—the first suggestion of Leonora's pimping—and badly misleads us by saying, " We saw plenty of her for the first month of our acquaintance, then she died, quite quietly—of heart trouble " (p. 51). The remark hardly prepares us for the comic shock of Leonora's finding her upon their return from the castle with her feet sticking out of a trunk, whose lid had closed upon her, " like the jaws of a gigantic alligator " (pp. 75-76)).

Dowell uses juxtapositions offered us by the digression to try to arouse our sense of pity for Ashburnham, but mostly he complicates our view of him. In the dining room scene, Ashburnham " gurgles "; in the castle he looks panic-stricken when Florence's finger touches his wrist; in neither case does he apparently say a word. We have to set this queer passiveness against Dowell's earlier suggestion that Ashburnham might be " a raging stallion " and his asserting that Ashburnham is a perfect English gentleman. And now Dowell tells us that Ashburnham is a sentimentalist whose infidelities are inspired " by the mad passion to find an ultimately satisfying woman " (p. 51). We learn that he has had to submit to Leonora's control of his estate, that he in fact does not have heart trouble, that he is truly, as Dowell had said in the dining room scene, " in a perfect devil of a fix " (p. 30) ; in short, that he is a victim of Leonora's " English Catholic conscience " which drove her to take over and " to fix things up " (p. 56). He is more to be pitied than blamed, even by the man he has deceived.

The scene not only sets the stage for Maisie's death and Florence's own victimizing of Ashburnham, but also foreshadows other events. Leonora's panic at the castle is placed against her striking Maisie Maidan and establishes the pattern of her angry, frustrated outbursts preparing us for her final moral breakdown when she lashes out against the " evil " of Nancy's innocence and beauty and offers her as a sacrificial victim for the preservation of her marriage. And perhaps, too, Maisie, with her innocence, in being offered by Leonora as a kind of toy for Ashburnham to play with, prepares us for Nancy, who resembles Maisie, who is as innocent as Maisie, though more intelligent, and who also is offered, though as a kind of treasure. Certainly the novel is full of such balancings.

There is even more one can say. There is, for example, the absolute skill with which Ford ties together the castle scene with its digressions. In the dining room scene, Dowell focuses our attention on Leonora's bracelet with the dangling golden key, which we discover twenty pages later she had just shortly before caught in Maisie's hair so deeply that Florence had had to extricate it. In the pictures which the scenes paint, our eyes are constantly directed to the wrists, the hands, the telling glances which communicate more than the relatively sparse dialogue does. And there is the ironic foreshortened view of the scene to come, as Dowell, on the way to the castle, laughs (the only time he does) at seeing one cow throwing another cow into a stream, an action which serves as an oblique hint of the human action to follow.

And so on and on. Gradually, as impressions are sorted out, and as the narrative shifts from public to private behavior, from moods of calm to those of panic and nightmare, from paralysis to breakdowns to outbursts and back to paralysis again, the design emerges.

Probably even before the end of Part I, we are aware that Ford is intentionally setting Florence and Leonora against Ashburnham and Dowell, that each of the women is from opposite sides of the same cloth and the two men from opposite sides of another cloth. Florence and Leonora, as different as they are, are essentially predatory females. Florence is an amoral materialist with a commercial frame of mind (she is the only one to come from a commercial family). Leonora is an efficient manager of the proprieties whose ambivalent passions ultimately lead to recklessness and disaster. She is a " sheer individualist," who cannot fathom Ashburnham, for his traditions are " entirely collective," prescribed as they are by " the feudal theory of an overlord doing his best by his dependents, the dependents meanwhile doing their best for the overlord " (p. 146). Ashburnham is finally able to find strength in the simplicities of his feudalism and sentimentalism. But Dowell, who seeks to emulate him, lacks both Ashburnham's moral stamina and inherited sense of honor, is relegated to being a nursemaid and solicitor, and remains at the end a mere shell of the Ashburnham traditions.

Once Florence is dead, Nancy steps in to make a four-some again. She is central to the novel's structure. The novel is divided into four parts, actually four frameworks, bound by crises in action or emotion. Each section moves carefully toward its own melodramatic climax. The first part ends with Maisie Maidan's death, the second with Florence's suicide, the third with Leonora's triumphant statement in India that she had finally recouped their fortunes, and the last with Ashburnham's suicide.

The novel revolves around its relatively few key scenes. Except when Dowell is in America settling the affairs of Florence and her uncle, he is a participant in almost every one of them, each one of which is presented in such a way as to allow other implications than his to be drawn. The major scenes, two or three of which may occur in a single day, are placed as follows:

Part I: (Early in July)[36] 1904	Florence meeting Leonora boxing Maisie's ears (chap. v; also mentioned in chap. i, Pt. iv). Ashburnhams and Dowells at first dinner (chaps. i, iii, v).
August 4, 1904	Trip to castle where Leonora realizes that Florence is about to become Ashburnham's mistress; followed by discovery of Maisie's death (chaps. iv, v, vi; also chap. i, Pt. iv).

[36] Dates in parentheses are approximate and are according to my working out of Ford's time scheme. For a discussion of the several inaccuracies in Ford's handling of time in this novel, see Richard W. Lid, "On the Time-Scheme of *The Good Soldier*," *English Fiction in Transition*, IV, no. 2 (1961), 9-10.

Part II: August 4, 1913 [37]	Ashburnham and Nancy to casino at Nauheim (trailed by Florence; also chap. I, Pt. III) ; Dowell meets Bagshawe; Florence's suicide (chap. II; also chap. I, Pt. I, and chap. I, Pt. III) .
Part III:	Except for the scene where Leonora allows Nancy to go with Ashburnham to the casino the night before they leave Nauheim (chap. II), this section is mostly a summary recapitulation, interspersed with snatches of dialogue, of the Ashburnhams' life before meeting the Dowells, though it culminates in the scene of Leonora announcing in India her successful restoration of their fortune (chap. V) .
Part IV: November 12, 1913	Leonora going to Nancy's room to persuade her to offer herself to Ashburnham and events leading up to that (chaps. III and IV; this day and following scene occur while Dowell is in America) .

[37] Events occurring between 1904 and 1913 are summarized with an occasional bit of dialogue. References to these years appear sporadically through the novel. Events include: trips of Ashburnham and the Dowells to Paris, once, at least, with Leonora (visits in 1904, 1905, 1906 mentioned, p. 98); Ashburnham throwing Jimmy out (December, 1904, p. 98); Florence's and Dowell's visit to La Tours (about 1912, pp. 13 and 16); Florence's talks with Leonora (pp. 191-194); Leonora's attempt at an affair with Bayham (pp. 9 and 196). Gose is inaccurate when he writes that "although the two couples were together only during the time they spent at the spa in Nauheim each summer, Florence soon became Edward's mistress." "The Strange Irregular Rhythm," (p. 495).

"One evening" (in November, 1913)	Nancy offers herself to Ashburnham (chap. v).
(Early December, 1913)	Nancy leaves (chap. vi).
(Late December, 1913)	Nancy's telegram and Ashburnham's suicide (chaps. i, vi; also chap. i, Pt. i).

This brief outline does no more than suggest the complexity of cross-references in the novel. For the most part, however, cross-references, advance views, and back-trackings are most common within chapters or blocks of action (as in the key castle scene) but are found to be relatively few between the two main structural units. This is to say that, in general, most events prior to Florence's suicide and most of the references to them are recounted in the first two parts, and the events following her suicide in the last two.[38] The first two parts center on Dowell's and Ashburnham's relationship with Florence, and the last two on their attachment to Nancy; throughout Leonora paces along the sidelines struggling to possess Ashburnham, while she talks endlessly in private sessions, first with Florence and then with Nancy.

---

[38] The only jumps ahead in the first two parts are references—some of them repeated—to Dowell's return to America, his receiving the cablegrams from Edward and Leonora, his arrival in England, Ashburnham's outburst to him, Ashburnham's death, and Leonora's revelations to him (woven throughout the novel, mostly by summary interspersed with dialogue). Parts III and IV contain references to the courtship and early married life of the Ashburnhams, Leonora boxing Maisie Maidan's ears, the trip to the castle at M—, Maisie's death, the talks between Leonora and Florence, Leonora's attempts at an affair with Bayham, Ashburnham's declaration of love to Nancy at the Casino in Nauheim and Florence's suicide. There are no more cross-references here than one might expect to find in a traditionally plotted novel, but, as I say, my listing does not suggest the complex repetitions and dislocations or the varying length of these references within the two main frameworks of *The Good Soldier*.

Such a structure makes clear that both Florence's promiscuity and Nancy's innocence play central roles in the destruction of " the extraordinarily safe castle " the foursome originally appears to be. But Florence's role, it turns out, is minor so far as Ashburnham's destruction is concerned; her disintegrating influence embraces Dowell and Leonora instead. Ashburnham is not to be ruined until he discovers his true passion for Nancy and is victimized along with her. All of the preliminary crises in the novel lead to the final climactic scene of Nancy's offering herself to Ashburnham, which is then followed by the coda of her departure, her telegram from Brindisi, Ashburnham's suicide, her madness, and her return to England.

4

The figurative language is carefully contrived to render and evaluate all of the action. The contradictory metaphors of the first chapter, though some are not directly mentioned again, are in effect structural images which help establish the ambiguities of pattern in the novel. Indeed, much of the imagery throughout is structural as it reveals the shifting impressions of Dowell superimposing present attitudes upon recollected ones. Contributory to both the effect of the moment and to the accumulated effect, the figurative language is drawn from the range of Dowell's experience. He searches for illustrations from nature, hunting, invalidism, common and domestic animals, games—with emphasis on " playing the game " (hockey, billiards, and whist in particular), household china and porcelain, opera, and heroic romances. He also evokes imagery of the heart, of fate and fortune, and of destruction and decay. Often exaggerated and contradictory, often either under- or overkeyed, the imagery reflects the imbalance of a man who has been an unseeing witness to the collapse from within of an apparently placid and indestructible way of life.

In a rather conventional way, some metaphors characterize and by repetition intensify our image of each personality. The three women are visualized in metaphors of bright light and whiteness in contrast with the dark inscrutable passions moving them. Shallow, flighty Florence, " a gay tremulous beam " (p. 15), " as radiant as the track of sunlight along the sea " (p. 30), seeks to leave the world " a little lighter than she had found it " (p. 40). Rushing into the hotel the night of her suicide, her face is " whiter than paper " against her black dress (p. 102), an image Dowell remembers later when he refers to her " personality of paper " (p. 121). On her deathbed she lies " Oh, extremely charming and clear-cut—looking with a puzzled expression at the electric-light bulb that hung from the ceiling, or perhaps through it, to the stars above " (p. 120), a picture which may be an oblique, sardonic reference to her having been " positively electric " in the castle scene. Leonora, more substantial than Florence, is " clean-run," " clear in outline " (pp. 205, 227), and in her black dinner dress (both Florence with her copper hair and Leonora with her blonde hair affect black) " seemed to stand out of her corsage as a white marble bust might out of a black Wedgewood vase " (p. 32). Nancy's whiteness is more ghostly and mysterious. Her white complexion against her black hair suggests the life-in-death she is to come to. She is a " spectre " (p. 201) who always wears white and in the moonlight reminds Dowell of " a phosphorescent fish in a cupboard " (p. 109).

Certain repeated figurative expressions offer little ironic

commentaries on the action or point to larger thematic
developments. Rodney Bayham is described as " rather
like a rabbit " (p. 239), an image of Leonora's second
husband that is perhaps prefigured by her statement:
" Edward has been dead only ten days and yet there are
rabbits on the lawn " (p. 105). Florence and Dowell on
the night of their elopement sit for several hours in the
woods " listening to a mocking-bird imitate an old tom-
cat " (p. 86), the perfect image, as we come to see later,
of Dowell's sexual sterility in relation to Ashburnham's
virility. Of more structural significance is Dowell's writing
that Florence's death is a relief to him like " an unbearably
heavy knapsack " falling from his shoulders (p. 120). It
is a simile he had used a few pages earlier to describe
what happens when a man finds his consummate passion.[39]
By recalling an image he had used with reference to Ashburnham's passion for Nancy at the time when he realizes
he loves her himself, Dowell is giving another hint of his
final grotesquerie: " But I guess that I myself, in my
fainter way, come into the category of the passionate, of
the headstrong, and the too-truthful. For I can't conceal
from myself the fact that I loved Edward Ashburnham—
and that I love him because he was just myself " (p. 253).
That he comes to see himself as even a pale reflection of
the excellency Ashburnham represented is his final illusion.

Occasionally Dowell's overstatements are misleading; his
remark that Leonora adored Ashburnham " with a passion
that was like an agony, and hated him with an agony that
was as bitter as the sea " (p. 26), proves to be only an
apparent exaggeration. Indeed, the reader seldom knows

---

[39] Dowell writes on p. 115 that after a man finds his consummate passion,
" he will travel over no more horizons; he will never again set the knapsack
over his shoulders; he will retire from those scenes. He will have gone out
of business." Ford had used the same simile in a similar context in *The
New Humpty-Dumpty*, p. 270.

when he can take Dowell's statements at their face value,
for the face value often shifts. On page 54 Dowell says
that "in boxing Mrs. Maidan's ears Leonora was just
striking the face of an intolerable universe," a view which
is Leonora's, distorted by her agonized discovery that
afternoon that Ashburnham was being blackmailed. Ten
pages later, the action is likened to a mother "hitting a
naughty child who had been stealing chocolates at an
inopportune moment," a view which must be read in
the context of the perfectly respectable appearance of
Maisie accompanying the Ashburnhams from India and
of Leonora's motherly attentions to her. Ashburnham
with Florence is a "poor wretch" (p. 70); with Leonora
he is a "noble nature" (p. 164)

In another development of pattern in the design, Dowell
sees Ashburnham in a series of images which become
increasingly more tragic and heroic. In the first, already
mentioned, Ashburnham is embracing Nancy on the palm
of God, while Florence stands alone. In the second, Dowell
seems "to see him stand, naked to the waist, his forearms
shielding his eyes, and flesh hanging from him in rags,"
as "Leonora and Nancy banded themselves to do execution, for the sake of humanity, upon the body of the man
who was at their disposal" (p. 239). In the third and
final one, he is "naked and reclining amidst darkness,
upon cold rocks, like one of the ancient Greek damned,
in Tartarus or wherever it was" (p. 252). Ashburnham's
plight is elevated to the universal level of classical legend
and tragedy, but at the same time, as with the exaggerated
commonplace metaphors applied to him earlier, it is difficult not to believe that Dowell, perhaps unconsciously,
belittles Ashburnham by overstating the significance of
his suffering and sacrifice. And yet, at the very end,
recounting Ashburnham's suicide, Dowell is calmer and

with studied reserve describes him as " the English gentleman " but also still " a sentimentalist, whose mind was
compounded of indifferent poems and novels " (pp. 255-
256) .

As Dowell writes, a similar reserve seems to take over
on at least one other level and leads him to certain insights
about social realities. He is constantly seeking out defini-
tions which will illuminate the heart of darkness opened
to him. Again the metaphors help to reflect the emerging
design. Near the beginning he believes that Ashburnham
was destined to be ruined by " tempestuous forces " (p.
52) , and he tries to enlist our sense of pity by asking,
" Is it possible that such a luckless devil should be so
tormented by blind and inscrutable destiny? " (p. 49).
Sometime later, when he is summarizing Ashburnham's
passionate affairs and has just finished considering the
one with the Spanish dancer La Dolciquita, Dowell interrupts to say that he has not titled this story " The Ashburnham Tragedy " because

> it is so sad, just because there was no current to draw things
> along to a swift and inevitable end. There is about this
> story none of the elevation that accompanies tragedy; there
> is about it no nemesis, no destiny. Here were two noble
> people—for I am convinced that both Edward and Leonora
> had noble natures—here then, were two noble natures,
> drifting down life, like fireships afloat on a lagoon and
> causing miseries, heartaches, agony of the mind, and death.
> And they themselves steadily deteriorated? And why? For
> what purpose? To point what lesson? It is all a darkness.
> (p. 164)

The denial of " blind and inscrutable destiny " here suggests that Dowell has come to see human forces at work.
But the paradox of " noble natures " being forces of
destruction does seem to suggest " the elevation that

195

accompanies tragedy," except that classical tragedy implies that the noble ones will be further ennobled by their sacrifice and death and hence give us assurance that man can transcend self and be better than he seems. Dowell leaves us with no such assurance. When he describes the last weeks before Nancy leaves, he comes to see that "there was a great deal of imbecility about the closing scenes of the Ashburnham tragedy" (p. 238). The saddest story has truly acquired the meaning of "shocking" and "wicked," but only in a grimly playful sense. Because imbecilities and madness are not elevating, Dowell's contradictory reversion to the term "tragedy" here forces us to seek a less classical definition. The imbecility is both in Ashburnham taking the "conventional line," by sending Nancy to India and her father, and in Leonora and Nancy ignoring it. Dowell finally realizes that it is not destiny or the forces of elevated tragedy but "conventions and traditions" that doom to extinction the qualities of Ashburnham's virtues.

> I dare say it worked out for the greatest good of the body politic. Conventions and traditions I suppose work blindly but surely for the preservation of the normal type; for the extinction of proud, resolute, and unusual individuals.
>
> Edward was the normal man, but there was too much of the sentimentalist about him and society does not need too many sentimentalists. Nancy was a splendid creature but she had about her a touch of madness. Society does not need individuals with touches of madness about them. So Edward and Nancy found themselves steam-rolled out and Leonora survives, the perfectly normal type, married to a man who is rather like a rabbit. (p. 238)

If Dowell comes to see so clearly the social realities, he still is unable to understand human motivations, for they remain unanswerable doubts. "Did the girl love

Edward, or didn't she?" he asks (p. 243). Did she love him either before or after Leonora shattered her illusions about Ashburnham? Dowell is "pretty certain" she loved him before, but does not know whether she did afterwards. He cannot even decide if she loved him when she went mad upon hearing about the suicide, or when she sent the telegram. "Because that may just as well have been for the sake of Leonora as for the sake of Edward. Or it may have been for the sake of both of them. I don't know. I know nothing. I am very tired" (p. 245). Leonora wanted to believe she did not, Ashburnham that she did. "I don't know. I leave it to you." He also leaves to us whether or not Edward was a "monster of selfishness" in wishing Nancy would still love him, although five thousand miles away (p. 246). Nancy is clearly the key here to the explication of the darkness and to the dilemmas which beset them all upon the release of passion.

First of all, Nancy in her innocence, corrupted by Leonora's management, is most instrumental in bringing Ashburnham to his pitiful end. In a careful *progression d'effet*, in what might be called the Nancy motif, Ford moves by hint and oblique reference toward the climactic scene. The first five of the six casual allusions to Nancy in the first two parts refer to her only as "the girl" or "the poor girl." [40] Her name is not mentioned until almost the end of Part II. Here Dowell reports her praise of Ashburnham's public virtues, and this is followed a few pages later at the beginning of Part III, just after Florence's suicide, by Dowell's unconscious remark about marrying the girl. Not until after this does the reader learn that it was on the same night that Ashburnham had first realized he loved Nancy. Moving to the center, Nancy involves herself and the others in moral tensions

[40] On pp. 20, 28, 58, 91, 94, and 95-96.

which precipitate the climax. Just before the climactic scene in Ashburnham's bedroom, we have the first direct mention of Nancy's madness (p. 233), a foreshadowing of our final view of her.

In loving Ashburnham, in allying herself with Leonora "with the swift cruelty of youth, and with the swift solidarity that attaches woman to woman" (p. 241), and in being loved by Ashburnham and Dowell, Nancy seems to bridge the gap between male honor and feminine possessiveness. Male honor is the embodiment of the order of the past, female possessiveness of the chaotic morality of the present.[41] When Nancy's idealization of Ashburnham is brought into conflict with Leonora's stories about his lechery, and when Leonora's needling of her and Ashburnham ends in his suicide, she breaks down into madness. Hence, the gap between the order of the past and the chaos of the present cannot be bridged, an interpretation the figurative language bears out.

Ashburnham finds release in death, and Leonora, her passion spent, seeks out the innocuous Rodney Bayham. But Nancy's madness is no release, for she is neither alive nor dead. Ultimately, it seems, she is symbolic of the plight the novel renders. Although Dowell at one point denies the forces of destiny, Nancy is certainly a nemesis for the four characters. She precipitates Florence's suicide, Leonora's moral breakdown (because Leonora cannot bear the thought of Nancy's possessing Ashburnham's soul),

---

[41] This is a popular idea with Ford. He had developed it earlier in the contrasting characters of Count and Countess Macdonald in *The New Humpty-Dumpty*. The idea is also important to our understanding of Sylvia and Christopher Tietjens. Ford later elaborated upon the idea just before writing *Some Do Not . . .* in *Women and Men* (1923), where he writes of the "monstrous regiment of women" who have banded together in "a sort of freemasonry to extort always more and more money from the unfortunate camel who bears them all upon his back. And behind his back they will be perpetually whispering their servants' discontent" (p. 25).

Ashburnham's suicide, and Dowell's miserable loneliness. As blind and as inscrutable as destiny, she brings out the best and the worst there is in all of them.

Except possibly for Ashburnham, Nancy at each reference is presented in sharper paradoxical terms than any of the others are. She is a maze of contradictions, and the sudden shifts between the extremes in her actions and emotions warn us that a profound shock will probably immobilize her. Her Catholic training coupled with her sordid childhood had combined to give her personality a combination " of saturnalia and discipline " (p. 125). She has " a tortured mouth, agonized eyes, and a quite extraordinary sense of fun " (p. 123). She is by turns " grotesque " and " beautiful," and both young and " as old as the hills." She can shift suddenly from talk of the saints to " tumbling all over the lawn with the St. Bernard puppy." She can ride furiously or sit quietly for hours nursing Leonora's headaches. " She was, in short, a miracle of patience who could be most miraculously impatient " (p. 124).

Most significantly, she is the epitome of the ambivalent sexual innocence and cruelty which plagues them all. She loves Ashburnham for " the public side of his record—for his good soldiering, for his saving lives at sea, for the excellent landlord that he was and the good sportsman " (p. 244). Once Leonora shatters her illusions about him, Nancy, in her complete sexual innocence and with the instinctive sexual cruelty of the adolescent girl—a part of the " immense and automatically working instinct that attaches . . . [women] to the interest of womanhood " (p. 244), allows herself to be offered to Ashburnham but without any awareness of what she is doing or saying. When she reads of Ashburnham's suicide, she becomes mad and speechless, except to repeat periodically " *Credo in*

199

unum Deum Omnipotentum," an ominous echo from the past, perhaps to remind us that she still believes in the god that was the gentle man Ashburnham, and in the God whom the world had irrevocably denied.

Finally, on the day before Dowell finishes his memoirs, Nancy repeats three times the word "shuttlecocks," drawn from her memory of having been "tossed backwards and forwards between the violent personalities of Edward and his wife" (p. 253). Again the *mot juste* which belittles and illuminates. The word exactly describes how the Ashburnhams have used her; ironically, both Leonora and Ashburnham also felt that the other two had used each of them as a shuttlecock. The paralysis of communication is final and absolute; like every other character in the novel, Nancy is an island unto herself. Even the endless, frenetic talks every night which dominate the last sections of the novel do not lead to any real communication. Instead they precipitate disaster, and, as Dowell complains, no one got what he wanted (p. 237). At the end, Nancy becomes the human embodiment of the unrealized passions underlying society, whose victim she is. Mad, without moral resources, she is perfectly proper, "utterly well behaved as far as her knife and fork go"; she looks beautiful, healthy, and poised, but she signifies nothing, is "a picture without a meaning" (p. 254). She is a personification of both the minuet and the prison, except that now the prison houses nothing but dead passions.

From the first, the reader has seen some of his way before him but has not discerned the end until he got there. The paradoxes of the first chapter have not been resolved but have been explained and revealed for what they are. The minuet *is* the prison, and the very forms and manners of public behavior which seem to give such stability and insurance against confusions are really a prison to the passions. Once passions are released, hell breaks loose. The whole last part of the book up to Nancy's departure includes an increasing number of references to hell, night, storm, half-lights, cruelty, torture, and agony, recalling the destructive images of the first chapter. Still, as Dowell reminds us, the minuet goes on, and outwardly in daytime everyone's behavior seems as calm and as reserved as ever (pp. 201-202).

Ashburnham is the only one who acts as though the minuet still has meaning. The only one to meet a test of moral courage, he refuses to let passion overthrow social order and remains a sentimentalist and a gentleman. The others render him obsolete, and all who remain are wasted by the expense of passion. Leonora breeds but does not love; Nancy is mindless; Dowell himself is merely a chaste eunuch, emotionally and sexually sterile. When his emotions do bubble to the surface, he can find release only in self-pity and lonely fears. He is a sentimentalist, as he says, but one who lacks every emotion of the man of passion and honor he emulates. At every turn, emotional and moral inertia and total meaninglessness—such is Ford's " unbiassed picture of the world we live in."

VII

PARADE'S END

1

IN NOVEMBER OF 1922, FORD LEFT AN ENGLAND HE HAD found unbearable since the war. Soon after, settled in his favorite Provence, he crystallized his intentions of writing a war novel, which he had not earlier felt equal to doing.[1] In *It Was The Nightingale* Ford explains at some length the genesis of *Parade's End*. The work he

> wanted to see done was something on an immense scale, a little cloudy in immediate attack but with the salient points

[1] Since the war, Ford had published *Thus to Revisit* (1921), a critical memoir, his poetic drama *A House* (1921), and one of his lesser novels, *The Marsden Case* (1923), apparently suggested by the life of W. R. S. Ralston, the first translator of Turgenev. Ford had also written but not published *That Same Poor Man*, a novel attacking the literary old guard in London. One of the characters is Croyd, a "writer who has served in the war as a sergeant and who returns to devote his energies and money to the promotion of lively letters in England. Like Moffat, the benefactor, Croyd is eventually turned against, as he had realized would happen, and in a rather fantastic conclusion to the novel, leaves the country." Frank MacShane, "The Pattern of Ford Madox Ford," *New Republic*, cxxxii (April 4, 1955), 16.

and the final impression extraordinarily clear. I wanted the Novelist in fact to appear in his really proud position as historian of his own time. Proust being dead I could see no one who was doing that. . . .[2]

The protagonist he sought must be one " in lasting tribulation—with a permanent shackle and ball on his leg." He could not have a physical defect, for he must go to war; his tribulation " must be something of a moral order and something inscrutable." He found his model in his long-time friend Arthur Marwood, who had worked with him on *The English Review* and had died just before the war. Marwood, " the heavy Yorkshire squire with his dark hair startlingly silver in places, his keen blue eyes, his florid complexion, his immense, expressive hands and his great shapelessness," " a man of infinite benevolence, comprehensions and knowledges," was the kind of major character Ford needed to carry his subject, which he saw as " the public events of a decade." Endowed with " the power of cool observation in tremendous crises," Marwood could serve perfectly well as Ford's sane central observer of a crumbling world.

There he was, large—an " elephant built out of meal sacks." Deliberate, slow in movement and extraordinarily omniscient. He was physically very strong and enduring. And he was, beneath the surface, extraordinarily passionate—with an abiding passion for the sort of truth that makes for intellectual accuracy in the public service. It was a fascinating task to find him a posthumous career.

Being tubercular, Marwood led a relatively passive life in the south of England—" the Permanent Official turned

[2] Ford discusses the genesis of *Parade's End* on pages 199-227 of *It Was the Nightingale,* from which the following summary is taken.

hermit, but unsoured! " [3] Ford, however, required a character who was " enough of a man of action to get into the
trenches and do what he was told. But he was to be too
essentially critical to initiate any daring sorties. Indeed
his activities were most markedly to be in the realm of
criticism." Marwood was the desired prototype; his story
had to be found elsewhere.

Coincidentally, it was Marwood who was indirectly
responsible for planting the germ of the story. Marwood
had told Ford of a mutual friend who had married a
woman because she had persuaded him she was with child
by him, but that he had discovered later that the child
might not have been his. Tortured by doubt, and by the
realization that his wife was continually unfaithful to him,
the friend was in constant agony. Because he was bound
by a gentlemanly sense of decency and because his wife
was a Roman Catholic, divorce was impossible. Ford was
also reminded of the story of Harold Munro's neighbor,
who, after his wife had left him for another man, fell in
love with another woman. In time his wife returned; when
she refused to divorce him, he committed suicide. Give a
man of Marwood's strength of character these tribulations,
put him in a war, and there was Ford's central character,
who " was to go through the public affairs of distracted
Europe with that private cannonball all the time dragging
at his ankle! " He would, however, not commit suicide;
he would " live his predicament down."

Ford realized that the war would intensify the agony
of his protagonist; he would be a true " *homo duplex*:
a poor fellow whose body is tied in one place but whose
mind and personality brood eternally over another distant

[3] Violet Hunt in *The Flurried Years*, p. 28, describes Marwood as " a
dandy in London and a farmer in Kent, where he would be sitting up all
night with pigs and handling compost."

locality." It was the anguish of worry within the individual consciousness which Ford saw as the most tragic lesson of war. It was worry which " feeds on itself and in the end so destroys the morale that less than a grasshopper becomes a burden. It is without predictable term; it is as menacing as the eye of a serpent; it causes unspeakable fatigue even as, remorselessly, it banishes rest." So powerfully did Ford feel this, he admittedly wrote a novel with a purpose. " It seemed to me that if the world could be got to see War from that angle there would be no more wars. . . ." The finished novel, though it may impress us with the undesirability of war, reveals its emphasis and meaning in quite different areas of human experience. The war presents us with but one of the battlegrounds of the action. More precisely, the subject is the collapse of the worthy past and the emergence of a *homo simplex*, for whom public and private tribulations are catalysts in a slow evolution toward serenity.

Ford makes it clear that he saw his novel as something more than a plea against future wars. First of all, his subject " was the world as it culminated in the war "—a " crumbling world." He even tells us that he was fascinated with the idea of using the world as his central character in " an immense novel in which all the characters should be great masses of people—or interests. You would have Interest A, remorselessly and under the stress of blind necessities, slowly or cataclysmically overwhelming Interest Z. Without the attraction of sympathy for a picturesque or upright individual." Ford realized that such a grandiose and inconceivable dream, if written, would be the culmination of the novel, but he did not feel prepared to write " without the attraction of human nature."

Ford nevertheless had become intensely interested in the novel of mass action which, through a wide range of characters, offered a panoramic or spectacular view of society without the benefit of a traditional central hero. The best early example is Flaubert's *Sentimental Education*, and Ford read that fourteen times.[4] Of Conrad's work he came to admire particularly his larger canvases like *Nostromo* (" the whole of a vast, imagined republic, where all humanity's passions, meannesses and failures from ideals may run riot "), *Under Western Eyes* (" all Russia forever alive in the background of a mass movement "), *The Secret Agent* (" the immense thriller with its enveloping background of a darkness enough to bury millions of lives . . . and with the eternal mother-woman dominating the whole of it "), and *The Nigger of the " Narcissus "* (" the only mass romance of the sea ").[5] As an Impressionist, himself gradually seeking larger and more representative canvases—in the Katherine Howard trilogy, *Mr. Fleight*, and *The New Humpty-Dumpty*—Ford may have had ambitions to write a novel without a hero. But temperamentally he was incapable of doing so. As almost every commentator on Ford has perceived, Ford's most representative novels are aesthetic projections of himself, or of what he saw himself to represent and his world to be.[6]

Ford needed a central figure to serve as a moral and psychological focus around which to weave his plots. He found that center, as we know, in his gentleman of honor, who is a kind of microcosm of the conscience of the national tradition. The other characters help illuminate him and in doing so illuminate themselves and the par-

[4] *Thus to Revisit*, p. 159.
[5] *Portraits from Life*, p. 68.
[6] Walter Allen, for example, believes that *The Good Soldier* and the Tietjens novels " are objective correlatives of Ford's own emotional situations. By pushing, as it were, his personal problem out of arm's reach and staging it in terms of characters other than himself and those closely associated with him, he depersonalized it, raised it to the level of the material of art." *The English Novel*, p. 397.

ticular issues treated, but Ford never wrote a novel like *Sentimental Education* or *Nostromo* in which the center is a nation or a whole society and the characters are illuminative radial lines toward that center. Ford's practice was rather to arrange around his central character both major and minor figures who help define the frames of mind or forces which oppose or support him, as I have already indicated with particular reference to *Mr. Fleight.* Hence, Tietjens, the prototype of the gentleman of honor, has to be from the ruling classes and from the best of those who have maintained the national conscience in practice as well as theory. With such a center, he can, however, present a panoramic picture of a society in transition and offer dramatically "the public record of a decade." Everything is to be seen in terms of and through the predicaments of this particular yet representative single character.

The plot of *Parade's End* focuses on the forces which lead to the protagonist's renunciation of his ruling class position in a corrupt, warlike world and to his reaffirmation of the value of personal integrity as the only basis for a revival of a worth-while world.[7] Christopher Tietjens, the younger son of a wealthy Yorkshire landowner, seems to have every quality and opportunity necessary for

---

[7] *Parade's End* is the title for the single volume edition published by Alfred A. Knopf in 1950. The volume includes *Some Do Not . . .* (1924), *No More Parades* (1925), *A Man Could Stand Up—*(1926), and *The Last Post* (1928). The title *Parade's End* was Ford's. Goldring in *Trained for Genius*, p. 258, writes: "In 1930, when the proposal was made to him to issue an omnibus volume of the Tietjens novels under the general title *The Tietjens Saga*, he wrote to a correspondent, in a letter quoted in the *Saturday Review of Literature*, 2nd August, 1941, deprecating the use of this title. 'I do not like the title *Tietjens Saga*,' he says, 'because in the first place Tietjens is a name difficult to pronounce and book-sellers would almost inevitably persuade readers that they mean *The Forsyte Saga* with great damage to my sales.' For a general title he suggested *Parade's End*, with the *Tietjens Saga* for a sub-title."

successful public service, but he attracts disaster because of his unrelenting stewardship of the traditional British virtues. He is bound to his promiscuous wife, Sylvia, whom he had married because of her claim that she was with child by him, and he is in love with Valentine Wannop, an intellectual who is a Latinist and a suffragette. For the sake of his son, who in fact might not be his, Tietjens agrees to take Sylvia back after her impulsive elopement to the Continent with a man named Perowne. Before she returns, he meets Valentine, and, though they make no overt declaration of their love, they are irresistibly drawn together by their ability to talk freely and openly with each other. As a result of several unfortunate coincidences and Christopher's refusal to admit or deny anything, he becomes a victim of malicious gossip. At the same time, Christopher's protégé in his government office, the ambitious, lower-middle-class opportunist Vincent Macmaster, falls in love with a Mrs. Edith Ethel Duchemin, whose clerical husband is a sexual psychopath. They begin an adulterous affair, and Macmaster, through Tietjens' generosity and the help of Edith Ethel, rises in social and political circles as rapidly as Tietjens falls.

Early in the war, Christopher, who had enlisted, suffers amnesia as a result of shell shock and is returned to England. Sylvia, who is thoroughly exasperated by his superiority, goodness, and the impenetrability of his emotions, continues her campaign of slander, lies, and accusations in order to break down his reserve. Through her efforts, the jealous enmity of Edith Ethel, now Mrs. Macmaster, and his own refusal to fake figures for the War Office, Tietjens is thoroughly discredited. Sylvia's repeated accusations that Valentine is her husband's mistress arouse a passion in him for Valentine so that on the day before he returns to the front he asks her to be his mistress.

She agrees at first, but that night they decide that they are among those who " do not." He does not write or see her again until Armistice Day.

 At the front, Tietjens is further pursued by tribulations, but he immerses himself in the numerous details of his menial job, in which he finds a measure of satisfaction. His sanity is threatened by psychopathic and alcoholic officers and by the troubles of the men in the ranks, who are all plagued by home worries similar to his own. Sylvia pursues him to the front lines. She is particularly frustrated, vindictive, and unbalanced at this time and precipitates a nightmarish episode which leads to Christopher's arrest and transfer to the trenches by General Campion, his godfather, who later, under Sylvia's continued needling, transfers Tietjens to the undignified post of accompanying German prisoners to prison camps. Under such constant strafing, Tietjens comes to realize that being with Valentine is his only hope for salvation, and he renounces his ruling class position, Sylvia, and his whole past.

Three weeks before the Armistice, Tietjens is discharged. He returns home friendless, ill, and penniless, but refuses to accept Groby, the family estate, from his older brother Mark or to take any of the family fortune. Valentine appears on Armistice Day, as do several officers from Tietjens' front line division, like ghosts from the past. One officer dies of a heart attack, another goes completely mad, and when Valentine and Christopher finally return to his empty house, Sylvia, who had previously taken almost all the furniture, is there, announces she has cancer and makes a dramatic though faked fall down the stairs. Christopher is tempted to go with her, but Valentine asserts herself, calls Sylvia a liar, and keeps him. Late in the night of Armistice Day Mark discovers that the Allies are not going to pursue the Germans into Germany; he vows then never to move or speak again.

Christopher, Valentine, and Mark and his mistress, Marie Léonie, move to a rural cottage where Christopher raises pigs and sells old furniture to wealthy Americans. Valentine is soon pregnant, and Marie nurses Mark, who is dying. Sylvia's last stand is to appear at the cottage one day while Christopher is away. She is trying to get Christopher and his ménage thrown out, but after she confronts Valentine, she is moved by the simplicity of their life, refuses to harm the unborn child, and finally agrees to divorce Christopher. After she leaves, Christopher appears for a moment. He has been to Groby and holds in his hand a chunk of Groby Great Tree, cut down with Sylvia's approval by the wealthy Americans who have leased the estate. Wearily, he goes to recover some lost pictures. Mark then speaks to Valentine, telling her to be kind to Christopher for the sake of her unborn child, and dies.

The English novel that might seem most nearly comparable to *Parade's End* as a social chronicle is Galsworthy's *Forsyte Saga*. Galsworthy's professed purpose was to present " an intimate incarnation of the disturbance that Beauty effects in the lives of men." [8] His " intimate incarnation " is like a family song which begins with a variation of themes on the sense of property and eventually trails off into the droning hum of Fleur's cry to be free, to be happy, and to bury the past. The original theme is now pitched in the minor key, as Soames sits under the yew trees in the cemetery which holds his family dead knowing that he has held on and that men of his spirit inevitably will. And yet he ends on the note of

[8] John Galsworthy, " Preface," *The Forsyte Saga*, Modern Standard Authors Edition (New York: Scribners, 1918), p. xii.

failure: the beauty and the loving in the world are forever to elude him. His failure is one of sensibility for
which he is not entirely responsible. He is the product
of an upper-middle-class sense of property, ingrained so
deeply that possession is the law of life. Only the artist,
Young Jolyon, the black sheep of the Forsytes, achieves
the serenity which beauty offers—in his water colors and
in his love for Irene and Jon. His detachment from the
family enables him to see where its weaknesses lie. " We
are, of course, all of us the slaves of property," he says
to Bosinney in his famous statement,

> " and I admit that it's a question of degree, but what I call
> a ' Forsyte ' is a man who is decidedly more than less a slave
> of property. He knows a good thing, he knows a safe thing,
> and his grip on property—it doesn't matter whether it be
> wives, houses, money or reputation—is his hall-mark." (p.
> 196)

The Forsytes are, in fact, half of England, those whose
wealth and security make everything possible. Galsworthy's obvious point is that beauty is not to be purchased. All of the true Forsytes of England are hence
predoomed to failure.

The trilogy is constructed upon meticulous patterns of
antitheses in characters, actions, and ideas, a technique
Ford criticized, thinking it more appropriate to the drama
than to the novel.[9] Thematically, the old is contrasted
with the new; individualism is set against the incursion
of the state (primarily in demanding income and inheritance taxes); property against art or, rather, security
against beauty; the age of the carriage against that of the
automobile; integration against disintegration. The story

[9] *Portraits from Life*, p. 139.

is told chronologically by a dramatic method in which its great number of scenes are rendered in dialogue, with the scenes set as economically as in stage directions. We see in the minds of selected characters only as much as will help to illuminate the scenes which precede or follow. The quality of the variety of antitheses in the novel is ironic, but instead of pointing up the ambiguities possible in the subject, the antitheses serve to elucidate, clarify, and even to classify the characters, actions, and ideas the novel represents. Galsworthy was endowed with a remarkable vision which enabled him to clarify the surface of the events of his day. The Forsytes of England stand revealed —their aims, ambitions, successes, failures, weaknesses and strengths—all defined, all perfectly understood, but without complexity, without penetration beneath the surface of observable human experience.

When set against *Parade's End*, Galsworthy's commercial family history seems pale, limited in imagination, extremely traditional in manner, and bound too closely to the period it pictures. Before Ford's tetralogy appeared in a single volume, it was often referred to as the "Tietjens' Saga." It is certainly closer than Galsworthy's several Forsyte novels to those great traditional tales of the north countries, of noble protagonists who are the friends, enemies, and playthings of the gods, who fight monsters and dragons for the grandeur of self, lady-love, and country, and who embody national and human aspirations toward perfection. The skeletal framework supporting the complexities of *Parade's End* is borrowed from the epic tradition, as several of Ford's earlier historical and contemporary novels had been borrowed from medieval legends.

Though the story of Tietjens' career is set against the panorama of a transitional period in which world war is

the culminating upheaval heralding disastrous shifts in
values, the fictional method is essentially dramatic. Ford's
treatment is internal, not external; psychological, not historical. The novel focuses on the trials and tribulations of
a single character and his resolution of them. In neither
his speech nor actions is Tietjens ever the pawn of a controlling idea; at least, his creator succeeds in surrounding
his story with the illusion of inevitability. Arthur Mizener
recognizes that

> Ford saw clearly that the lyric effects of dialogue and medi-
> tation, no matter how brilliant, were sterile unless they grew
> out of the solid ground of character and action. His success
> in making them do so [in *Parade's End*] is an almost unique
> achievement in the 20th Century novel, and a very great
> one.[10]

Each of the first three novels in particular has much
of the intensity of the dramatic novel (in Edwin Muir's
terms) in treating time as fate, in placing emphasis on
causality, and in being spatially limited.[11] But the world
Parade's End renders is not "static" as in many novels
of James and Conrad or, indeed, as in a good deal of
English fiction; that is, it is not a world in which the
characters have to explore and formulate their moral
identity with relation to what is present but not yet appre-
hended. Lord Jim needs to redeem himself from an act of
cowardice to return to the solidarity of mankind; Heyst
destroys himself because of his lifelong denial of humanity
(at least, in principle) ; Strether discovers he has not lived,
has not got out of life what is there. Their worlds remain
in order to be discovered. Especially in the novels of
James, characters and relationships change: they come to

---

[10] "A Large Fiction," *The Kenyon Review*, XIII (Winter, 1951), 146.
[11] *The Structure of the Novel* (London: Hogarth, 1938), pp. 41-61.

realize with Kate Croy at the end of their affairs that they " are not as they were." The dramatic affair has worked itself out in a social scene (space) which itself does not shift. Such is true, of course, of *The Good Soldier*. But in *Parade's End* characters change (especially Tietjens) as the world changes, for Ford is dealing with shifts in both space and time and with a theme that could be handled adequately only by a sequence novel of a length commensurate with the changes it represents, as is true of *War and Peace*. Tietjens' change is one of fortune, but it also involves a shift in his view of life to one that will allow him to live in harmony with his own soul, a discovery which defines the nature of the central struggle within Tietjens. At the beginning of the novel his notions of harmony—of what is done by a member of the family of Groby, of the ruling classes, of the Edwardian gentleman —are being severely tested by Sylvia's elopement with Perowne, followed by her request to return. She, and the politicians at Whitehall, and the war destroy that harmony, but in its place Tietjens finds a new one with Valentine and in his role as a small producer. He discovers the only serenity possible for a man of talent and feeling whose old world has crashed around him.

2

Christopher Tietjens is the culmination and prototype of Ford's gentlemen of honor. Like the earlier models, he is the naive, self-effacing altruist, bound by a moral commitment to the duties of his aristocratic position, and like them he is inspired by a consuming desire for serenity and perfection. He is the " Christ-bearer," the living embodiment of the conscience of his nation and race. Consequently, he is insufferable to others, who inevitably persecute and test him. He most of all resembles the eighteenth-century " natural " aristocrat as described by Edmund Burke in his *Appeal from the New to the Old Whigs*:

> To be bred in a place of estimation; to see nothing low and sordid from one's infancy; to be taught to respect one's self; to be habituated to the censorial inspection of the public eye; to look early to public opinion; to stand upon such elevated ground as to be enabled to take a large view of the widespread and infinitely diversified combinations of men and affairs in a large society; to have leisure to read, to reflect, to converse; to be enabled to draw the court and attention of the wise and learned wherever they are to be found;—to be habituated in armies to command and to obey; to be taught to despise danger in the pursuit of honour and duty; to be formed to the greatest degree of vigilance, foresight, and circumspection, in a state of things in which no fault is committed with impunity, and the slightest mistakes draw on the most ruinous consequences—to be led to a guarded and regulated conduct, from a sense that you are considered as an instructor of your fellow-citizens in their highest concerns, and that you act as a reconciler between God and man—to be employed as an administrator of law and justice, and to be thereby amongst the first benefactors of mankind—to be a professor of high science or of liberal and ingenuous art—to be amongst rich traders, who from their success are presumed to have sharp and vigorous understandings, and to possess the virtues of diligence, order, constancy, and regularity, and to have cultivated an habitual regard to commutative justice—these are the circumstances of men, that form what I should call a *natural* aristocracy, without which there is no nation.[12]

[12] Edmund Burke, *Works* (rev. ed., Boston: Little, Brown, 1866), IV, 175.

". . . without which there is no nation" are words which clearly describe the prophetic warnings of Ford through Tietjens. Burke assumes there must be a harmony between the public and private selves, between the performance of public duties and the convictions of conscience, before the ruling class can fulfill its proper function within the hierarchy of nature's order of reconciling God and man. The defection of the ruling class is disaster for the state. That is the essence of the traditional indoctrination of the British schoolboy. Tietjens at one point wryly explains himself to General Campion:

> "Ruggles told my father what he did because it is not a good thing to belong to the seventeenth or eighteenth centuries in the twentieth. Or really, because it is not good to have taken one's public school's ethical system seriously. I am really, sir, the English public schoolboy. That's an eighteenth-century product. What with the love of truth that—God help me!—they rammed into me at Clifton and the belief that Arnold forced upon Rugby that the vilest of sins—the vilest of all sins—is to peach to the headmaster! That's me, sir. Other men get over their schooling. I never have. I remain adolescent. These things are obsessions with me. Complexes, sir!" [13]

Like Ford's other honorable protagonists, Tietjens attempts a literal translation of these ideals to everyday life, but since he is more severely tested than they by the chaotic forces of moral corruption, instinctive sexuality, insanity, and war, he is driven to profounder agonies of doubt and introspective re-examination.

The conflict within Tietjens centers in the struggle between his public and private selves. His story is instructive. "Throughout the tetralogy," E. V. Walter perceives,

[13] *Parade's End*, p. 490. All future references in this chapter are to this edition and are placed within parentheses.

" Ford's art breathes life into the ancient political truth that the state is the soul writ large and the self is the republic in microcosm." [14] The image of self and the image of nation ideally mirror each other, but when the national ideals become corrupt and hollow, the image of the moral self has to be maintained on its own basis. The only direction is underground. The only hope is anonymity. The natural aristocrat as hero becomes the nonheroic simple-lifer and small producer who is the warden of the lost virtues which under his care will be regenerated and someday returned to the world. Tietjens is nearly mad before he goes underground with his feudal, pre-nine-teenth-century ideals to seek a new beginning. Although our final view of him, standing before Mark's bed holding a chunk of Groby Great Tree is that of a weary, forgetful man who looks " like a dejected bulldog " (p. 835) , he has apparently achieved his desire to be an Anglican saint, " the quality of being in harmony with your own soul," and hence with God (p. 496) . He has achieved the initial step in the renewal of the virtuous state.

To readers of Ford, Tietjens' public self is familiar, despite certain differences between him and earlier pro-tagonists. Unlike Sergius Macdonald, Tietjens is totally English, being the son of a Yorkshireman and a saintly woman from the south of England. Unlike George Moffat, he is from the wealthy landed gentry. From his father's side of the house he has acquired his stolid exterior and his commitment to the character and duties of the ruling class; from his mother's side, his emotionalism, his senti-mentality, his saintliness. His sufferings stem from his desire to live up to both heritages. Brought up in a world and a class where the ordered life ran smoothly and what

[14] " The Political Sense of Ford Madox Ford," p. 17.

complaints one had could be handled by letters to the *Times,* Tietjens conscientiously assumes his rightful duties as a public servant without concern for rumblings that might come from below and with complete assurance that lesser servants like the police " don't touch people like us " (p. 45). He has absolutely no self-interest as far as personal glory goes. To the lower ranks he is patronizing but just. He guides the fortunes of the lower-middle-class Macmaster just for the sake of helping him, and later at the front out of a sense of duty to his military superiors he broods over Macmaster's nephew, Captain McKechnie, and keeps him from going totally insane.

By his omniscient faculty of " right intuitions " (p. 93), and by his almost frightful ability to keep his emotions under apparent control, Tietjens insults and exasperates others. The desire to tear away his mask of impenetrability leads them to denounce and persecute him. But Tietjens sees no need to justify his actions, for he knows that a man of his class does what he wants and takes what he gets for it.

> Why, if he, Christopher Tietjens of Groby, had the need to justify himself, what did it stand for to be Christopher Tietjens of Groby? That was the unthinkable thought.
>
> Obviously he was not immune from the seven deadly sins, in the way of a man. One might lie, yet not bear false witness against a neighbour; one might kill, yet not without fitting provocation or for self-interest; one might conceive of theft as reiving cattle from the false Scots which was the Yorkshireman's duty; one might fornicate, obviously, as long as you did not fuss about it unhealthily. That was the right of the Seigneur in a world of Other Ranks. He hadn't personally committed any of these sins to any great extent. One reserved the right so to do and to take the consequences. . . . (p. 350)

He had adopted his extreme reserve believing that it was "a habit of behaviour [. . .] the best in the world for the normal life," although he realizes that "in the face of death [. . .]; in the face of madness, passion, dishonour or—and particularly—prolonged mental strain," he might break (pp. 178-179).

Before Sylvia, who causes him to face all of these, he never removes his mask. She has started or broadcast most of the vicious gossip about him. She insults, shocks, and strikes him, but he remains imperturbable. In the long, painful scene in *Some Do Not . . .*, which begins by her throwing her salad plate at him, she is desperately trying to get up enough nerve to tell him his father had committed suicide from a broken heart because he believed Tietjens was living on a woman's money and had had a child by Valentine Wannop, whose father had been Mr. Tietjens' best friend. Tietjens answers: "Oh! Ah! Yes! . . . I suspected that. I knew it, really. I suppose the poor dear knows better now. Or perhaps he doesn't. . . . It doesn't matter" (p. 178). There seems to be every psychological justification for her having berated him earlier in the scene:

> "If," Sylvia went on with her denunciation, "you had once in our lives said to me: 'You whore! You bitch! You killed my mother. May you rot in hell for it. . . .' If you'd only once said something like it . . . about the child! About Perowne! . . . you might have done something to bring us together. . . ." (p. 172)

With Sylvia, Tietjens is taking what he gets for having seduced her on a train; she had "bitched" him into a marriage of honor by declaring she was with child by him, although it may have been by a man named Drake. Sylvia herself is not certain and is ignorant about how to find out (p. 176). Though Tietjens had been dazzled by her beauty, his emotions were never deeply involved, and he can cooly tell her it makes no difference that she has ruined him.

> "You had been let in for it by some brute. I have always held that a woman who has been let down by one man has the right—has the duty for the sake of her child—to let down a man. It becomes woman against man: against one man. I happened to be that one man: it was the will of God. But you were within your rights. I will never go back on that. Nothing will make me, ever!" (p. 174)

With increasing fury and desperation Sylvia tries to break down Tietjens' defenses, for he is the only man she has desired whose inner self she could neither penetrate nor possess. He had succumbed to her beauty in a moment of physical passion, but he had never accepted her as a woman, the instinctive woman who needs both a man's body and soul. To her he is an ox, " repulsive: like a swollen animal " (p. 29), who is " the soul of truth like a stiff Dutch doll " (p. 32); on the other hand, he is like Christ in his detachment and eternal forgiving. She can fathom neither side of that paradox. Though she is the one who is most instrumental in ruining his public reputation, she fails in bringing him to his knees.

Tietjens is equally baffling to others. From their first meeting, Edith Ethel sees him as " the male, threatening, clumsily odious and external," and she hates him as a " nebulous monster " (p. 93). To Campion, who is protective and sentimental over him, he is a Dreyfus by virtue of his " positive genius for getting into the most disgusting messes " (p. 409). Later Campion charges Tietjens with being a " disaster to every one who has to do with you. You are as conceited as a hog; you are as obstinate as a bullock. . . . You drive me mad. . . . And you have ruined the life of that beautiful woman . . ." (p. 481) . To Marie Léonie, Tietjens is Apollo to Mark's Jupiter (p. 694) , and a " mealsack " (Valentine's label for him) who nonetheless " had some of the spirit of Chantecler beneath his rolling shoulders of a farmyard boar " (p. 701) . At the end both Mark and Sylvia realize he is the Anglican saint he desired to be (pp. 731, 806) .

Ford's earlier gentlemen of honor suffered for their purity of motive and sacrificed fortune and self for the sake of their simple, traditional ideals. But compared with Tietjens they seem somewhat remote and wooden, like figures in a romantic melodrama or musical comedy. They are saved by Ford's sense of comedy, by his awareness of the muddles they precipitate, and by his brilliance in rendering those muddles and using them for serious social comment. Atlhough there is some rendering of their con-scious thoughts as ordered by the author-narrator, there is no rendering of their consciousness as experienced from moment to moment. With Tietjens there is—not consis-tently or exclusively but enough to give him a dimension of reality that the earlier protagonists generally lack. His consciousness, the private self working on several levels, records, reflects, and evaluates the trials of contemporary society as Ford envisioned them. For the kind of epic panorama Ford was writing, he needed to see his gentle-man of honor in a time of catastrophic upheaval of the civilized world and from both the internal and external vantage points of several characters who illustrate the various faces of the devil—or of the angels—confronting him. Tietjens, always at the center, is projected by means of a genuinely multiple vision.

3

Tietjens increasingly fears that his public self will fail him, allowing his emotions to take over. Intellectually he perceives the nature of the enemies conspiring against his convictions, his excellence, his whole way of life. He is aware that the Tietjens clan is under a curse pronounced when the family took over Groby from a Catholic family on the accession of William and Mary. The curse appears to have had its effect, for every Tietjens squire since then has " died of a broken neck or of a broken heart; for all the fifteen thousand acres of good farming land and iron land, and for all the heather on the top of it . . ." (p. 177). Tietjens also knows that he is doomed to persecution, for " in such a world as this, an idealist—or perhaps it's only a sentimentalist—must be stoned to death " (p. 237). As a vestige of the eighteenth century he is bound to be crushed by the twentieth. He realizes the prophetic relevance in the ceremony disbanding a battalion:

> " Well, the end of the show was to be: the adjutant would stand the battalion at ease; the band would play *Land of Hope and Glory*, and then the adjutant would say: *There will be no more parades.* . . . Don't you see how symbolical it was—the band playing *Land of Hope and Glory*, and then the adjutant saying *There will be no more parades?* . . . For there won't. There won't, there damn well won't. . . . No more Hope, no more Glory, no more parades for you and me any more. Nor for the country . . . nor for the world, I dare say . . . None . . . Gone . . . Na poo, finny! No . . . more . . . parades! " (pp. 306-307)

The forces working against Tietjens strike at his intellect perhaps even more than they do at his emotions. Or it is the attacks on his intellect that create his emotional trials. Ford as author-narrator tells us at one point that in every man there is a balance of two minds, " the one checking the other; thus emotion stands against reason, intellect corrects passion and first impressions act a little, but very little, before quick reflection " (p. 87). On one level, Tietjens' story dramatizes the breakthrough of the intellect by the emotions. His intellectual awareness that there will be " no more parades " has to become an emotional reality before he can face a world without parade and live in harmony with it.

His internal dissension presages the falling apart of his established world. Sex, or, perhaps more accurately, instinctive sexuality, seems the motive power behind the varied assaults on his intellect and emotions.[15] But sex can be used as a weapon to preserve as well as to destroy. Since the time of *A Call* and *The New Humpty-Dumpty* Ford had been fascinated with opposite types of feminine sexual passion. On the one hand, there is the cruelty of the jealous or frustrated woman to *possess* a man body and soul. On the other, there is the tenderness of the intelligent woman to *ally* herself with him both body and soul. In *Some Do Not . . .* Ford makes clearer than ever before that he is placing one passionate disposition against another. Tietjens thinks to himself:

[15] Ford was obviously familiar with Freudian psychology. He writes about and occasionally attempts to project the unconscious thoughts of his characters; he refers at one point to the " sublimal consciousness " and several times to " frustration," " inhibition," " mad doctors," " complexes "; and Sylvia declares in her first scene that she pins her faith, in part, on Freud (p. 37). Her remark leads the reader to suspect that Ford saw Freudian psychology as one of the destructive elements in modern life. Miss Jeaffreson in *The Marsden Case* is an amateur Freudian who " analyzes " the hero and his sister. At one point (p. 355) the hero goes to " the Straightener," as does the narrator at another.

But, positively, she [Valentine] and Sylvia were the only two human beings he had met for years whom he could respect: the one for sheer efficiency in killing; the other for having the constructive desire and knowing how to set about it. Kill or cure! The two functions of man. If you wanted something killed you'd go to Sylvia Tietjens in the sure faith that she would kill it: emotion, hope, ideal; kill it quick and sure. If you wanted something kept alive you'd go to Valentine: she'd find something to do for it. . . . The two types of mind: remorseless enemy, sure screen, dagger . . . sheath! (p. 128)

Tietjens arouses passion in both women, and, as he predicts, one sets out to destroy his public self in order to possess and then destroy his inner self, while the other rather ignores his public self, sees him as he is, and saves him.

Society naturally reflects these opposing impulses so that even before Sylvia and Valentine are introduced directly, implications of sexual destructiveness in society are evident. On the train to Rye, Tietjens, plagued with thoughts of Sylvia, excoriates the English and Dante Gabriel Rossetti, Macmaster's favorite poet and the subject of his monograph, for their " attempts to justify fornication " (p. 17). Tietjens assures his companion that he stands " for monogamy and chastity. And for no talking about it " (p. 18). Soon after, when Macmaster questions his statement that there will be a war, Tietjens says,

" War, my good fellow, [. . .] is inevitable and with this country plumb centre in the middle of it. Simply because you fellows are such damn hypocrites. There's not a country in the world that trusts us. We're always, as it were, committing adultery—like your fellow!—with the name of Heaven on our lips." (p. 20)

Although the remark is petulant, it suggests the correlation between sexual promiscuity and political immorality developed throughout the novel. A vulgar incursion of sex into a purlieu of the ruling class, the golf club, occurs when two drunken lechers brag publicly of their sexual exploits and have to be reprimanded by Campion. Sandbach, Campion's brother-in-law, is another yet more dangerous representative of the salacious frame of mind taking over the society of the good people. He is the son of an ennobled mayor of Middleborough with whose commercial family the landed Tietjens' had been constantly at odds. Sandbach's gossip with its elaborations and dirty innuendoes infuriates Tietjens, although he realizes " that it was natural for an unborn fellow like Sandbach to betray the solidarity that should exist between men " (p. 77). On the other hand, Campion and Waterhouse, the cabinet minister, people of Tietjens' own class, take it for granted that Tietjens has a mistress and treat him as an equal, though they complain of his making a public display of her.

Even before the war, Tietjens' two women imperil the balance between his intellect and passion. The tension between them begins when he falls in love with Valentine just after he has agreed to take Sylvia back. With the perfect assurance of an English gentleman, he can accept the gossip that surrounds him. He knows he could prove it a lie, but refuses for the sake of his child because " it was better for a boy to have a rip of a father than a whore for mother! " (p. 77). As his affection for Valentine grows, he views with increasing horror the thought of returning to Sylvia; it must be, he thinks, God's retribution upon him for having seduced her. " Perhaps God then, after all, visits thus heavily sexual offenses " (p. 121). Returning to the Wannop cottage through the early

morning fog after depositing the suffragette Gertie with
a neighboring parson, Tietjens discovers that Valentine
is a woman with whom he can talk easily, although he feels
frustration and resentment at the north country convention which prevents him from showing his feelings or his
concern for her as she guides the horse. He has a momentary urge to free himself from that convention, to ally
himself with her "warm and clinging" south country
personality.

> He had then forty-eight and three-quarter hours. Let them
> be a holiday! A holiday from himself above all; a holiday
> from his standards, from his convention with himself. From
> clear observation, from exact thought, from knocking over
> all the skittles of the exactitudes of others, from the suppres-
> sion of emotions. . . . From all the weariness that made him
> intolerable to himself. . . . (p. 129)

But after the general's car has struck Mrs. Wannop's horse
and he waits by himself for the knacker, he realizes that
"principles are like a skeleton map of a country—you
know whether you're going east or north" (p. 144).

It is Tietjens' fate to be involved in the complex worries
of others which supplement and reflect his own. All together, they illustrate the nerve-wracked incoherence of
a world without principles, of people with only fragments
of little but corroding concerns and with no view of life
as a whole. When Tietjens goes to war, he discovers the
incredible home worries, generally sexual in nature, and
sometimes bordering on madness, which beset men of all
ranks. The shell-shocked Captain McKechnie refuses on
a matter of principle to divorce his adulterous wife; the
alcoholic colonel, whose command Tietjens has to assume,
collapses under the strain of family arguments at home
over his father's estate.

But perhaps the most frightful picture Tietjens carries through the war is the one of O Nine Morgan, with his face half torn away by a shell fragment, appearing in the doorway of Tietjens' hut, saying " Ere's another bloomin' casualty," and dying in the pool of his own blood at Tietjens' feet. Shortly before, Tietjens had refused him leave to return to Wales to reclaim his wife from a local prizefighter, because the prizefighter would certainly have killed him.

O Nine Morgan presents Tietjens with another reflection or echo of his own plight and ultimately becomes a central symbol for the breakdown of Tietjens' feudal personality. There is, first of all, Tietjens' growing awareness of identity with the " other Ranks." That his " inner mentality " will plague him with the thought that as an *officer* he was responsible for O Nine Morgan's death seems to Tietjens to be the " absurd end of the earth " (p. 355).[16] He admits that " in literalness " he had been responsible for the man's death. The memory of O Nine Morgan's wondrous eyes when he, " God-Tietjens," had passed judgment on him evokes thoughts of all the dead in the war that he had seen and could imagine, a blackness of mood that came at odd times. " In this case it was because of one fellow, a dirty enough man, not even very willing, not in the least endearing, certainly contemplating desertion. . . . But your dead . . . *yours* . . . your own. As if joined to your identity by a black cord . . ." (p. 356) . In effect, Tietjens had decided for O Nine Morgan what he has chosen for himself.

So he [O Nine Morgan] was better dead. Or perhaps not. Is death better than discovering that your wife is a whore and

---

[16] It also occurs to Tietjens at this point that on that very day he had been forced to talk of his relations with his wife to a superior officer of his own class—another unthinkable condescension (p. 356) .

being done in by her cully? *Gwell Angau na gwillth,* their own regimental badge bore the words. *"Death is better than dishonour."* . . . No, not death, *angau* means pain. Anguish! Anguish is better than dishonour. The devil it is! Well, that fellow would have got both. Anguish and dishonour. Dishonour from his wife and anguish when the prize-fighter hit him. . . . That was no doubt why his half-face grinned at the roof. The gory side of it had turned brown. Already! Like a mummy of a Pharoah, *that* half looked. . . . He was born to be a blooming casualty. Either by shell-fire or by the fist of the prize-fighter. . . . (p. 310)

Plagued by both anguish and dishonor himself, Tietjens naturally associates the memory of O Nine Morgan with Sylvia, sexual cruelty, war brutality, and all the forces of destruction. The Welsh soldier, Tietjens supposes, had been impotent, which would account for his wife turning to the prizefighter. Tietjens sees himself as a eunuch " by temperament," which would account for his refusal to sleep with Valentine and for the adulteries and recriminations of Sylvia. Usually Sylvia or thoughts on sex and death evoke the image of O Nine Morgan.

The crisis comes during one of his several painful interviews with Campion, when the General asks why he does not divorce Sylvia. This excites in him a panic of fatigue and worry.

Fragments of scenes of fighting, voices, names, went before his eyes and ears. Elaborate problems. . . . The whole map of the embattled world ran out in front of him—as large as a field. An embossed map in greenish *papier mâché*—a ten-acre field of embossed *papier mâché*, with the blood of O Nine Morgan blurring luminously over it. (pp. 492-493)

He suddenly remembers having sat on the Montaigne Noire in Belgium nineteen months earlier during the German shelling of Poperinghe, and he recalls his anger and despair at this example of " Prussian brutality." This internal monologue is framed by the vision of the bloody map, for it is referred to in almost the same words at the end of the passage (p. 494). The skeleton map of the principles showing east and north that he had counted on earlier has been defaced by the blood of the dead in the war. Toryism is dead. It is at this point that Tietjens asks himself, " *Why* the devil am I so anxious to shield that whore? It's not reasonable! It is an obsession! " (p. 495). There is now no mental obstacle preventing his being with Valentine. On Armistice Day he can declare with conviction that " the war had made a man of him " by making him coarser and harder, and that he " would no longer stand unbearable things." November 11, 1918, began a new age. " Feudalism was finished; its last vestiges were gone. It held no place for him. He was going—he was damn well going!—to make a place in it for . . . A man could now stand up on a hill, so he and she could surely get into some hole together! " (p. 668).

The " moral," " inscrutable " tribulations which plague Tietjens' sensitive consciousness through his involvement with all of his sexually distraught and mentally disturbed comrades reflect and give meaning to his own personal agony. Immediately after O Nine Morgan's death, Tietjens is made aware that the whole battalion knows of that unfortunate soldier's home worries. " Thank God, Sylvia can't get here," he says (p. 311). At that very moment she *is* there, ready " to pull all the strings of all the showerbaths " in order to bring Tietjens " to heel." She is not quite certain why she has come, breaking her apparent vow to spend the duration of the conflict in a convent reading prewar romantic novels, but she is " at the end of her tether " and determined that she and

Tietjens will live under the same roof again (p. 384-385). She commits the unpardonable Tory sin of washing her dirty linen in public. She realizes it is stupid to do so, that Tietjens will only harden his resolve not to give in, but she is not fully responsible. She persecutes him relentlessly, chaotically, without premeditation, saying horrible things on the spur of the moment that she does not really want to say, driven by her instinctive need for the total possession of Tietjens' maleness. She is depressed because she feels she has been betrayed by a battalion and that the war has stolen his attentions from her (pp. 399, 438). She makes crude complaints about Tietjens to Campion, who lists them methodically on a sheet of paper—" Colonel's horse: Sheets: Jesus Christ: Wannop girl: Socialism? " (p. 489)—with which he confronts Tietjens after the night of Sylvia's making which had led to Tietjens' arrest and which was to result in a transfer to the front lines. The whole episode is a comic reversal of Sylvia's intention, a trick which is to be characteristic of her fate.

Sylvia is the most fierce, persistent, and representative antagonist of Tietjens' intellect. She had gone off with a dull brute like Perowne " in a violent fit of sexual hatred, from her husband's mind " (p. 389). Her purpose had been to humiliate Tietjens, but she had been bested by his silence and by her own humiliation " at having found no one better than an oaf like Perowne " (p. 390). The affair had ended sordidly, and though she was defiant before her mother, Father Consett, and later Tietjens, she realized that this method had failed her. She then vows, more out of caprice than shame, to remain chaste in the future. It is Father Consett who warns that Sylvia's " hell on earth " will be when Tietjens falls in love with another woman. " *Then* she'll tear the house down. The world will echo with her wrongs " (p. 42).

Sylvia's passionate jealousy of Valentine, in addition to her intense desire to destroy Tietjens' reserve, brings her to the front lines. As she looks across the lobby at her placid husband, she tells Perowne, who, ironically, is there pleading to have her sleep with him: " If that man would throw his handkerchief to me, I would follow him round the world in my shift " (p. 386). But with tragi-comic frustration she realizes that trying to put some emotion in him is " like trying to move an immense mattress filled with feathers " (p. 406). She recalls to herself the time she had beaten her dying bulldog in a moment of sexual passion for Tietjens and then had left it outside to freeze to death. ". . . The last stud-white bulldog of that breed. . . . As Christopher is the last stud-white hope of the Groby Tory breed. . . . Modeling himself on our Lord . . ." (p. 417). She remembers her affair of passion with Drake and craves to recapture the pleasure of the mental torture his sexual brutality gave to her—but this time she craves to experience it with Tietjens. In fact, she leaves Tietjens at the end of his tether and haunted by the fear that his mind is breaking (p. 485).

Her love-hatred for her husband works at cross-purposes with itself and defeats her. She is remarkably aware of her motives but chaotic in her methods, her frustrated desires leading her to acts of desperation, which cause confusion and disorder. She realizes it is not sporting to persecute Tietjens " before the servants," for " it was like whipping a dying bulldog " (p. 381). He has spoiled her for other men by the virtue of his intellect, which allows him to " explain things to her " (p. 418), but at the same time it is against his intellect that she is fighting to win his passion. Her passion drives her to break all the rules of the game of sexual pursuit, and she is a helpless victim of her instinctive feelings. Her displays become more and more vulgar, her lies more and more obvious. Her direct attack on Tietjens on Armistice night fails and ends, by another painful though comic turnabout for Sylvia, in her public humiliation during her suit of restitution of conjugal rights. Finally, she appears at the country cottage to spy, hoping to gather the facts she needs to corroborate her increasingly reckless lying.

There is much that is pitiable in her failure to make Tietjens the man she wants him to be and to make him submit to her as a woman. Her belief that God had changed sides at the cutting down of Groby Great Tree, her realization that Tietjens had found contentment with Valentine in his simple life, her increasing awareness of the spirit of Father Consett hovering over her, and her disgust with her own vulgarity, give her the courage to confront Valentine to tell her she would not harm her unborn child " with its littleness " (p. 827). Sylvia has had finally to admit that unwittingly she had forced Tietjens underground and to his salvation. There is a poignant bitterness in her question, " What was she given beauty— the dangerous remains of beauty!—for if not to impress it on the unimpressible! " (p. 806). Valentine with her ability to see people as they are realizes that Sylvia is, for all of her show, " timid " and " noble " (p. 827).

4

On another level, Sylvia is Society, that wealthy, generally high-born group which out of boredom has gone *fanti* and whose comings and goings appear in the illustrated journals. The women of this set were man-mad, although usually continent except under the influence of "inexperience or champagne." Like them, Sylvia

> *had* to have men at her feet; that was, as it were, the price of her—purely social—daily bread as it was the price of the daily bread of her intimates. She was, and had been for many years, absolutely continent. And so very likely were, and had been, all her Moiras, and Megs, and Lady Marjories—but she was perfectly aware that they had to have, above their assemblies as it were, a light vapour of the airs and habits of the brothel. (p. 150)

Unlike most of them, who succumbed to passion, made hasty marriages, and faded into obscurity, Sylvia was lucky in getting Tietjens, with whom she had had a brief affair before meeting Drake, a married man. She was then indifferent to Tietjens, unable to understand why others thought him so brilliant. " His actions and opinions seemed simply the products of caprice—like her own; and, since she knew that most of her own manifestations were a matter of contrariety, she abandoned the habit of thinking much about him " (pp. 153-154). But slowly she had gained respect for his knowledge of life and for his predictions, which always turned out right. And slowly his very excellence, his superiority, his treating her with impeccable honor, and his willingness to forgive her everything, aroused in her the passion that brought her close to madness, for she needed to have this man at her feet as she had always had any man she ever desired.

Valentine, on the other hand, is from a well-born, though impoverished, family of intellectuals. Her father had been a Latinist, the closest friend of Christopher's father; her mother, acording to Christopher, is the only great English novelist since the eighteenth century. Brought up in an atmosphere of advanced Victorian idealism, Valentine sees the world as " a place of renunciations, of high endeavour and sacrifice " (p. 229). Along with her young friends, she advocates an " enlightened promiscuity," but really feels " that sexual incontinence [is] extremely ugly and chastity to be prized in the egg-and-spoon race that life [is] " (p. 264). Her innocence and idealism are to be severely tested by her experience as an Ealing maid when she hears from the drunken cook of the bestial, animal side of sexual passion. She still clings, however, to the illusion that " far from the world of Ealing and its county councillors who over-ate and neighed like stallions, there were bright colonies of beings, chaste, beautiful in thought, altruist and circumspect " (p. 231). She suffers her final " great sexual shock " when Edith Ethel asks her how to get rid of a baby, and Valentine realizes that the passion of Edith Ethel and Macmaster for each other was not " one of the beautiful things of life " (pp. 230-231).

Her feelings are further complicated by her suspicion that the baby may be Christopher's, for, like everyone else, she had suspected that he was Edith Ethel's lover. Because Edith Ethel's coarse epithets against the father are the same ones she later uses against Tietjens, Valentine feels her suspicions are confirmed, but she finally gains assurance that Tietjens has deserted Edith Ethel, that he is not the father, and that he is now available for her. For a time, in the " darkened world of her sexual tumult," Valentine brings herself to say in words almost echoing those of Tietjens, " Chastity: napoo finny! Like every-thing else! " (pp. 265-266). She knows that she and Christopher are in love with each other and that they are both suffering. She waits for a word from him. When he does not give it in their long interview at Macmaster's before he leaves for the army, she reclaims her faith in chastity and in " her image of the world as a place of virtues and endeavours " (p. 267) .

Valentine remains chaste until Tietjens returns from the war, but her view of the world " of virtues and endeavours " is further tested so that even before he is back she is ready to leave her sordid impecunity and her intellectually degrading job as a physical instructor to dullish middle class girls. Vaguely, she seeks release and dreams of reading Aeschylus by the Aegean sea (pp. 514, 816). Both she and Tietjens have witnessed the gradual coarsening of the assured world of their youth, a process which is brilliantly rendered in the last sections of *Some Do Not . . .* by Mrs. Wannop's queries about a sensational article she has been commissioned to write on war babies and by the drunken exploits of Valentine's Communist brother Edward. This increasing indifference to past ideals is set beside Valentine's and Tietjens' consuming though some-what intellectualized love for each other and brings them to the realization that they are among those who " do not." But inevitably both are affected by all of the cheapening of human values on every level of life and are forced to reappraise their own values.

In addition to Valentine's sexual awakening, in Ealing and through Edith Ethel, and complementary to it, there is a growing awareness of the failure of the advanced Victorianism of her parents to provide for either her physical or her intellectual needs. Her father had been a popular and revered scholar, " an Oxford Disraelian Conservative Imperialist " (p. 135) , who had taught Valentine that a pure mind comes from a healthy body, but he had left his family impoverished. Valentine has a deep affection for her talented, preoccupied, inaccurate mother, but until Mark's promise of an annuity she had had to support her and her brother and to do her mother's voluminous

secretarial work. On Armistice Day, Valentine tells Miss
Wanostrocht, the headmistress and one of Mr. Wannop's
disciples:

> "Look here, I disapprove of this whole thing: of what my
> father has brought me to! Those people . . . the brilliant
> Victorians talked all the time through their hats. They
> evolved a theory from anywhere and then went brilliantly
> mad over it. Perfectly recklessly. . . ." (p. 534)

This outburst is precipitated by Valentine's anguish at
the news of Christopher's return, by her doubts about their
future together, and by her reawakened love for him,
which she had tried to forget, in spite of the " insult " of
his not writing her since he had left for the front two years
earlier. Hearing the sirens and cannon of the Armistice
celebration, she realizes she must leave her nunlike existence and have fun (p. 513). She sees something prophetic
in the rushing of her girls to leave the athletic field to join
the celebration when she had been charged to keep them
at their " Physical Jerks " and then to march them in an
orderly fashion back to their classes. At the Mistress'
conference earlier that morning, Valentine, again echoing
Tietjens, had wondered why the students, why " they,"
were not going to be allowed a moment of triumph or
celebration.

> If, at this parting of the ways, at this crack across the table
> of History, the School—the World, the future mothers of
> Europe—got out of hand, would they ever come back? The
> Authorities—Authority all over the world—was afraid of
> that; more afraid of that than of any other thing. Wasn't it
> a possibility that there was to be no more Respect? None
> for constituted Authority and Consecrated Experience?
>   And, listening to the fears of those careworn, faded, ill-
> nourished gentlewomen, Valentine had found herself specu-
> lating.

" No more respect . . . For the Equator! For the Metric
system. For Sir Walter Scott! Or George Washington! Or
Abraham Lincoln! Or the Seventh Commandment! " (pp.
510-511)

" You might arrive anywhere," she adds, " —at county
families taking to trade; gentlefolk selling for profit! All
the unthinkable sorts of things! " The nightmare of the
Armistice celebration places her in Tietjens' arms for good
and at the same time heralds the degrading death agonies
of the Victorian idealisms and all the past.

5

When Tietjens returns from the war, he is ill, distraught,
and still suffering from a partial loss of memory. He is
worn out by the muddles he has unwittingly and with the
best of motives brought about. His personal trials, his
involvement in the lives of others, and the horror of the
sights, sounds, and smells of war have exhausted him.
He is resentful of the Whitehall " boodlers," who, seeing
the game as more important than the players, had mis-
managed the war. He is drained of his capacity to feel
any emotion at all.[17]

Out of his frightful, debilitating tribulations comes one
consuming need—that for communication, the desperate
desire to talk, to enjoy intellectual companionship. It is
the intellectual's reaction to the intellectual paralysis

[17] Ford had written in *England and the English*, pp. 180-181: "After long
periods of illness, of mourning, of mental distress, no news of the outside
world and no ecstasy of verse will hold the mind; events and thoughts pass
through the tired consciousness leaving no trace, as the smoke of orchard
fire passes through apple boughs. Then Nature may assert a sway of her
own."

imposed by all the Sylvias, opportunists. boodlers, sex-obsessed hypocritical moralizers, in short, by the twentieth century and by those who had taken over on August 4, 1914, when the Germans invaded Belgium near Gemminich. Tietjens never forgets that " the thing is to be able to stick to the integrity of your character, whatever earthquake sets the house tumbling over your head " (p. 454). This is a curiously ironic statement from a man who has been brought close to material and mental ruin by the persistent exercise of an integrity that he refuses to relinquish. But his suffering does not destroy him; instead it creates within him a new vision and a new dedication.

On one morning of great personal anguish while still at the front lines, he hears the bugler practicing a Purcell air and recalls Herrick's " exact, quiet words " and thinks of the seventeenth century, " the only satisfactory age in England," with its " quiet fields, Anglican sainthood, accuracy of thought, heavy-leaved, timbered hedge-rows, slowly creeping plough-lands moving up the slopes." He is reassured that the land remains, a thought which evokes George Herbert's parish.

> The name *Bemerton* suddenly came on to his tongue. Yes, Bemerton, Bemerton, Bemerton was George Herbert's parsonage. Bemerton, outside Salisbury. . . . The cradle of the race as far as our race was worth thinking about. He imagined himself standing up on a little hill, a lean contemplative parson, looking at the land sloping down to Salisbury spire. A large, clumsily bound seventeenth-century testament, Greek, beneath his elbow. . . . Imagine standing up on a hill! It was the unthinkable thing there! (pp. 564-567)

Later, when thoughts of Valentine begin to obsess him during extensive bombing raids, he realizes a " country parsonage was not for him " (p. 603) because Valentine's mind is of infinitely greater value, " the exact mind, the impatience of solecisms and facile generalizations! "

> She was, in effect, the only person in the world that he wanted to hear speak. Certainly the only person in the world that he wanted to talk to. The only clear intelligence! . . . The repose that his mind needed from the crackling of thorns under all the pots of the world. . . . From the eternal, imbecile " Pampamperipam Pam Pamperi Pam Pam! " of the German guns that all the while continued. (p. 604)

As a safeguard against the insanity that threatens them, both Tietjens and Valentine before their reunion seek for the exact words that will objectify their thoughts and feelings. During one of his psychological crises in the trenches Tietjens tries to write out in the manner of an official report to headquarters an account of the last day of his first leave. He cannot complete it, for he discovers " that this writing gave no sort of psychological pointers " (p. 348), but having written it, he realizes that Sylvia had forced him into Valentine's arms (p. 349). On Armistice Day upon the news of Tietjens' return, Valentine, though she does not put it into writing, tries to articulate the nature and depth of her connection to the " grey bear," the " grey problem," whom for the past two years she had been trying to forget. She finally brings herself to state baldly:

> " Chuck it. You're in love with a married man who's a Society wife and you're upset because the Titled Lady has put into your head the idea that you might ' come together again.' After ten years! "
>
> But immediately she protested:

"No. *No.* No! It isn't that. It's all right the habit of putting things incisively, but it's misleading to put things too crudely." (pp. 520-521)

"Comic things, words, as applied to states of feelings" (p. 525), she says shortly after, but she persists until she comes to see that Tietjens upon his discharge had not put it up to Edith Ethel to call her. She knows then she will go to him in spite of the labels of "fornicatrix" and "adultress" that others will attach to her. In their ruminations they are talking to themselves; what they both need, they are aware, is to talk to each other, to be able to argue again over quotations from Ovid and Catullus. Only then, Ford the artist is telling us, can a man "stand up."

By the end of the tetralogy, though Tietjens has not yet fully recovered the balance between reason and passion, the conditions for his doing so are finally present. Valentine protects both his intellect and his emotions from distractions so that he can do the work he has to do. Her mind, possessing a saving sense of order, embraces both the past and the present. She is the clear intellect and the eternal, life-giving mother, who retains the proper balance between mind and heart. Neither she nor Christopher give up the dream of Bemerton parsonage; if they have the money when the time comes, they will buy a living for their son there. The unborn Chrissie is to be the inheritor of a new age of order and spiritual harmony which will arrive when madness has spent itself.

In order to have Valentine and all that she represents for him, Tietjens has to renounce public life as he has known it. His renunciation is not an escape from the world. It is rather a denial of its corrupt ways, resulting, after suffering and persecution, from a detachment of spirit that can help him to discard what is debased, ineffectual, and dangerous, and allow him to discover the healthy core of a satisfactory human existence. He had, in fact, before the war, despite all of his assurance, felt singularly un-attached, often the fate of a younger son in an upper class feudal family. He seemed to have been

born to be a sort of lonely buffalo outside the herd[.] Not artist, not soldier, not bureaucrat, not certainly indispens-able anywhere; apparently not even sound in the eyes of these dim-minded specialists. An exact observer. . . . (p. 128)

"An exact observer" he is, seeking more and more for clarity of meaning. During his brief command of the drunken colonel's front line battalion, Tietjens insists on maintaining communication with neighboring units, a policy which " was perhaps the dominant idea of Tietjens, perhaps the main idea that he got out of warfare " (p. 624). It was the single conviction he would carry through the rest of his army service and adapt to his life with Valentine. Love, he discovers, is the opportunity for inti-mate conversations. " You seduced a young woman in order to be able to finish your talks with her. You could not do that without living with her. You could not live with her without seducing her; but that was the by-product " (p. 629). He denies he is a " Hamlet of the Trenches. No, by God he was not. . . . He was perfectly ready for action. Ready to command a battalion " (p. 630). And later to become a dealer in old furniture and a small producer. Like Gringoire, Ford's projection of himself in *No Enemy*, Tietjens was to come back from the war

with the serene resignation of a man with no other imagin-able destiny before him. It was to be more toil and more toil and more toil. He did not, apparently, ask for—certainly he did not imagine—any other future. So that resignation is not the right word. Serenity is. . . . (p. 193)

With all of the novel's emphasis on the importance for Tietjens of accurate communication, on striving for perfection, and on the discipline of careful methods of work, *Parade's End* may be read as a parable on the artist in contemporary society. Ford's own insistence on *le mot juste*, his pride in being an artist in words, his belief that the artist is a sensitized instrument who by recording men's ways can save mankind, Ford's own war experiences as we know them, his disillusionment on his return from the war as recorded in *It Was The Nightingale* and later in *No Enemy*, and his experiment with the trials and simplicities of rural life after the war in order to seek new beginnings—all these point with some validity to the observation that Tietjens is a projection and perhaps an idealization of his author. "An art is the highest form of communication between person and person," [18] Ford believed, and both Tietjens and Valentine might be called artists in living who find life's secret in the exact word and in the clear intellect, as both are symbolized, in Tietjens' consciousness, by the figure of George Herbert.

William Carlos Williams reads *Parade's End* as a poet and sees it as Ford's testament to the necessity of accurate expression, to the belief that " disrespect for the word . . . spells disaster."

To use the enormous weapon of the written word, to speak accurately that is (in contradiction to the big crude lie) what Ford is building here. For Ford's novels are written with a convinced idea of respect for the meaning of words—

[18] *The March of Literature*, p. 4.

and what a magnificent use they are put to in his hands! Whereas the other position is not conceivable except as disrespect for the word's meaning.

With specific reference to *Parade's End*, Williams sees Valentine and Sylvia as representing, respectively, devotion and disrespect for the exact word:

> The word keeps the same form as the characters' deeds or the writer's concept of them. Sylvia is the dead past in all its affecting glamor. . . . Valentine Wannop is the reattachment of the word to the object—it is obligatory that the protagonist (Tietjens) should fall in love with her, she is Persephone, the rebirth, the re-assertion—from which we today are at a nadir, the lowest ebb.
>
> Sylvia is the lie, boldfaced, the big crude lie, the denial . . . that is now having its moment. . . .[19]

The serenity that Tietjens achieves after Sylvia is all but defeated is recorded in *The Last Post*, but with a curious indirection. The last rendering of his consciousness occurs in two brief passages near the end of *A Man Could Stand Up*—(pp. 657-658, 665-669). Tietjens does not appear until the next to last page in *The Last Post* to take part in the " present action " of that novel, and then he is only given one sentence. The " present action " involves the appearance of Sylvia and several of her cohorts at the cottage where Valentine, Christopher, Mark, and Marie Léonie live. It is the day of Mark's death and Sylvia's final defeat.

Ford said he did not like *The Last Post* and that he wrote it only to satisfy his friend Isabel Paterson's desire to know what happened to Tietjens. Curiously he seems to disavow it when in *It Was The Nightingale* he refers

[19] Williams, " *Parade's End*," pp. 159-160.

to his trilogy.[20] He writes in his " Dedicatory Letter " to the novel that his intention was to give us " a slice of one of Christopher's later days so that you may know how more or less he at present stands. For in this world of ours though lives may end Affairs do not." [21] So far as Tietjens' day is concerned, the novel offers a very slim slice, but thematically *The Last Post* is a necessary and important part of the whole saga.

Christopher is still at the center, being viewed variously through the consciousnesses of Mark, Marie Léonie, Valentine, Sylvia, and, briefly, through Michael Mark, his son, and Cramp, a carpenter. Mark's is the most detached, the most significant view. Approaching death, having foresworn the world, he is close in his objective judgment to a Jupiter, as Marie Léonie calls him. As Christopher's stepbrother he is hewn from the same block, but he is a purer Tietjens, for his mother, old Mr. Tietjens' first wife, was a northerner. In one sense, he, not Christopher, is the last Tory. Mark is the exhausted remnant of the once great ruling class. He was, as he says, born tired. He had never wanted to manage Groby and was satisfied with being the indispensable public official and having Marie Léonie serve him his mutton chops and rum toddies.

Both Christopher and Mark renounce the postwar world on matters of principle, but with a difference. Mark's immobility and his refusal to communicate represent the ravages of the disordered, immoral betrayal of the Tietjens', and hence Britain's, heritage. Mark embodies the part of Christopher that has gone inactive. Christopher

---

[20] *It Was the Nightingale*, p. 208. See Goldring, *Trained for Genius*, p. 258, for Ford's statement: " I strongly wish to omit *Last Post* from the [omnibus] edition. I do not like the book and have never liked it and always intended to end up with *A Man Could Stand Up*."

[21] *The Last Post* (New York: The Literary Guild of America, 1928), p. vi. Published in England by Duckworth in the same year under the title *Last Post*.

is no longer omniscient. He has stripped from him or he himself has denied every sign of his Tory-Groby inheritance except his personal integrity; he now mingles with the " Other Ranks "; he has become nearly anonymous, a result, Mark conjectures, of " a sort of craving for mortification of the spirit "—" a manifestation of the confounded saintliness that he got from his soft mother " (pp. 740-741).

Mark turns over to Valentine a world that has become for the Tietjens " inefficient and venial," and " fusionless and dishonest " (p. 740). Mark tells her on Armistice Day, before he learns the Allies' decision, that if England did not pursue the Germans into Berlin it would be both a sin against God and an intellectual sin; the ruling class had betrayed the fundamental principle that if you do what you want you must take what you get for it; " to abandon that logic was to abandon clearness of mind: it was mental cowardice." Valentine questions the suffering resulting from such logic, to which he answers:

> " Yes, you are afraid of suffering. . . . But England is necessary to the world. . . . To my world. . . . Well, make it your world and it may go to rack and ruin how it will. I am done with it. But then . . . do you accept the responsibility! " (p. 775)

Mark still, however, has one attachment to life. He wants to see Christopher released from bondage to Sylvia. Sylvia's " sex ferocity," as Mark calls it (p. 829), and her total lack of system in trying to gain the attentions of Christopher's mind had been a mortal enemy to the Tietjens' family. However, by her recklessness she had driven Christopher into the saving arms of Valentine. Finally, when Sylvia admits defeat and agrees to a divorce, Mark thinks:

Well, if Sylvia had come to that his, Mark's, occupation was
gone. He would no longer have to go on willing against her;
she would drop into the sea in the wake of their family
vessel and be lost to view. . . . But damn it, she must have
suffered to be brought to that extreme. . . . Poor bitch!
Poor bitch! The riding had done it. . . . (p. 830)

Mark is now assured that Christopher has " achieved a
position in which he might—with just a little more to
it—anticipate jogging away to the end of time, leaving
descendants to carry on the country without swank "
(p. 831).

6

" I think," Ford wrote to Percival Hinton in 1930,
" *The Good Soldier* is my best book technically, unless
you read the Tietjens books as one novel, in which case
the whole design appears. But I think the Tietjens books
will probably ' date ' a good deal, where the other may—
and indeed need—not." [22] The " whole design " of *Parade's
End* is a reflection of the cycle it portrays, moving from
an already shaky prewar *status quo* to its disintegration
and a suggested eventual reintegration. Ford believed in
the cyclical theory of the rise and fall and rebirth of ideals
and principles. "Arts rise and die again, systems rise and
die again, faiths are born only to die and to rise once
more; the only thing constant and undying is the human
crowd." [23] Mark Tietjens reflects this view when he notes
in his summation that the breed had not changed, only
the times (p. 762), and Sylvia echoes it (p. 802). *Parade's*

[22] Quoted in Goldring, *Trained for Genius*, p. 245.
[23] *England and the English*, p. 56n.

End shows what happened when the orderly, self-assured eighteenth century, preserved within the aphorisms, conventions, and ideals of the ruling classes, had to face the twentieth century, which finally in the great war produced the moral and intellectual chaos the nineteenth century had engendered. But the eighteenth-century virtues were not all destroyed; they were simply forced underground. The best of them still offer the necessary basis for personal survival in a fragmented, meaningless society.

John McCormick considers Ford to have been the only war novelist " to advance the form of the novel in the decade after the war was fought," though the Tietjens series, he believes, " contains grave lapses and remains a minor effort," in part because " Ford was defeated by his attempt to marry social conservatism to technical experiment."

> His social perceptions tend to negate his artist's conscience, and *vice versa*; his defence of a social system which produced people like Sylvia Tietjens and General Campion led him into anomalies which no amount of artistry could resolve. He demonstrated brilliantly Tietjens' ambiguous feeling about the war, but his honesty in perceiving the corruption of Tory values after the war axiomatically made the post-war Tietjens into a quaint " character " of slight literary reality.[24]

This view is based upon the assumption that " the catastrophe of the First World War " led the novelist to the discovery " that new techniques were required to express the new fragmentation of society " and " that the novel was the unique instrument of the imagination for dealing with catastrophe " (p. 41). But apparently for McCormick this is not true for a resynthesis, such as Ford makes

[24] *Catastrophe and Imagination*, pp. 217-221.

in *Parade's End.* *A Farewell to Arms*, attempting no resynthesis, is the " only excellent novel of the first war in English because, unlike other novelists, Hemingway made the connection between the fact of the war and an intellectually defensible idea of the war." (p. 221).

It is probably dangerous for a novelist who hopes to be taken seriously in the present day to construct a plan for survival so that his story ends " happily " or, at least, not hopelessly. The question would rather seem to be whether the terms of survival evolve naturally out the plot or out of the total conception which gave the work its form. Both *A Farewell to Arms* and *Parade's End* would suffer with different endings. It is not necessary to agree with either Hemingway's or Ford's interpretation of the consequences of catastrophe and love, but it is necessary to approach both without limiting conceptions, whether they be political, social, or moral. At least, one must first face each work on its own terms.

Parade's End is not, strictly speaking, a war novel, even though it uses and interprets the war as the final holocaust of the Tory decline. Neither does it defend Sylvia or Campion or the social system which produced them, as McCormick charges. Tietjens proves it does not by the fact that he denies their society by shedding his feudal prerogatives, his Toryism, and all the causes of his suffering. He retains his humane virtues, which are a necessity for any revival of society if it is not to be lawless. The pass to which society had brought itself by the end of the second decade of the twentieth century left little hope, but Ford with his acute historical sense perceived the possibility of society's regenerating itself by a return to a language of truth, clarity, and precision, and to a balance of reason and passion. Only by the individual's seeking for emotional and intellectual harmony within his

own soul can social and moral order be restored or even
hoped for. That, oversimplified, is Ford's message through
Christopher, and it seems to be both a morally and intellectually defensible one.

In spite of its weaknesses, I think that *Parade's End*
has an integrity of its own and succeeds in becoming a
cogent, impressive work of art. Though it lacks the compression and tightly knit structure of *The Good Soldier,*
it has a remarkably intricate and ordered pattern of
its own.

Whereas *The Good Soldier* is almost Ford's shortest
novel and is nearly perfect, *Parade's End* is his longest
novel, and it is too long. A purely subjective, but I submit
none the less valid, reaction is that the reader feels that
The Good Soldier is exactly the right length, while he is
relieved to finally reach the last page of *Parade's End.* NO!
This feeling may result partially from the extreme complexity with which Ford handles time and from his increasing indirectness in presenting action. The tetralogy
is certainly weakened by several coincidental gatherings
of characters and by some overlong expository passages
(particularly the one treating the alcoholic colonel, pp.
578-585). Some distended scenes, though interesting for
their techniques, are out of proportion (such as the interview between Tietjens and Colonel Levin, pp. 323-340).
There are too many not always effective allusions to titles
and occasional ineptnesses in style: " purplishest " (p.
656); " [. . .] when [. . .] Mr. Duchemin [. . .] and his three
assistants went together along a road the hearts of any
malefactors whom in the mist they chanced to encounter
went pit-a-pat " (pp. 85-86).

Probably Ford has to pay the price of his fascinating
experiment of presenting the postwar Christopher without
once going into his consciousness. Mark's resolving several

of the dilemmas which had plagued Christopher does not mean that Christopher has necessarily solved them. Christopher had long before satisfied himself that Michael Mark was his own son, but we have to assume that he still believes his father committed suicide and that he does not forgive either his father or Mark. Perhaps Christopher's consciousness has little more to tell us, but by the end of *The Last Post* he seems too impersonal and remote. We miss *his* view of his new life with Valentine. Disengaged from Christopher's consciousness, the reader tends to lose much of his feeling of identification with him. On the other hand, the method succeeds in rendering Christopher's postwar anonymity. Even his memory is now more like that of the average man's, for he need no longer hold onto it with his previous tenacity as a defense against Sylvia and against the Sandbachs and Campions of the world.[25]

Ford achieved in *Parade's End* an impressive though not flawless fusion of themes and techniques. He did this by carefully juxtaposing private lives, which also embody representative social attitudes, against Armageddon and the upheaval of society. His earlier panoramic novels had prepared him for the problems of that form. The epic chronicle of Christopher Tietjens is inspired by a grander conception than the earlier works of its kind, but its methods, except for the addition of the internal monologue, are mostly the same, though intensified and extended. Like Mr. Fleight and Sergius Macdonald, Tietjens is the center around which the other illuminative characters move. These characters function variously as representatives of the official ruling classes (Mark, Campion, Waterhouse,

---

[25] Tietjens, however, retains his gift of prophecy, at least in the eyes of Valentine. She is assured that his dream of Chrissie's becoming a new George Herbert will come true. She believes that Tietjens was " always right. But previous " (p. 815).

and Fittleworth as the landed gentry; the officials of Whitehall, the *arriviste* Macmaster, the commercialist Sandbach as the new governing class); of leisure class society (Mrs. Satterthwaite, Sylvia, the social-climbing gossip Ruggles); of the intellectuals (the Wannops); of the military (Campion and the regular army colonel in *A Man Could Stand Up*—); and of the "Other Ranks" (McKechnie, O Nine Morgan, Sergeant-Major Cowley, Cramp, and Gunning). The people on these various levels of society concern themselves more intimately with Tietjens' conflicts than their earlier prototypes often did with the conflicts of their protagonists.

The careers and fortunes of the characters shift in relation to each other like adjacent elevators going in opposite directions. As Macmaster rises in prestige, Tietjens falls; as Sylvia loses Tietjens, Valentine gains him; as McKechnie goes mad and Macmaster suffers a nervous breakdown causing his death, Tietjens, though sometimes close to madness, retains his sanity. As Christopher relinquishes successively his official position, his fortune, and Groby, Mark, though he also finally abandons his official position, becomes the embodiment of the Groby-Tory virtues and attributes which, except for the intellect, are paralyzed and destined to die. But as Mark rejects the world, his brother is able to accept it on its most minimal basis, where the seed of the new life is. And finally, in terms of the body politic, the new order of opportunism, mediocrity, and compromise with principles takes over as the old order retreats.

The Christopher-Sylvia-Valentine triangle, outlined earlier in this chapter, comprises the novel's major design, as the two women with all that they represent vie for Christopher with all that he represents. Sylvia is the major disintegrative force. Her allies are McKechnie, the drunken colonel, Edith Ethel, Sandbach, even Macmaster himself, and all those who betray honor, release uncontrollable passions, and cause disorder, insanity, and war to triumph. The vision of the death of O Nine Morgan within Christopher's imagination develops into an expansive symbol suggesting the blood bath which helps to submerge Christopher's traditional sense of duty and responsibility. The principal symbol of reintegration is Valentine, along with Christopher's mother, and the memory of the tradition through George Herbert. There is also the Sergeant-Major who dreams of a time when a "man will be able to stand up on a bleedin' 'ill . . ." (p. 570).

As in *The Good Soldier*, the point of view offers the basis for the time-shift and cannot be separated from it.

> . . . the time shift is, as Ford uses it, a large-scale interior monologue, the interior monologue of the narrating intelligence. Both devices are used to take events out of the chronological pattern and to arrange them in a pattern of meaning: the interior monologue arranges them in the pattern of their meaning for the character who thinks about them, the time shift arranges them in the pattern of their meaning for the novel as a whole.[26]

Several narrative methods are used. Ford as the third person author-narrator assumes the freedom of the first person rambling narrator ranging over the affair he is recounting, presenting action in the apparently disjointed manner in which memory strikes the consciousness. The result is an extremely complex, often confusing, but quite carefully patterned complexity which conveys impressions of the immediate present at the same time that it clarifies the meaning of the affair and suggests universal experience.

[26] Mizener, "A Large Fiction," p. 143.

Ford occasionally assumes the expository function of the traditional novelist, usually to give the biography of a character, or briefly and deftly to set a scene, or to explain something (such as the life of a typical regular army man), but most often exposition is handled through the consciousness of a character. In some scenes Ford assumes the role of the objective reporter allowing himself an occasional glimpse into one character or another. The best example of this technique is the scene between Sylvia, her mother, and Father Consett early in *Some Do Not . . .*, where we enjoy a very few momentary intrusions into Mrs. Satterthwaite's thoughts but all the while see as in a theater the contest between Sylvia and the priest. As Sylvia is observed only from the outside here, Ford is able to " get in " the first impression he wishes us to have of the harsh, brash, bored, reckless, somewhat blasphemous person she is. After this, whenever we are allowed to see into her consciousness, we see her pain and horror and gain a measure of pity for her. Less often, Ford will present a scene through the consciousness of more than one character; this device is used notably in the early scenes with Macmaster and Edith Ethel and in some of those with Christopher and General Campion.

As the effaced narrator Ford shifts between two methods. He may relate only conscious thoughts pointing to the situation at hand and working according to the more or less logical patterns of associative thinking in the manner of the Jamesian central intelligence. As in Mark's final ruminations, past events are recalled and often dramatized, sometimes partially, sometimes completely, as the consciousness under scrutiny observed or felt or feels about them. Or Ford may render the subconscious thoughts as they are projected into the consciousness of a character by all the devious routes of the associative process. This

technique has come to be called the interior monologue
and, by extension, the stream of consciousness. Using it
either in soliloquies or interspersed with dialogue, Ford
usually saves this device for characters in times of mental
or emotional stress. A natural enough development of
Ford's earlier techniques, it seems to have been arrived at
independently. Ford declares that at this time he had not
read Proust, Joyce, or Virginia Woolf. This is possible.
The Good Soldier, which directly paves the way for the
stream of consciousness method, was published in the same
year as Dorothy Richardson's *Pointed Roofs* and Virginia
Woolf's *The Voyage Out*, a year after *Dubliners*, and a
year before *The Portrait of the Artist as a Young Man*.
The point will concern the literary historian. What Ford
seemed actually to have been doing was adapting and
extending methods perfected by James and Conrad.[27]

The author-narrator's method in handling time is generally to select single events which comprise the present
action and then to play freely in dialogue or within the
thoughts of characters upon the memories and impressions

[27] William York Tindall states baldly that Ford based his method on that
of *What Maisie Knew* and that "with hints from Conrad, Proust, and
others" Ford wrote *Parade's End*. Ford's "stream of consciousness, unselected, complicated by the simultaneous overflow of sensation, thought,
and memory, seems more immediate and completer, though less excellent,
than James' decorous selections." *Forces in Modern British Literature:
1885-1946* (New York: Knopf, 1947), p. 309.

Using Robert Humphrey's distinction, John McCormick notes that "in
stream-of-consciousness proper, the novelist places first emphasis on the
exploration of 'pre-speech levels of consciousness for the purpose, primarily,
of revealing the psychic being of his characters.' The novelist is concerned
not with formulated thought but with the margins of thought. Interior
monologue, direct or indirect, is most frequently confused with stream-of-
consciousness, and again Humphrey's distinction is valuable: interior monologue, indirect when the author guides us through the character's mind,
direct when the author effaces himself, is 'the technique . . . for representing
the psychic content and processes of character, partly or entirely unuttered,
just as these processes exist at various levels of conscious control before
they are formulated for deliberate speech.'" *Catastrophe and Imagination*,
p. 60.

of past events as they impinge on the present. *Parade's End* dramatizes separated moments of present action. The first part of *Some Do Not . . .* takes place in July, 1912, during Tietjens' and Macmaster's trip to Rye and their stay there of about a week; most of the key events are rendered (the scene on the golf links, Tietjens with Campion, the Duchemin breakfast, Valentine and Tietjens traveling through the fog); others are handled through memory (Tietjens having dinner with Waterhouse and the events of that evening). Concurrently Sylvia is in Lobscheid. The second part, occuring on an August day in 1916, starts before lunch and ends early the next morning. *No More Parades* covers about three days, " three months " later (p. 299), probably early in 1917. On the first day O Nine Morgan is killed; the second day Tietjens spends with Sylvia, both attending the tea at Lady Saches'; on the third day General Campion has his long interview with Tietjens which results in his being transferred to the front lines. *A Man Could Stand Up—* begins and ends on Armistice Day, but is interrupted by a recounting of Tietjens' few days as a battalion commander, " months and months " earlier (p. 543). *The Last Post* recounts the last day of Mark's life, probably in the summer of 1920 or 1921.[28]

This method naturally underdramatizes the suspense that is characteristic in a novel of action chronologically narrated. Important information is introduced casually, such as the fact that Tietjens had been intimate with Sylvia before their marriage. Several important climactic

---

[28] Ford gives no hints as to the date of Mark's death in *The Last Post*, but enough time has to have elapsed since Armistice Day for the move to the cottage, for Sylvia to have gone to court, and for Tietjens to have settled in his business and to be already betrayed by his American partner Schatzweiler. If Ford were sticking literally to a decade, the date, of course, would be 1922.

scenes are presented indirectly: notably, the last night of Christopher's first leave rendered through Christopher's consciousness; the night of Sylvia's visit to Rouen, handled by dialogue in a scene between Tietjens and Colonel Levin; and the most significant climax of the whole series, the events on the night of Armistice Day, presented through the minds of Marie Léonie, Sylvia, and Valentine.

Ford does not, however, relinquish psychological suspense. Often he moves through nervous, nightmarish scenes to points of emotional climax. Practically every scene in *Some Do Not . . .* is so handled. Even the relatively quiet, jog-trot scene between Christopher and Valentine in the fog is climaxed by the accident with Campion's car. The key scenes of Sylvia in Rouen, of Armistice Day, and of Mark's last day achieve their nightmarish atmospheres because of all the people who appear like ghostly reminders of the past. Ruminations and internal monologues together with present action build up to climactic scenes through *progression d'effet*. A more traditional novelist would certainly have capitalized on the scene where Sylvia announces she has cancer. Ford does not avoid it because it is melodramatic. By reflecting the scene through the memories of three persons he can juxtapose the action and the three interpretations of it with Sylvia's final attempt to intimidate Christopher, which does lead to a melodramatic climax. After a preparatory section from Sylvia's point of view, he renders through Valentine the final confrontation of the two women, towards which much of the novel moves.

As is characteristic of Ford's less ambitious novels, action is developed within large blocks which themselves are separated into smaller component blocks. In *Parade's End* the blocks are determined by each of the four novels, although there are more overlappings and cross-references

than is true of the parts of *The Good Soldier*, for example.
Some Do Not . . . details Christopher's rejections of adultery (convention still suppresses emotion), of his official
position on a matter of principle, an action with which
Sylvia has nothing to do directly; of his family, of Groby
or Groby money, and of his club, for all of which Sylvia
is in some way responsible. *No More Parades*, in which
Valentine does not actually appear, heralds the end of
" swank," of the comforting assurances of the conventions
and the displays of the prescribed behavior and attitudes
of the genteel life. In *A Man Could Stand Up*—, in which
Sylvia does not actually appear, Tietjens discovers through
the horrors of war, personal tribulations, and thoughts of
Valentine a basis for a pattern of order in a new dream
of the clear intellect and intimate, exact conversation.
The Last Post is the swan song of the governing class:
Sylvia, bored, and Mark, tired, sink with the family vessel,
while Christopher and Valentine become the transitional
figures for the inevitable reintegration. They are, as E. V.
Walter calls them, the new Adam and Eve.[29]

The impressions drawn from the complex mass of the
novel's rendered experiences are given as they gather themselves in particular moments in individual consciousnesses.
Events become important only as characters perceive or
feel them. Characters talk on one level, think on another;
do one thing, feel another. Duplicate cerebration (with
Tietjens sometimes triple) leads to numerous reflexive
references. At one point Tietjens thinks concurrently of
Sylvia and Captain McKechnie, thinks about and talks
to another officer, writes a sonnet, and prepares the papers
for a draft (pp. 314-319). In the trenches he must deal
with the nightmare of the present, the ambiguities and
horrors of the past, and the hopes and plans for the future.

29 " The Political Sense of Ford Madox Ford," p. 19.

Internal monologues allow extensive juxtapositions of characters, scenes, and words for the development of *progressions d'effet*. Christopher looking at the dead O Nine Morgan thinks amid the shell bursts of how McKechnie (whom he knows then as Mackenzie) could know an uncle of his, of how Valentine would look if she saw him there, of his having forgot to send a runner to the orderly room, of wondering how McKechnie was withstanding the strafe, of Morgan's shattered face and his own attempts to recall Valentine's face, of the fact that he has had no letters from home except some circulars from old furniture dealers, of Heine's *"Du bist eine Blume,"* of Valentine as a primrose, of the fact that he had never kissed her and must be a eunuch " by temperament " in contrast to Morgan, who is one physically, of whether or not Morgan was better dead, of the Welsh motto " Death is better than Dishonour," and of Pontardulais, Morgan's home village (pp. 308-310). This passage, which dramatizes Tietjens' fatigue and precarious disorder of mind, precedes the disastrous arrival of Sylvia.

The numberless repetitions and repetitions with variations of words, phrases, images, and allusions to scenes and thoughts create a complex series of reflexive references which serve various purposes in the weaving of the novel's pattern. Although it would be difficult to prove that Ford made or placed all of them deliberately, it is clear that he paid his usual close attention to the details on every level of his narrative.

Certain key words and phrases occur repeatedly. The repetitions within a scene may be merely complementary and illuminative. The bloody hunting pictures in the Lobscheid scene when Sylvia is first introduced, the repetitions and reflections of " surface coarseness " in the last pages of *Some Do Not . . .* , the brown study of the troops

in the dugout and the trenches, and the several references
to the depressing mud are a few examples of repetitions
which strengthen and cohere the impression of the scene
in which they appear. Of course, some repetitions serve
to characterize. Sylvia is the thoroughbred, the bitch, the
serpent. To Christopher she is " as full of blood and as
cruel as the usual degenerate Derby winner. In-bred for
generations for one purpose: to madden men of one type"
(p. 121). To Mark, she is " as thin as an eel, as full of
vice as a mare that's a wrong 'un, completely disloyal,
and dressed like any Paris cocotte" (p. 738), but as a
bitch her role is " to perpetuate the breed"; that is what
bitches " are for in the scale of things" (p. 731). Christopher also sees Sylvia as an eel (p. 143); she is usually
in some snakelike position, and Christopher remembers
her most vividly wearing a golden sheath gown, itself a
contrast to the nunlike grey outfit or blue school uniform
Valentine often wears.

Most evident of the noncharacterizing phrases are the
repetitions of the titles in various contexts. Each title is
carefully chosen to suggest the central issue of each novel.
In *Some Do Not . . .* , for example, the title is used five
times. Macmaster realizes he will never achieve the comforting prerogatives of the ruling class Tietjens and then
quotes to himself Ford Madox Ford:

> The gods to each ascribe a differing lot:
> Some enter at the portal. Some do not! (p. 22) [30]

Another reference distinguishes Tietjens from the fly-
driver, who " wouldn't leave my little wooden 'ut, nor miss

---

[30] The lines are adapted from Ford's *Mister Bosphorus and the Muses*
(London: Duckworth, 1923), p. 57, where the lines read:
    " The Gods to each ascribe a differing lot!
    Some rest on snowy bosoms! Some do not!"

my breakfast, for no beast. . . . Some do and some . . . do not " (p. 144). The staff officer whom Tietjens tells he wants to go to the front answers, " Some do. Some do not " (p. 225). Another reference is put into the mouth of a tramp who observes the weeping Valentine leaving Christopher after agreeing to become his mistress. " 'That's women!' [. . .] 'Some do!' He spat into the grass; said, 'Ah!' then added: ' Some do not!' ' " (p. 280). Ford manages a very carefully cadenced close to the chapter, but the point of view is broken and by a *cliché* (" He imagined himself the monarch of that landscape "), and the device is uncomfortably reminiscent of the raven's commentary in *The Shifting of the Fire*. Finally, when Christopher and Valentine decide not to become lovers, there is an allusion to the title (p. 283), and the varied pattern of the recurring phrase, woven through the novel like a familiar theme, is complete.

A more bitter and ironic comment is made by the repetition of a phrase borrowed from a character of Henry James. Christopher, like Ford's other aristocratic gentlemen, thinks at one point that he hates no man but wonders why humanity in the mass becomes " a phenomenon so hideous."

You look at a dozen men, each of them not by any means detestable and not uninteresting, for each of them would have technical details of their affairs to impart; you formed them into a Government or a club and at once, with oppressions, inaccuracies, gossip, backbiting, lying, corruptions and vileness, you had the combination of wolf, tiger, weasel and louse-covered ape that was human society. And he remembered the words of some Russian: " Cats and monkeys. Monkeys and cats. All humanity is there." (p. 79) [31]

[31] The " cats and monkeys " quotation comes from James's " The Madonna of the Future," where it is phrased: " Cats and monkeys, monkeys and

Mrs. Wannop repeats the "cats and monkeys" allusion when she is trying to reassure Tietjens that he should disregard the "wilderness of cats and monkeys howling and squalling your personal reputation away" and remember that "the only thing that matters is to do good work" (pp. 118-119; also p. 123). Tietjens takes her advice when he is persuaded to discard any concern for his personal reputation, but there is little assurance at the end that he does not still believe that the masses of humanity are cats and monkeys.

Various other repetitions suggest formal patterns. Often early references are foreshadowings. Christopher's future life is prefigured as he admires the simple domesticity in the cottages of the Wannops, then of his sister, and then of the parson who temporarily hides the suffragette Gertie. When Christopher learns he is to be transferred to the trenches, he fears the mud, and he is later to be buried in it during an enemy strafe. Sometimes, one character's thoughts are reflected or picked up by another one. Valentine's remark on Armistice Day that county families might have to take to trade or gentlefolk sell for profit (p. 511) is later reflected in Sylvia's realization that "her world was waning. It was the fact that her friend Bobbie's husband, Sir Gabriel Blantyre—formerly Bosenheir—was cutting down expenses like a lunatic. In her world there was the writing on the wall" (pp. 808-809). Situations may echo or balance each other. Everyone Tietjens takes under his wing uses him or deceives him: Sylvia, Macmaster, McKechnie, and finally Schatzweiler, his American partner. The scene of Tietjens and Macmaster riding in the perfectly appointed train arguing over Rossetti is set

cats—all human life is there!" Ford in his book on James ascribes the quotation to Turgenev, but I have not come across it in my reading of Turgenev.

against that of Valentine's leading Tietjens in the cart
through the fog as they argue over Latin quotations.
As Valentine dances with Tietjens on Armistice Day, the
reader recalls Sylvia's dancing with him during her appearance at the front. All these kinds of repetitions, each one
so artfully balanced with the other and each one so skillfully juxtaposed to the different contexts in which it
appears, are like capillary frameworks within the larger
structure.

Certain obsessive images which plague the principal
characters and define the nature of their psychological
crises are also structural. Father Consett's threat of exor-
cism and his prophecy of Sylvia's eventually becoming
reckless and vulgar are always in the back of her superstitious mind. The shade of the priest constantly pursues
her, and, despite her attempt in Rouen to make a foolish
bargain with his spirit, he ultimately prevents her planned
attack to torment the pregnant Valentine.[32] Sylvia, like
Mark and Valentine, realizes that God eventually would
have to allow Christopher's fortunes to improve, and she
suspects that Father Consett had interceded with God on
her husband's behalf (p. 807). The silver candlesticks and
dark oak-panelled walls of the Duchemin rectory, and
Edith Ethel looking in the reflected light " like a mad
block of marble, with staring, dark eyes and mad hair "
(p. 229) asking Valentine how to get rid of a baby, is
a picture which torments Valentine. The moment had
meant for her her first awareness of the harsh, vulgar side

---

[32] In Rouen, tormenting Christopher, Sylvia had denied to herself that
she was vulgar. "If I am vulgar I'm vulgar with a purpose. Then it's not
vulgarity. It may be vice. Or viciousness. . . . But if you commit a mortal
sin with your eyes open it's not vulgarity. You chance hell fire for ever. . . .
Good enough!" (p. 416). At Christopher's cottage she has to admit that
because of her public displays and her wheedling of information from
Christopher's servants, she has been vulgar (p. 805).

of Edith Ethel's nature and the denial of her naive belief of chasteness in high places. The picture is a symbol of Valentine's " sexual shock." It returns to her when Edith Ethel charges her with having a child by Christopher (p. 260) and when Christopher is telling her of Macmaster's knighthood party (" The tallest silver candlesticks of course. . . . You remember, silver candlesticks and dark oak " [p. 284]) just after he and Valentine have agreed it would be too " untidy," " ugly," and " private " to become lovers. This is a kind of illuminative and complex ironic conjunction that Ford enjoyed making and that during the writing of *The Good Soldier* he learned to handle with great subtlety and force.

Both sights and sounds recur in Christopher's nightmare ordeal. He is never certain if the subterranean sounds of the soldier's picks and the phrase " *Bringt der Hauptmann eine Kerze*," which he hears under his dugout, are real or imaginary. The recurring figure of O Nine Morgan is a more complex illusion than I have suggested, for Tietjens associates his death not only with his blood but also with his eyes. The eye is associated with the inward eye of conscience, for Tietjens feels responsible for Morgan's death as he does for one of his officer's losing an eye as he was carrying him to safety. He cannot escape the image of Morgan's eyes (" the mystified eyes of the subject races," p. 484) when he asked for leave or of the one eye in his shattered face as it looked at the roof of the hut. In the only scene of combat in which we see Tietjens, he prepares to stab a German soldier who has his eyes shot out. An echo is sounded when Campion tells Tietjens of the time he had been unable to face the eyes of his Glamorganshire battalion after he had lost half a company over a fault of his own (p. 473).

Less obsessive but still significant are the numerous

poetic quotations and snatches from songs, some of them repeated, which reflect the hopes, fears, and ideas of several characters and illustrate either their ties to their cultural tradition or their break from it. The drunken bugler on the church steps across from Mark's rocms on Armistice night playing "The Last Post" and later Cramp's oldest son playing the same parade call for the dead near his thatched shelter, portend for Mark the regretful end of the Tietjens of Groby. On the other hand, Christopher's hearing the bugler play Purcell's music to Herbert's poem evokes thoughts in him that inspire his reaffirmation.

Repeated epithets applied by characters to themselves and others have particular thematic significance. The most attention is naturally paid to Tietjens. Sylvia cannot help believing that by his refusal to condemn her he desires to model himself on Jesus Christ, a charge he greets with such horror that she uses it in her campaign against him. Campion is properly shocked by her allegation; the skeptical Mark feels that Christ probably would not give up a responsibility to Groby (p. 741). Sergeant-Major Cowley, who Sylvia realizes is wise in the way Father Consett was wise, challenges her remark that Tietjens can save others but not himself by reminding her: "We couldn't say exactly that of the captain. . . . For I fancy it was said of our Redeemer. . . . But we 'ave said that if ever there was a poor bloke the captain could 'elp, 'elp 'im 'e would . . ." (p. 404). Valentine recognizes his Christlike qualities and knows that he must be intolerable to women like Sylvia, but she also sees him as a "grey problem," a "grey grizzley," a "great motionless carp," a "mealsack," and an "elephant." Because Christopher can tell her things he tells no one else, she is aware that he is a creature of self-doubts and questionings, a view of himself he never allows Sylvia.[33]

Christopher's desire, as he words it, is to be an Anglican saint like his mother, by which he means simply one who is in harmony with his own soul and one who can touch pitch and not be defiled. Of course, he does touch pitch, but, ironically it draws him closer to his salvation. His initial offhand pride in his omniscience and his feelings of omnipotence that being a member of the ruling class gives him become a trial and a burden when he is faced during the war with deciding men's fates. He dreams of being a rural parson, but as he and Mark realize, he could not in all conscience be a minister of God and in his desires lust after Valentine (pp. 746-747). Christopher as conceived by Ford is probably quite literally the " Christbearer," certainly not Christ himself or even a Christ figure. His real need is to discover within himself intellectual and emotional harmony and to live as simply and as conscientiously as he can according to the spirit if not the letter of the Sermon on the Mount. Ford is writing a psychological novel which may be read as a political, but not so easily as a religious, parable. But Christopher cannot be divorced from the Christian tradition. Because he accepts it rather literally he is bound to be accused of emulating Christ and to be persecuted by those who have forsaken the Christian message for personal glory or material comfort or mere entertainment.

[33] Valentine " had suddenly a clear view of him as a man extraordinarily clearsighted in the affairs of others, in great affairs, but in his own so simple as to be almost a baby " (p. 236).

7

The various, seemingly endless, complex patterns of repetitions and echoes serve not only to tie together intimately the series of rendered moments and crises of experience but also to suggest inferential meanings beyond those of the plotted action. No literal realism results. The effect is that of a heightened reality achieved by exaggerations of characters and motives in order to make them representative and to give the record of a decade both a focus and a multiple dimension. In one sense, Ford achieved something similar to " an immense novel in which all the characters should be great masses of people—or interests." [34] In *The March of Literature* Ford prefaces his treatment of the contemporary conscious literary artists by noting:

> And from now on we shall have to observe in our projection the rules of impressionism. We are writing, that is to say, no longer in any measure the biographies of writers; *we must use them as if they were natural objects* bringing in a touch from one here and from another there so that there may result not a picture of men, but an impression of a world movement. (p. 802, my italics)

We have seen that from his earliest fiction Ford treated his characters somewhat like natural objects—allying or contrasting one to the other in order to dramatize different shades of personal or social frames of mind. This method is particularly convenient in the panoramic novels in which Ford attempts a detailed picture of certain areas of the political, literary, or social life of his day. Using

[34] *It Was the Nightingale*, p. 215.

the " perfectly direct, simple, and sentimental soul " (p. 119) of Christopher Tietjens, Tory gentleman of honor, as the center around which to range other representative characters, notably Sylvia as the destroyer and Valentine as the preserver of life, and by exaggerating, through simplification, the principal qualities of their temperaments, Ford achieves a curious depersonalization which allows *Parade's End* to be easily read as allegory.

J. J. Firebaugh has given the fullest allegorical reading to date. He sees *Parade's End* as " an allegory of social decay " resulting finally in Christopher and Valentine living together as a synthesis of the political Left and Right.[35] Although Firebaugh is an able interpreter, it seems to me he makes too much of assigning to Valentine the allegorical role of " the social radical " (p. 26). She is not essentially a radical at all. Poverty had forced her to become " a slavey " in Ealing, and the sexual horror of that experience had forced her to become a suffragette (p. 82). But her militant activity for women's rights is most distasteful to her and merely a stage she goes through; and she remains basically the Latinist, pacifist, and sensitive intellectual who, like Tietjens, has to suffer through several of the horrors and crudities of life before she can shed the delusive, outmoded ideals of her heritage. The allegory can be read in more expansive terms, and rather than limit it to the fusion of what are after all ambiguous political positions, it may be more accurate to see it as a rediscovery through personal tribulation of the necessary traditional bases of public honor, and of a re-establishment of harmony between the public and private selves. Only then can society " carry on the country without swank " and with some semblance of emotional balance, intellectual clarity, and order.

[35] " Tietjens and the Tradition," *Pacific Spectator*, VI (Winter, 1952), 23.

Parade's End, though it is a kind of messianic saga, avoids remarkably well the lifeless abstractions sometimes characteristic of allegory. Through his intentionally complicated methods of the time-shift and the direct rendering of consciousness, through his constant attention to material and psychological details and to their artful placement, and through his imagery, Ford achieves the impression of life being lived, of the continuity of human experience as a mosaic of memory, intelligence, and passion. This successful fusion of the abstract with the myriad specific facts of psychological experience which create a credible sense of life is an accomplishment of the major novels of Ford's middle period. Although *Parade's End* is somewhat marred by prolixity and perhaps by the extreme remoteness of the protagonist in the final novel, Ford succeeds in rendering the desperate human situations of the decade it covers and in giving them coherence, vitality, and a prophetic significance.

VIII

THE LAST NOVELS

1

OF FORD'S LAST FIVE NOVELS, FOUR ARE THEMATICALLY interesting, for they continue his record of his age into the third and fourth decades of the century and beyond. They render the moral and psychological frustrations of American or Americanized protagonists in a world of big business, gangsters, speakeasies, depression, and Communist ascendancy. The satire *When the Wicked Man* (1931) seems to be Ford's answer to *Babbitt*. *The Rash Act* (1933) and *Henry for Hugh* (1934) are companion novels comprising a subtle and extended parable of a composite British-American personality who manages under the influence of love and Provence to achieve victory over despair. *Vive Le Roy* (1936), although essentially a spy thriller and potboiler, wishfully projects into the future France's adoption of Ford's ideal state of small producers. The other novel is Ford's last historical romance, *A Little Less Than Gods* (1928), a tale of intrigue and near incest set against Napoleon's final bid for power. Weakened by extremely complex and coincidental plots, the last novels are facilely written by an author who is more and more reticent to approach an action directly. Dialogues and soliloquies become increasingly elliptical and disjointed. The time-shift and Ford's other customary techniques have become so automatic that they are sometimes used independently of the needs of the story.

When the Wicked Man is an ironic tale of the American nineteen-twenties dramatizing the moral collapse of the postwar world. Through its protagonist, Joe Notterdam, the novel shows us the final breakdown and disappearance of the traditional conscience of the gentleman of honor. English-born, but having made his fortune in America, Notterdam is a self-made man, the president of an old, respected publishing firm. Although he slowly becomes enmeshed in a morally deteriorating web of graft, alcohol, women, and deceit, he is declared a hero because he protects the widow of a young writer and kills a notorious American gangster. In reality, he is a soul racked by conscience. He has been cuckolded by Kratch, his long-time business partner and senior shareholder in the publishing firm, although Kratch and Notterdam's wife, Elspeth, have for years deprived themselves of their love for each other because of their tremendous respect for Notterdam. Kratch, ill and worn out, leaves for Europe to take a long rest. Notterdam, while drunk, signs a lifetime contract for the novels of a writer named Porter, who had been born in the same English village as he. Notterdam is persuaded by Kratch's secretary, Henrietta Felise, to appease his dying partner by cancelling the contract. As a result, Porter commits suicide, but Notterdam and Henrietta manage to make it appear that the novelist died a natural death just before the arrival of fame. His last novel is boomed and becomes a best-seller. Notterdam becomes hopelessly involved. He allows a senator to be bribed in order to pass a bill beneficial to his firm; he worries about his drinking but drinks more and more. He is pursued and persecuted by Porter's fiery, alcoholic, Creole widow, who is herself the mistress of a gangster. Notterdam and Henrietta fall in love, but he cannot bring himself to tell her that Elspeth will not divorce him because of the affair she thinks he is having with Mrs. Porter. On the night before sailing to Europe to visit Kratch, he drunkenly seduces Henrietta. In Paris he tells the bedridden, destitute Kratch to take Elspeth and gives him money. Finally, in the English village of his birth, he attempts a drunken seduction of Mrs. Porter, who is there writing her husband's memoirs and is now engaged to another man. They are interrupted by the pursuing gangster, who suddenly appears at the door. Notterdam shoots and kills him. In expiation he vows to give up Henrietta and alcohol. By the end of the voyage home he is drinking champagne. When he arrives in New York, he is a national hero, and Henrietta is there with open arms to greet him.

Notterdam is plagued by his *doppelgänger*, the image of his other ravaged self that his superstitious mind sees in times of drunkenness or emotional panic. He ascribes his fate to the inscrutability of destiny and to the fact that he is a descendant of Nostradamus. But, as heretofore in Ford's novels, his dilemma is the inevitable result of the muddles he has brought about. Notterdam illustrates Ford's conviction that it is almost impossible to have a working conscience and be involved in a large-scale commercial enterprise. At one point Notterdam rationalizes that he was performing a patriotic duty in pushing the small publishers out of business.

They cumbered the ground and interfered with that economy of output which called not merely for small profits and quick returns, as the old saying had it, but immense expenditure of capital on publicity, mass production, the carefully and long-prepared creation of markets where no markets existed—all the brain-work that had made of American Business the scientifically constructed edifice that it was.[1]

Notterdam realizes that cancelling Porter's contract is a betrayal of the honor due one's townsman, one's countryman, one's fellow man. Although he sees himself falling into " an abysm of dishonour " (p. 315), he cannot help himself, and when he tries to seduce Porter's widow in her husband's childhood home, his betrayal is irrevocable and expiation impossible. Without the counterweight of honor, one has to succumb to " The Machine." While in jail for a short time after he has killed the gangster and before being cleared, he considers repentance and reform:

How do you reform yourself?
Don't do what you did before.
That however is impracticable. It is impossible. Cables beginning to come from the House told him: EDUCATIONAL SCHEME PASSED SENATE. . . . HAVE SECURED CRAKES THREE NEXT. . . . HOBBS TEXTBOOK OF ECONOMIC TEXTBOOKS SOLD FOUR THOUSAND ON COAST. . . . PORTER BEGINNING TO MOVE FAST. . . . REAL EMPRESS FAUSTINA GETTING OVER.
The machine in fact continued and was too strong for you. You cannot get rid of bribery, poaching, pure blah—or even profiting from the results of murder. The House was going to profit very greatly by his having murdered Porter.
What are you to do then in middle middle-age? Begin a new career? Stop work? Suppress lewd works like the

[1] *When the Wicked Man* (New York: Liveright, 1931), p. 133.

EMPRESS FAUSTINA? What then? Open a shooting
gallery on the publicity of having shot McKeown [the
gangster]? Like making a profit out of the publicity gained
by the suicide of Porter?

What then? The machine will continue with you or without you. You cannot stop humanity or the onrush of New
York. (pp. 345-346)

The frustrations inherent in a commercially dominated
world also plague but do not destroy the protagonist of the
companion novels *The Rash Act* and *Henry for Hugh*.
Against the setting of the depression Ford places a complex
plot of double identity. Both Henry Martin Aluin Smith,
a destitute American, and Hugh Monckton Allard Smith,
president of a large British automobile concern, who look
and act alike, contemplate suicide on the same day. The
night before, they meet in a Riviera nightclub and renew
an old acquaintance they had had when both served in
the British army. By a series of circumstances Henry fails
and Hugh succeeds in " the rash act." Henry, whom Hugh
had made his heir the night before, assume's Hugh's name
and position. Everyone except one girl Henry had be-
friended, Eudoxie, believes he is Hugh. She helps him
to maintain the ruse. Henry as Hugh is beset by his own
past and that of Hugh's. He is troubled by his conscience
and the fear of assuming Hugh's personality at the cost
of his own. Eventually it is discovered that he and Hugh
have the same great grandfather but that their grand-
fathers were brothers. Because Henry's father was the
son of the great grandfather's oldest son, Henry is the
direct heir, Hugh a member of " the cadet branch." When
he realizes this and gains a controlling share and management of the Monckton Company through the wills of
Hugh and Hugh's aunt, who has discovered Henry's true
identity, he can accept the responsibility and also reclaim

his American citizenship, his own name, and his own identity.

Both novels, *The Rash Act* especially, are reminiscent of Hemingway's *The Sun Also Rises* and seem to be almost a parody of it. Henry thinks he may be a member of the lost generation. His life had been pointless enough. As a young man he had interrupted his Rhodes scholarship for fear of becoming too British, and he had given up as distasteful working for his father, the head of a large American candy firm. His marriage had been a failure, his wife proving to be a Lesbian. She had divorced him in order to live with another woman he had at one time wanted to marry. The divorce settlement had taken practically all of his money. When the depression made his investments worthless, there seemed to be nothing to do but commit suicide.

On the other hand, Hugh, Henry's double, is still wealthy, for his great company was not affected by the depression. Sterile because of a war injury, Hugh is nevertheless passionately in love with a Swedish actress married to a shiftless, idealistic poet.[2] When she deserts him, he turns to suicide. An injury Henry suffered in his suicide attempt supposedly has made him sterile also. He nonetheless has acquired from Hugh a *maîtresse en titre*, a young girl who had the hotel room adjoining Hugh's. Also rejected (by an ex-governor of Cochin-Saigon), she and Hugh had commiserated with each other. Henry saves her from suicide the night after his own attempt, and she accepts him as Hugh and shares his bed. Henry, however, is in love with Eudoxie, who is married to a dope peddler, then in prison. Eudoxie herself peddles adulterated cocaine while operating a prosperous beauty and health salon for

[2] Henry had also once been in love with a Swedish actress whose husband was a violinist and dope addict.

wealthy American women. Eventually, a new doctor tells Henry he is not sterile after all. When Eudoxie gets her divorce, they are free to marry. Henry's provisional mistress had sometime earlier married Henry's Communist secretary.

Although given to such overcontrived exaggeration, Ford understood the postwar conditions that elicited the note of despair. But he is still the incurable idealist. The Smith novels stand in relation to *When the Wicked Man* as the Tietjens saga does to *The Good Soldier*. Twice in his writing career, Ford followed a relatively short, bitter, ironic analysis of his age with a lengthy novel which in addition to his analysis outlined the conditions necessary for survival. Unlike Notterdam, Henry, an altruist by nature, does not betray his conscience. Immobilized by " a life without recognizable landmarks," by " the dreariest sort of attachments," and by his " drifting into bored or warmed-up adultery because it was the fashion of the times," Henry cannot face poverty, although he can make elaborate and romantic preparations for death by drowning.[3] He is really only seeking a challenge. When the boat he plans to jump from is in danger of being capsized by a sudden tornadic wind, he fights to save it and his own life. Shortly after, safely on land, he comes upon Hugh's body and exchanges his passport for the one clutched in Hugh's hand, an action which proves to be his real " rash act." That is almost his final act until he is brought out of his inertia by " the monstrous regiment of women " which surrounds him.[4] Through the efforts of Eudoxie and Hugh's Aunt Elizabeth, Henry is able to take over the Monckton empire in his own name.

[3] The quoted phrases are from *The Rash Act* (London: Cape, 1933), pp. 276, 72, and 67 respectively.
[4] *Henry for Hugh*, p. 250.

Eudoxie tells him that what she and Aunt Elizabeth have done is merely " the preparation of servants " and that " from now on " he is master (p. 321). She reminds him

". . . that the note of one's life must continue to be renunciation. . . . But the accepting of new burdens, though attended with the trappings of glory [. . .] is in itself a higher renunciation than the hermit's retirement to a cell and a diet of herbs and water. . . ." (p. 322)

The postwar male seems to have lost almost completely his initiative to act. Henry, born in the nineteenth century but fated to live in the twentieth, realizes that he was born in an age of " resolution " to live in an age of " mental confusion." [5] He is not able to adjust by himself to the demands of the transition. Ford always had faith that the best kind of woman could save a man.[6] But whereas Tietjens, for example, is inspired by Valentine to pull himself out of his despair and pain to pursue a course of

[5] *The Rash Act*, p. 32.

[6] Violet Hunt states that when she first knew Ford she " was full, not of Love, but of Loving-kindness, and obsessed by the permanent illusion of all women that they can Save. His [Ford's] friends, Conrad, Marwood, Byles, dear Dollie Radford—not so much mine—had dinned it into me.

" But, in fact, Woman has always been powerless to save, and there is no such thing as Loving-kindness between her and Man. It is bound to be Love, or nothing, with a dash of hate. The sexes are ravening beasts when once you come to brass tacks. And as, in the ancestral poem I have already quoted, 'Of Love once sown, who knoweth what the crop is?' if it is an ill one—a crop of dragon's teeth—it is left for Her to reap the dreary harvest. As for salvage, it is well known that the shipwrecked mariner turns against his rescuer; and sailors, wise and primitive men, will let a man drown lest he live to do them injury." *The Flurried Years*, p. 66.

I cannot resist quoting here from a letter of Violet Hunt probably to Ethel Colburn Mayne in the possession of Mr. Edward Naumburg, Jr. of New York. This illuminating letter about Violet Hunt's reaction to *Some Do Not . . .* is obviously a first draft; it is incomplete, undated, and apparently never was sent. " Miss Dickinson who was over here yesterday says it's [sic] psychology is splendid and will have it that Ford draws me in *Sylvia*. I do fancy, apart from her beauty, he has come to look on me as like that and it seems rather terrible but a matter of no importance really."

definite action, Henry has to be literally forced out of his lethargy by women and given a responsibility he cannot refuse. Eudoxie is Ford's final portrait of the managing woman, although she is more like Lady Savylle of the romantic farce *The Panel* than either Pauline Leicester in *A Call* or Leonora Ashburnham. Eudoxie is not required to maintain the proprieties but to encourage an irresolute man to meet her desires for his well-being, as Lady Savylle had had to arrange matters so that Edward Foster would marry her. Because Henry Smith is essentially a man of honor and an American born to action, he will make a good manager of Monckton's. He has first to be led to a course of action and to be made aware he is not sterile like Hugh.

Any overt, direct statement of the themes of these slow-moving novels is difficult to make. The themes are somewhat muted, though it is clear that Henry in his own identity, once discovered, will carry on as a benevolent American capitalist the virtues of Ford's typical gentleman of honor. The analogous attitudes and experiences of Henry and Hugh suggest the continuity of the tradition. Curiously enough, as " the chief proprietor of a great firm " Henry acquires the aristocratic manner. He gives a " hard-boiled " answer to a man who is seeking a contract to make a film about the Monckton factory. " Perhaps Henry Martin was not going to let him have it. Suitors to you have not the right to ask you questions." [7] He is exercising the new " *droits de seigneur* "—the class prerogatives of the capitalist.

The parallel identities of Henry and Hugh are another manifestation in Ford's fiction of the other-self and the double-identity. Ford's earlier novels offer us portraits of brothers or step-brothers who complement each other or

[7] *Henry for Hugh*, p. 332.

serve as foils for one another. *The Benefactor* and *Parade's End* offer a relatively close similarity. George Moffat and Christopher Tietjens are idealistic, altruistic, persecuted by those they help, and plagued by muddles they have unwittingly created as a result of their good intentions. Gregory Moffat and Mark Tietjens are similar to their brothers in reserve, but are more practical, more detached, more successful. They offer to help their brothers, who generally refuse. There is no envy between them. Usually the stable brothers have a great deal of affection and respect for their chivalric brothers, who seem rather to take them for granted. The most detached and sardonic of all the practical brothers is Mr. Blood in *Mr. Fleight*, who uses Mr. Fleight's scandal in order to get the public to forget the divorce scandal in which his gentle twin brother had been innocently involved.[8] Even the relationship between Dowell and Ashburnham in *The Good Soldier* seems remotely similar to that between these sets of brothers, although it is of course not parallel. Violet Hunt remarks on the resemblance between Ford and both Dowell and Ashburnham and suggests that Ford in his treatment of them was projecting two sides of his own personality.[9] Gringoire in the mostly autobiographical *No Enemy* is a projection of Ford, the narrator, as an artist and small producer. In a way, Henry and Hugh and the Moffat, Blood, and Tietjens brothers or near brothers give the impression of being composite though complex single characters divided for fictional purposes into two more or less simple characters.[10] In the later novels, the other-

---

[8] Mr. Bettesworth in *The Portrait* has a wild younger brother; Don Kelleg (*An English Girl*) and the Young Lovell have half-brothers. They serve merely as dramatic foils or contrasts to the protagonists.

[9] Goldring, *Trained for Genius*, p. 174.

[10] According to Goldring, Ford's relationship with his brother was somewhat analogous to that of the brothers in these novels. As a child Oliver was noted

self sometimes becomes an actual double-identity. Henry Smith is faced with his dilemma over the wisdom of assuming his double's life, Walter Leroy with the coincidence of his exact resemblance to the dead King of France.

The divided-self, the other-self contained within a single character, is evident in Ford's awareness of the mind's several levels of consciousness (especially emphasized in Christopher Tietjens) and in his recognition of the divided personality in which persons of " strong natures " contain opposing rather than complementary selves. Valentine in *Parade's End* calls them " doublings."

> And Valentine knew that Edith Ethel really loved beauty, circumspection, urbanity. It was no hypocrisy that made her advocate the Atalanta race of chastity. But, also, as Valentine Wannop saw it, humanity has these doublings of strong natures; just as the urbane and grave Spanish nation must find its outlet in the shrieking lusts of the bullring or the circumspect, laborious and admirable city typist must find her derivative in the cruder lusts of certain novelists, so Edith Ethel must break down into physical sexualities—and into shrieked coarseness of fishwives. How else, indeed, do we have saints? Surely, alone, by the ultimate victory of the one tendency over the other! (p. 268)

for his varied though unspecified escapades for which he never seemed to have been punished. " Throughout his life he seems to have had all those qualities of humour and gaiety which enable a man to steal a horse and get away with it. Ford, on the other hand, could never so much as look over a hedge without provoking an outburst of denunciation. In spite of their difference of temperament, the two brothers got along reasonably well, and no trace of jealousy, at least on Ford's part, seems ever to have affected their relations." *Trained for Genius*, p. 42.

Ford describes Oliver, in *It Was the Nightingale*, pp. 271-277, as " a gifted and in many ways extraordinary fellow " and " a mad genius " who was " the sparkling jewel of the family whilst I was its ugly duckling." " Man About Town, Army Officer, Actor, Stockbroker, Painter, Author [. . .] valise manufacturer," Oliver seems to have been endowed with several qualities Ford lacked and may have desired. Ford's own assumption of his various personae suggests that this may be so. To this extent, and perhaps no further, Ford utilized the relationship of his brother and himself in his novels.

Such doublings are also evident in William Sorrell, Sylvia Tietjens, Leonora and Edward Ashburnham, and less clearly in several other early characters who show two sides to their natures: Katya Lascarides in *A Call*, Bransdon in *The Simple Life Limited*, and the hero of *The Young Lovell*. In protagonists like Moffat, Tietjens, and Notterdam, the division usually manifests itself as a struggle of conscience.

The divided-self torn by guilt and remorse has been a significant contemporary theme from the great Russian novelists and Conrad to Kafka and Graham Greene. Ford, although he does probe beneath superficial emotions and motives, seldom explores the psychological depths or works out the universal implications of guilt as these writers do. And yet, he does clearly define one cause for modern man's sense of guilt: the loss of the ballast of high principles, resulting from a separation of what man has been taught from what he can honestly believe in. Ford's protagonists seldom suffer from guilt, but when they do, it is generally for their somehow having failed to play the game which tradition or society demands of them. George Moffat in *The Benefactor*, afraid of the sense of guilt that might consume him if he betrays his code of honor, gives up Clara Brede. And for the same reason, Ashburnham sends Nancy away. Ford's protagonists are ultimately able to protect themselves from guilt because their essential moral strength is gained by their ties to tradition, but it is no blind devotion to the past that saves them. Like Christopher Tietjens and Sorrell, they have to discover non-conventional but more fundamental attitudes and ways of life in order to maintain their integrity and achieve serenity in the world as it is. It is a process of renouncing or shuffling off whatever frustrates or attempts to destroy them. Some of Ford's characters are defeated, but they gain moral victories (Moffat and Ashburnham, for example). The only one who does not is Joe Notterdam; he feels guilt because he has relinquished all the precepts of his tradition under the pressures of a materialistic, commercial culture.

A recurring underlying theme, related to Ford's use of the brother figures, is that of incest. Although Ford characteristically treats of the trials of his protagonists on discovering their real loves after an unfortunate engagement or marriage, he occasionally explores the frustrations of an impossible love. According to Ford, there is a faint suggestion of an incestuous passion in *The Inheritors*.[11] In *The Simple Life Limited* Hamnett Gubb marries his half-sister Ophelia to remove her from the influence of the colony, but the union is never consummated and in fact they never live together. Ashburnham's rejection of Nancy is largely due to his horror at the thought that she is his ward and that he regards her as his daughter. Mark Tietjens carries the fear that Valentine is his and Christopher's half-sister, until he realizes shortly before his death that their father had not committed suicide and hence Valentine was not his daughter.

> So Valentine was not his [Old Tietjens'] daughter and there was no incest. It is all very well to say that you care little about incest. The Greeks made a hell of a tragic row about it. . . . Certainly it was a weight off the chest. He had always been able to look Christopher in the eyes—but he would be able to do it better than ever now. Comfortably!

---

[11] Ford writes in his commentary on *The Sisters*, " Tiger, Tiger," *The Bookman*, LXVI (January, 1928), 498: "And curiously enough ' The Inheritors,' the first of our collaborations to be published, has a faint and fantastic suggestion of—unrequited—love between brother and sister. It was as much as anything, because of this, that Conrad fiercely—almost fanatically—insisted in collaborating in this book."

It is uncomfortable to look a man in the eyes and think:
You sleep between incestuous sheets.[12]

Ford's last historical romance, *A Little Less Than Gods*,
offers his most direct and serious handling of the incestuous relationship. Ford claims that both he and
Conrad separately had long planned a Napoleonic tale.
Conrad finally started his in *Suspense*, which he never
completed. According to Ford, Conrad was planning in it,
as in his early unfinished novel *The Sisters*, "to risk"
treating love affairs that would prove to be incestuous.[13]
There is not enough explicit evidence in these fragments
to indicate Conrad's intentions along these lines. Ford,
in any event, carried out the same intention in *A Little
Less Than Gods*, though it can be said that he never faced
the problem honestly or profoundly. George Feilding, the
hero, unknowingly falls in love with his half-sister, Hélène
Frejus. She discovers the relationship first but cannot
bring herself to tell him. She tries avoiding him, but when
he does find her and she receives his embrace with horror,
he surmises the truth. After the excitement of the final
scenes, Hélène goes into a convent as the hero sails for
America, probably to marry the daughter of a wealthy
American acquaintance.

Ford's fascination with a taboo subject may have been
one expression of his revolt against his Victorian elders.
He was always sensitive to the foibles and aberrations
which characterized the social disintegration of his times.
A transitional figure between the "resolutions" of the
nineteenth century and the "mental confusion" of the
twentieth, he was receptive to the influences of both. In
choosing to treat the topics of incest, Lesbianism, drunkenness, dope addiction, and gangsterism, he adopted the

[12] *Parade's End*, p. 832.   [13] "Tiger, Tiger," p. 498.

modern note. Never apologizing, he approaches these subjects with a kind of resigned detachment and accepts them
as facts of contemporary life. They help give to his novels
of the nineteen-twenties and thirties an impression of
modernity, though it is not always an impression that
rings true.

When the Wicked Man and the Smith novels display a
certain lack of proportion in their sometimes exaggerated
emphasis on these moral delinquencies, as though Ford
had used them so his novels would sell better. But he had
not basically changed his tactics from those in his earlier
novels in which political corruption, commercial selfishness, and personal heartlessness define the separation of
society from its most splendid traditions. He never fore-
went the assurances his Pre-Raphaelite and Victorian
inheritance had given him. His faith in the small producer,
in a clear and exact language, and in the need for the
conscientious employment of one's true talents reflected
the Victorian confidence in a moral regeneration of society.
His hope was to offer answers, and to define honorable
means for their attainment, to an age that had grown
accustomed to disaster and dishonor.

2

Of the last novels, Ford seems to have taken the
greatest care with the writing of *The Rash Act* and *Henry
for Hugh*. On the flyleaf preceding the title page of *Henry
for Hugh* the publishers quote Ford as saying that he
thinks this is his best novel to date and that he has put
everything he knows about writing into it, a statement
that Ford, with his characteristic confidence in his present

endeavor, makes of several of his novels. Certainly in the
Smith novels, as in the other final novels, Ford is still the
master of presenting scenes and of slowly, almost slyly,
unfolding them through the consciousness of a character
or narrator who employs all the devices of the time-shift
and the *progression d'effet*. Perhaps in an attempt to veil
the inherent improbabilities of a sustained plot treating
almost identical doubles, Ford moves very slowly in the
Smith novels. Because he tried to make the second novel
independent of the first, *Henry for Hugh* contains a good
deal of repetition, which retards the action even further.
Ford's method allows Henry Smith, the primary central
intelligence, an opportunity to ponder at great length the
significance of the numerous coincidences which confront
him, but after the initial scenes leading to his assumption of Hugh's identity, he becomes passive and prolix,
although in his ruminations he sometimes recalls an
amusing or revealing episode from his past. In spite of
all the details given us by Henry's impressions of events,
the method is indirect and somewhat capricious, and the
plot device is too shaky to hold the story together for six
hundred pages. Assuredly, Ford needs the space to explain
the alliance of the two personalities, but the novels lack
the dramatic intensity typical of his earlier work. However, neither here nor in his other late novels has Ford
lost the ability to beguile the reader by withholding telling
details and revelations until the exact moment he needs
them, though sometimes he does allow the method to
degenerate into a trick. In *Vive Le Roy*, for example, an
excruciating *progression d'effet* appropriate to a thriller
builds up to an interview between the long-separated hero
and heroine, but it is neither rendered nor reported.

Using an English-born American who suffers total moral
deterioration in *When the Wicked Man*, and transferring

to an American the positive and traditional qualities of a worthy Englishman in the Smith novels, Ford expresses his conviction that the seed of the future lies in America. The Americans in the last novels are more credible as Americans than earlier portraits of such people as Dowell and Mrs. De Bray Pape, who leases Groby, but they still are not easy to accept, are close to being caricatures, and seem to have been inspired by literary rather than by actual models. But if Ford does not show any deep understanding of the details of American life or business, there is, even so, an imaginative truth in his portrayal of Americans and of the dilemmas of an acquisitive, industrious nation, still young, energetic, and iconoclastic.

In *When the Wicked Man,* or wherever American business men appear, Ford tries to capture, not always successfully, the harsh, earthy figurative slang of American speech and the fast-paced, nervous rhythms of the practical, overworked man of business. Ford must have assumed that " swell " was the principal American epithet, for it appears throughout the American novels and five times on the first page of *Vive Le Roy.* Occasionally there will be sentences like: " He could not well be canned at that hour and it would have taken a hell of a lot of booze between yesterday and the morning to drive him clean loco." [14] But most of the last novels, and especially *The Rash Act* and *Henry for Hugh,* are written in a leisurely, limpid style of notable mellowness and with a subtlety of nuance that is also characteristic of Ford's final memoirs and book-length philosophical musings. By this time Ford had caught so exactly the " vernacular of an extreme quietness " that his later style often achieves an enervating casualness which both disarms and attracts the reader.

[14] *When the Wicked Man,* p. 154.

His later style at its best can be observed in the revisions he made in words, sentences, and rhythms for the 1935 edition of *Ladies Whose Bright Eyes*, a novel about a businessman—British, to be sure, but with his own commercial, colloquial language. The several stylistic changes made in the revised edition, most evident in the first half and in the very last section of the novel, are appropriate to Ford's revised understanding of Sorrell. The language achieves more conciseness of expression; compound-complex sentences often become two complex sentences; "and" at the beginning of many sentences is omitted; paragraphs are split—one paragraph of 270 words is split and condensed into 141 words; unnecessary and burdensome words, phrases, and sentences are omitted; brief passages are deleted. Rhythms are more carefully adapted to action and to Sorrell's perception of events. While the intimate conversational style that Ford sought is often too evident and forced in the early edition, in the revision the style is less slangy and stenographic, more impressionistic and convincing. Thus, for example, " It was very nearly as big and quite as spic-and-span as Windsor itself " (1911 ed., p. 64) becomes " It was nearly as big as Windsor " (1935 ed., p. 68) ; or

> The sound of the singing died away, and in his intense weariness Mr. Sorrell dropped asleep.
>
> . . . .
>
> He was always very dizzy and stupid upon awakening, so that when he was gently shaken he had not the least idea where he was. (p. 67)

becomes in the 1935 edition simply:

> The sound of the singing died away. . . .
> He was gently shaken. He did not know where he was. (p. 70)

Perhaps the most valuable change is that, through certain stylistic innovations, Sorrell's character is shown more directly, is seen more clearly, and is developed more consistently. Often direct discourse has been shifted to indirect, and sentences have been fragmented or interrupted by ellipses to represent mental processes rather than statements about them, as in the passage describing Sorrell's final emergence from his delerium, where Ford adapts his cadences to Sorrell's semi-conscious perception as it is shaped by pain, fear, and memory, and thus achieves a more credible, precise, and lively impression than the original edition manages to do. Intrusive, obvious remarks by the author-narrator to describe states of mind have been cut out. Sorrell's more inane wisecracks, his contemptuous remarks about the lower orders, everything which belittles him in the earlier edition have been deleted.

The best short passage displaying Ford's later ability to mirror states of mind and to adapt his rhythms to them is perhaps the following one describing a procession:

> The gate of the workhouse fell back; there came out a white figure carrying on high a crucifix. Then there were several little boys in white, swinging brass censers with brass chains. Some workmen ran out of the adjoining fields, and some women in grey dresses. There came out from the convent a man in purple vestments, and behind him two more in white linen surplices that shook in the breeze. And after that the nuns—a great number of nuns, two and two, in black habits with coifs waving like swan's wings. The sound of singing came to him, melodious and triumphant.
>
> " God bless my soul! " Mr. Sorrell said, " I thought religious processions were forbidden by law! "
>
> And he remembered very strongly now that when the Roman Catholics had attempted to carry the Sacrament through the streets of London, there had been a great outcry

some years before, and the thing was stopped—quite rightly, as he thought. (pp. 65-66)

The 1935 edition reads:

The gate of the workhouse fell back. There came out a white figure, bearing on high a crucifix. . . . Several little boys in white, swinging brass censers on brass chains. . . . Workmen ran out of the adjoining ploughlands; some women in grey dresses. From the workhouse came a man in purple vestments; behind him two more in white surplices that shook in the breeze. . . . And after that there were nuns. . . . Great numbers of nuns, two and two. In black habits with coifs waving like the wings of swans. The sound of singing came to him; melodious and triumphant.

Mr Sorrell had thought that religious processions were forbidden by law. . . . When Roman Catholics had attempted to carry the Sacrament through the streets of Southwark some years before there had been a great public outcry. (p. 69)

All the changes Ford made for the revised edition are the workmanlike emendations of a craftsman who prided himself on being an Impressionist. They give focus, they simplify, they convince. Ultimately, they lend depth and credibility to the new seriousness with which Ford came to view Sorrell and the resolution of his plight.

3

Ford's return to his early fantasy of William Sorrell is significant because it allowed him to reshape his themes in terms of his later ideas. It can be considered his final statement, though it is not essentially different from that made by *Parade's End*, or *The Rash Act* and *Henry for Hugh*, or several other novels. Dionissia's exhortation to Sorrell about "new beginnings" and the need for faith is a reflection of Christopher Tietjens' awareness of the regenerative value of hard, simple work. Similarly, Eudoxie persuades Henry Smith of the value of the "renunciation" of "accepting new burdens" and warns him to use his power scrupulously. They all are brought to discovering their own identity. They all reject the atrophied knowledge and conventions of their contemporaries. They all come to realize their ignorance of how things are made or done because everything has been done or made for them; consequently, they all must seek to use what knowledge their talents have given them. Hence, Sorrell goes to Russia to build bridges, Tietjens sells antiques, and Smith takes over a factory.

During the last decade of his life Ford's creative energies were concentrated on his nonfiction, in which he could develop more fully and directly his views on life and art. These books reinforced the moral criticism and historical arguments he had worked out in his mature novels, starting with *Parade's End*, and recapitulated the thoughts and feelings of his lifetime. The records of his age that he offered in his novels become in these final personal-literary-philosophical works more literally a record of his mind and sensibility as it ranged over the present and the past and projected his hopes for the future. Because he realized that the social, moral, and literary traditions he knew were in danger of being forgotten, he saw it as his duty to leave an account of them for future generations.[15]

The eight books of nonfiction published between 1929 and 1938, though related, fall naturally into three types: autobiography, literary history, and moral-philosophical

---

[15] See Ford's dedications to *Return to Yesterday* and *Great Trade Route*.

essays. Ford considered *Return to Yesterday* (1931) and *It Was the Nightingale* (1933) as his collective autobiography rather than as reminiscences such as he had written in *Memories and Impressions* and *Thus to Revisit*. *Return to Yesterday* recounts Ford's impressions of his early life and ideas and offers his final account of the collaboration with Conrad and the fullest record of his editorship of *The English Review*. In *It Was the Nightingale* (originally titled *Towards Tomorrow*) he describes his postwar period as a market gardner in Sussex, his reasons for leaving England, the genesis of *Parade's End*, and his second editorial venture with *The Transatlantic Review*.[16] *Portraits from Life* (1937) is a collection, originally written for *The American Mercury*, of critical reminiscences of eleven writers he knew.[17] Though it repeats much of what he had written earlier, the book does add critical insights and offers Ford's final evaluations of these literary acquaintances of his.

The English Novel (1929) is a short but characteristic summary of Ford's views on English fiction, which, as would be expected, pays tribute to the tradition of the serious art novel in which Ford worked. But it was in his final book, the monumental *The March of Literature* (1938), in which he drew upon his lifetime of reading, of study, of love of literature and the arts. It is Ford's benevolent apologia for his life as a literary artist and represents, perhaps more than any other single work of his, his wide learning in the literatures of the world. He argues the prominence of Mediterranean over Nordic literature because the southern writers generally cared

---

[16] The holograph copy of *It Was the Nightingale*. owned by Mr. Edward Naumburg, Jr., is titled *Towards Tomorrow*.

[17] James, Conrad, Hardy, Wells, Crane, D. H. Lawrence, Galsworthy, Hudson, Dreiser, Swinburne, and Turgenev (whom Ford says he met in early childhood).

about art as method, as technique, rather than as merely a vehicle for ideas and feelings. At the same time, by his comparative method, which allows him to draw analogies among the several literatures of the world, he emphasizes the " true internationalism of letters," a conviction which he had always held and which had been one of the principal ideas behind *The Transatlantic Review*.

Most significant to an understanding of his themes are the three volumes which develop his social and moral criticism. *No Enemy* (1929) illustrates and defends the life of the artist and small producer and justifies Christopher Tietjens' and Ford's own dedication to the simple life and the salvation it seemed to offer amid the treacheries and despairs of postwar England. But that rural experiment failed, and Ford turned later to the south of France, where, as he tells us in *Provence* (1935), the people and the climate made the life of the small producer more practicable. In *Provence* and *Great Trade Route* (1937) Ford champions the Mediterranean over the Nordic civilization and offers his final vision of the ideal community of small states that I outlined above in Chapter IV.

All these later texts comprise Ford's testament of faith. In all of them he works along the lines of his " generous emotions " and foresees that it is only by the exercise of his noblest qualities of mind and temperament that man can survive. He does not expect that human nature will change much, but he is convinced that, once the complex machinery of the overorganized state is discarded and the professional politician is left without a job, each man will then be able to provide for himself, to live where he is happiest, and to limit his natural feelings of jealousy and envy to growing a more productive garden or building a better house than his neighbor. When this stage is achieved, each man in his own way will be an artist, and the artist's imagination, his clarity of language, and his allegiance to the great aesthetic and human traditions will govern men's actions and direct their goals.

Since the passing of the " Great Figure " from all areas of public, intellectual and moral life, and the loss of all-embracing, comforting views of life as a whole, the only hope Ford offers for the salvation of society is to seize a fragment of what is left and with faith and integrity to construct out of it a new world of moral and psychological harmony in which the balance of power is always with the individual and not with the cartels, the state, or the superficial social conventions. The small producer must stay small, and life must be contained within a comprehensible scale if man in the mass is not to be destroyed by his own wolfishness.

Novels like *Mr. Fleight, The Good Soldier*, and *When the Wicked Man* are Ford's trenchant, ironic, even bitter portraits of the complex frustrations and compromises of his day. They are moral protests without direct preaching. But closer to his temperament, which maintained a traditional sense of personal honor, and to his Victorian heritage, which felt the necessity of offering saving solutions, are his pleas for integrity, altruism, and the positive virtues he develops in his affirmative novels and in much of his nonfiction. Ford may not have convinced our generation with the solutions he offers, but he presents them without sermonizing, through the consciousness of his characters, so that the reader can take them or leave them.

Although Ford's fiction is remarkably faithful to his critical strictures against moral intrusions by the author, he could not always, as a novelist, meet the challenge of his critical theories. As one might expect, the novels that show the most obvious expression of his themes are not usually his best work. *An English Girl, The Simple Life Limited, The New Humpty-Dumpty,* and *When the Wicked Man* are burdened by coincidences and the machinery of overmelodramatic plots, often carelessly constructed or contrived too neatly by the demands of a preconceived idea. Ford admired James for his " apparent digressions," but several of Ford's novels are weakened by digressions and extended expositions that fail to pass the test of justification. The reader of Ford's work cannot help being struck by the constant restatements of theme and the repetitions of key phrases or images: the " raging stallion," " the stuff to fill graveyards," " *homo homini lupis,*" " grim, inscrutable Destiny," and others. For a conscious stylist and artist, he wrote too fast and too much. He allowed too many infelicities of style and taste, and too frequent lapses into tiresomeness, slickness, and unnecessary complexity of manner.

To one who has read all of Ford's novels, there is a special point in Conrad's reminder to Ford, in a letter referred to earlier and written during the collaboration, that " the value of creative work of any kind is in the *whole* of it. . . . [The] phrasing, expression—technique in short—has importance only when the conception of the whole has a significance of its own apart from the details that go to make it up." Ford is not always so careful in constructing the whole of his novels as he is in creating particular scenes. He can skillfully prepare a scene and juxtapose it with those surrounding it for the maximum effect. Yet brilliant scenes or gatherings of scenes do not necessarily make for a successful formal unity. Thus, a novel like *The Rash Act* and its sequel *Henry for Hugh* can contain several scenes which catch the shimmering haze or the " vibrating reality " of life—Henry in his boat before and after the storm which prevents his suicide or

Henry waking up in Hugh's room—but still be marred by an exaggerated indirectness and a length which arrives almost at the point of paralysis. *A Little Less Than Gods* has some splendidly realized scenes of Napoleon (shifting between efficiency and slothfulness, or between being considerate and tyrannical), of the indignant but essentially weak Wellington, and between Henry Feilding and his half-sister Hélène, but the plot dealing with Napoleon's last hundred days and that dealing with the incestuous attraction have only a tenuous relation to each other.

And yet, overall, in both his fiction and nonfiction, Ford leaves an impressionistic, technically adroit, and entertaining record of his age as seen from the perspective of his intelligent, literate, and humane temperament. Since his energies were not always saved for his fiction, his novels are uneven in quality, but when he drew on his own trials of love, scandal, or war and saw them in terms of the moral, social, and psychological issues of his era, he could write penetrating, carefully ordered novels that achieve in practice what he preached in theory. Then, too, he managed not only to subdue his fondness for melodrama, or to use it for complex ironic effects, but also to render his characters with a good deal of psychological truth. Always, with the help of his comic vision, he could dramatize the grotesque in life and the ironic confusions of human beings involved in their own muddles. His finest achievements in technique were in novels in which he managed chronology, narrative point of view, and language to create direct and sustained impressions of life. In both his first and third person narrations, he brought the myriad perceptions of the mind under the control of art by capturing the rhythms of the consciousness in the act of perception and by revealing order and design in experience through his woven patterns of image and metaphor. Sometimes, in his Katherine Howard trilogy, in such fantasies as *Ladies Whose Bright Eyes*, or in social comedies like *A Call*, he succeeded in constructing unified and revealing if for the most part only clever or intricate plots. In *The Good Soldier* and *Parade's End*, in which he achieves formal excellence through an imaginative fusion of theme and technique, Ford brought to this century exceptional novels of impassioned insight and integrity that both for their art and their truth we cannot ignore or soon forget.

BIBLIOGRAPHY

I. Ford Madox Ford: A Selected Bibliography

The Brown Owl: A Fairy Story. London: T. Fisher Unwin, 1892.

The Feather. London: T. Fisher Unwin, 1892.

The Shifting of the Fire. London: T. Fisher Unwin, 1892.

The Queen Who Flew: A Fairy Tale. London: Bliss, Sands and Foster, 1894.

"D. G. Rossetti and His Family Letters," *Living Age,* ccix (April 4, 1896), 53-59.

Ford Madox Brown: A Record of His Life and Work. London: Longmans, Green, 1896.

"Millais and Rossetti Exhibitions," *Fortnightly,* lxix (February, 1898), 189-196.

"Sir Edward Burne-Jones," *Living Age,* ccxxix (October 8, 1898), 110-121.

The Inheritors: An Extravagant Story. With Joseph Conrad. London: William Heinemann, 1901.

Rossetti: A Critical Essay on His Art. London: Duckworth, and New York: Sutton [1902] My references are to the Chicago: Rand, McNally [1915] edition.

Romance. With Joseph Conrad. London: Smith, Elder, 1903.

"Collected Poems of Christina Rossetti," *Living Age,* ccxli (April 16, 1904), 158-167.

The Benefactor: A Tale of a Small Circle. London: Brown, Langham, 1905.

Hans Holbein the Younger: A Critical Monograph. London: Duckworth [1905].

The Fifth Queen: And How She Came to Court. London: Alston Rivers, 1906.

Privy Seal: His Last Venture. London: Alston Rivers, 1907.

An English Girl: A Romance. London: Methuen [1907].

The Pre-Raphaelite Brotherhood: A Critical Monograph. London: Duckworth [1907].

England and the English: An Interpretation. New York: McClure, Phillips, 1907.

The Fifth Queen Crowned: A Romance. London: Eveleigh Nash, 1908.

Mr. Apollo: A Just Possible Story. London: Methuen, 1908.

The 'Half-Moon': A Romance of the Old World and the New. London: Eveleigh Nash, 1909.

A Call: The Tale of Two Passions. London: Chatto and Windus, 1910.

The Portrait. London: Methuen, 1910.

Memories and Impressions: A Study in Atmospheres. New York: Harper and Brothers, 1911. Published in England under the title *Ancient Lights and Certain New Reflections: Being the Memories of a Young Man.* London: Chapman and Hall, 1911.

The Simple Life Limited. Under the pseudonym Daniel Chaucer. London and New York: John Lane, 1911.

Ladies Whose Bright Eyes: A Romance. London: Constable, 1911. Revised edition without sub-title: Philadelphia and London: J. B. Lippincott, 1935.

The Critical Attitude. London: Duckworth, 1911.

The Panel: A Sheer Comedy. London: Constable, 1912. Published in America, slightly revised, under the title *Ring for Nancy: A Sheer Comedy.* Indianapolis: Bobbs-Merrill [1913], and New York: Grosset and Dunlap, 1913.

The New Humpty-Dumpty. Under the pseudonym Daniel Chaucer. London and New York: John Lane, 1912.

Mr. Fleight. London: Howard Latimer, 1913.

The Young Lovell: A Romance. London: Chatto and Windus, 1913.

Henry James: A Critical Study. London: Martin Secker, 1913. My references are to the New York: Albert and Charles Boni, 1915 edition.

Collected Poems. London: Max Goschen, 1914.

The Good Soldier: A Tale of Passion. London and New York: John Lane, 1915. My references are to the New York: Alfred A. Knopf, 1951 edition, or to its paperback reprint: New York: Vintage Books, 1957, both of which include "An Interpretation" by Mark Schorer.

When Blood Is Their Argument: An Analysis of Prussian Culture. New York and London: Hodder and Stoughton, 1915.

Between St. Denis and St. George: A Sketch of Three Civilisations. London: Hodder and Stoughton, 1915.

A House. No. 21 of *The Chapbook: A Monthly Miscellany.* London: The Poetry Bookshop, March, 1921.

Thus to Revisit: Some Reminiscences. London: Chapman and Hall, 1921.

The Marsden Case: A Romance. London: Duckworth, 1923.

Women and Men. Paris: Three Mountains Press, 1923.

Mister Bosphorus and the Muses: Or a Short History of Poetry in Britain. London: Duckworth, 1923.

The Nature of a Crime. With Joseph Conrad. London: Duckworth, 1924.

Joseph Conrad: A Personal Remembrance. London: Duckworth, 1924.

Some Do Not . . . . London: Duckworth, 1924, and New York: Albert and Charles Boni, 1924.

No More Parades. London: Duckworth, 1925, and New York: Albert and Charles Boni, 1925.

A Man Could Stand Up—. London: Duckworth, 1926, and New York: Albert and Charles Boni, 1926.

The Last Post. New York: Literary Guild of America, 1928. Published in England under the title *Last Post.* London: Duckworth, 1928.

A Little Less Than Gods: A Romance. New York: Viking Press, 1928.

"Tiger, Tiger," *The Bookman,* LXVI (January, 1928), 495-498.

"On Conrad's Vocabulary," *The Bookman,* LXVII (June, 1928), 405-408.

No Enemy: A Tale of Reconstruction. New York: Macaulay, 1929.

The English Novel From the Earliest Days to the Death of Joseph Conrad. Philadelphia and London: J. B. Lippincott, 1929.

Return to Yesterday. London: Victor Gollancz, 1931. My references are to the New York: Horace Liveright, 1932 edition.

When the Wicked Man. New York: Horace Liveright, 1931.

The Rash Act. London: Jonathan Cape, 1933.

It Was the Nightingale. Philadelphia and London: J. B. Lippincott, 1933.

Henry for Hugh. Philadelphia and London: J. B. Lippincott, 1934.

Provence: From Minstrels to the Machine. Philadelphia and London: J. B. Lippincott, 1935. My references are to the London: Allen and Unwin, 1938 edition.

" Techniques," *Southern Review*, I (July, 1935), 20-35.

Vive Le Roy. Philadelphia and London: J. B. Lippincott, 1936.

Portraits from Life: Memories and Criticisms. Boston: Houghton Mifflin, 1937. Published in England under the title *Mightier Than the Sword: Memories and Criticisms.* London: Allen and Unwin, 1938.

Great Trade Route. New York: Oxford University Press, 1937.

The March of Literature From Confucius' Day to Our Own. New York: The Dial Press, 1938.

Parade's End. Introduction by Robie Macauley. New York: Albert A. Knopf, 1950. (The Christopher Tietjens tetralogy in one volume.)

II. Secondary Sources [1]

Allen, Walter. *The English Novel: A Short Critical History.* New York: E. P. Dutton, 1955.

Baugh, Albert C., and others. *A Literary History of England.* New York: Appleton-Century-Crofts, 1948.

Beach, Joseph Warren. *The Twentieth Century Novel.* New York: Appleton-Century-Crofts, 1932.

Blackmur, R. P. " The King Over the Water: Notes on the Novels of F. M. Hueffer," *The Princeton University Library Chronicle*, IX (April, 1948), 123-127.

Bowen, Stella. *Drawn from Life.* London: Collins, 1941,

Brown, E. K. " James and Conrad," *Yale Review*, XXXV (Winter, 1945), 265-285.

Burke, Edmund. *Works.* Revised ed. Vol. IV. Boston: Little, Brown, 1866.

Conrad, Joseph. *Letters to William Blackwood and David S. Meldrum.* Edited by William Blackburn. Durham, North Carolina: Duke University Press, 1958.

[1] I note here only the references I have used. For an annotated checklist of material on Ford, see *English Fiction in Transition*, I (Spring-Summer, 1958), 2-19; and supplements: I (Fall, 1958), 35; II (Spring, 1959), 41-43; and periodically thereafter.

————. *Notes on Life and Letters*. London: J. M. Dent and Sons, 1921.

————. *Prefaces to His Works*. With an essay by Edward Garnett. London: J. M. Dent and Sons, 1937.

Crankshaw, Edward. "Ford Madox Ford," *The National Review*, CXXXI (August, 1948), 160-167.

————. *Joseph Conrad: Some Aspects of the Art of the Novel*. London: John Lane, 1936.

Douglas, Norman. *Late Harvest*. London: Lindsay Drummond, 1946.

Firebaugh, J. J. "Tietjens and the Tradition," *Pacific Spectator*, VI (Winter, 1952), 23-32.

Flaubert, Gustave. *Letters*. Edited by Richard Rumbold. Translated by J. M. Cohen. London: George Wiedenfeld and Nicolson, 1950.

Galsworthy, John. *The Forsyte Saga*. "Modern Standard Authors Edition." New York: Charles Scribner's Sons, 1918.

Garnett, David. *The Golden Echo*. London: Chatto and Windus, 1954.

The Germ. Reprint by Thomas B. Mosher. Portland, Maine, 1898.

Goldring, Douglas. *South Lodge: Reminiscences of Violet Hunt, Ford Madox Ford and the English Review Circle*. London: Constable, 1943.

————. *Trained for Genius: The Life and Writings of Ford Madox Ford*. New York: E. P. Dutton, 1949. Published in England under the title *The Last Pre-Raphaelite*. London: Macdonald, 1948.

Gose, Elliott B. "The Strange Irregular Rhythm: An Analysis of *The Good Soldier*," *PMLA*, LXXII (June, 1957), 494-509.

Greene, Graham. "Dark Backward: A Footnote," *London Mercury*, XXXII (October, 1935), 562-565.

————. *The Lost Childhood and Other Essays*. New York: Viking Press, 1952.

Greenslet, Ferris. *Under the Bridge*. Boston: Houghton Mifflin, 1943.

Guerard, Albert J. *Conrad the Novelist*. Cambridge, Massachusetts: Harvard University Press, 1958.

Harkness, Bruce. "The Handling of Time in the Novels of Joseph Conrad." Unpublished Ph. D. dissertation, Department of English, University of Chicago, 1950.

Haugh, Robert F. *Joseph Conrad: Discovery in Design*. Norman: University of Oklahoma Press, 1957.

Hicks, Granville, Richard Aldington, and others. "Homage to Ford Madox Ford; A Symposium." *New Directions: 1942*. Norfolk, Connecticut: New Directions, 1942, pp. 443-494.

Hunt, Violet. *The Flurried Years*. London: Hurst and Blackett, 1926. Published in America under the title *I Have This to Say*. New York: Boni and Liveright, 1926.

Hunt, William Holman. *Pre-Raphaelitism and the Pre-Raphaelite Brotherhood*. Vol. I. New York: Macmillan, 1905.

Jackson, Holbrook. *The Eighteen Nineties*. Middlesex: Hammondsworth, 1950.

James, Henry. *The Art of Fiction and Other Essays*. Edited by Morris Roberts. New York: Oxford University Press, 1948.

————. *The Portrait of a Lady*. New York: The Modern Library, n. d.

Jean-Aubry, G. *The Life and Letters of Joseph Conrad.* 2 vols. Garden City, New York: Doubleday, 1927.
––––––. *The Sea Dreamer: A Definitive Biography of Joseph Conrad.* Garden City, New York: Doubleday, 1957.
Jepson, Edgar. *Memoirs of an Edwardian.* London: Richards, 1937.
Joyce, James. *A Portrait of the Artist as a Young Man.* New York: Modern Library, 1928.
Kazin, Alfred. " The Anger of Flaubert," *New Yorker,* xxx (September 11, 1954), 134-139.
Kenner, Hugh. *Gnomon.* New York: McDowell, Oblensky, 1958.
––––––. "He Wrote of Giants," *The Kenyon Review,* xi (Autumn, 1949), 696-699.
––––––. *The Poetry of Ezra Pound.* Norfolk, Connecticut: New Directions, n. d.
Lewisohn, Ludwig (ed.). *A Modern Book of Criticism.* New York: Modern Library, 1919.
Lid, R. W. "Tietjens in Disguise," *The Kenyon Review,* xxii (Spring, 1960), 265-276.
––––––. "Time in the Novels of Ford Madox Ford." Unpublished Ph. D. dissertation, Department of English, University of Michigan, 1958.
––––––. " On the Time-Scheme of *The Good Soldier,*" *English Fiction in Transition,* iv, no. 2 (1961), 9-10.
Lubbock, Percy. *The Craft of Fiction.* New York: Peter Smith, 1947.
Macauley, Robie. " The Good Ford," *The Kenyon Review,* xi (Spring, 1949), 269-288. A revised portion of this essay appears as an introduction to *Parade's End.* New York: Alfred A. Knopf, 1950.
McCormick, John. *Catastrophe and Imagination: An Interpretation of the Recent English and American Novel.* London and New York: Longmans, Green, 1957.
MacShane, Frank. "The Pattern of Ford Madox Ford," *New Republic,* cxxxii (April 4, 1955), 16-17.
Marrot, H. V. *The Life and Letters of John Galsworthy.* London: William Heinemann, 1935.
Marshall, Archibald. *Out and About.* New York: E. P. Dutton, 1934.
Meixner, John A. " The Saddest Story," *The Kenyon Review,* xxii (Spring, 1960), 234-264.
Meyerhoff, Hans. *Time in Literature.* Berkeley and Los Angeles: University of California Press, 1955.
Mizener, Arthur. "A Large Fiction," *The Kenyon Review,* xiii (Winter, 1951), 142-147.
Monroe, Harriet. *A Poet's Life.* New York: Macmillan, 1938.
Muir, Edwin. *The Structure of the Novel.* London: The Hogarth Press, 1938.
Naumburg, Edward, Jr. "A Catalogue of a Ford Madox Ford Collection," *The Princeton University Library Chronicle,* ix (April, 1948), 134-165.
––––––. "A Collector Looks at Ford Madox Ford," *The Princeton University Library Chronicle,* ix (April, 1948), 105-118.
[Patmore, Coventry.] " Pre-Raphaelite Exhibition," *Saturday Review,* iv (July 4, 1857), 11-12.

Pound, Ezra. Interview. St. Elizabeth's Hospital, Washington, D. C., February 5, 1951.
———. *Letters: 1907-1941*. Edited by D. D. Paige. New York: Harcourt Brace, 1950.
Rossetti, Dante Gabriel. *The House of Life*. Edited with an introduction by Paull Franklin Baum. Cambridge, Massachusetts: Harvard University Press, 1928.
———. *Works*. Edited by William Michael Rossetti. London: Ellis, 1911.
Rossetti, William Michael (ed.). *Family Letters with a Memoir*. Vol. I. Boston: Roberts Brothers, 1895.
Schorer, Mark. "The Good Novelist in *The Good Soldier*," *The Princeton University Library Chronicle*, IX (April, 1948), 128-133. Reprinted in *Horizon*, XX (August, 1949), 132-138, and with revisions as "An Interpretation," which serves as an introduction to the 1951 Knopf and 1957 Vintage Books editions of *The Good Soldier*.
Tate, Allen. "Techniques of Fiction," in *Forms of Modern Fiction*. Edited by William Van O'Connor. Minneapolis: University of Minnesota Press, 1948, pp. 30-45.
Tillotson, Geoffrey. *Criticism and the Nineteenth Century*. London: Athlone Press, 1951.
Tindall, William York. *Forces in Modern British Literature: 1885-1946*. New York: Alfred A. Knopf, 1947.
Turgenev, Ivan. *Liza*. Translated by W. R. S. Ralston. London: J. M. Dent, 1914.
Walter, H. V. "The Political Sense of Ford Madox Ford," *New Republic*, CXXXIV (March 26, 1956), 17-19.
Wells, H. G. *Experiment in Autobiography*. New York: Macmillan, 1934.
Wilde, Oscar. *Works*. New York: Walter S. Black, 1927.
Williams, William Carlos. "*Parade's End*," *Sewanee Review*, LIX (January-March, 1951), 154-161.
Zabel, Morton Dauwen. *Craft and Character: Texts, Method, and Vocation in Modern Fiction*. New York: Viking Press, 1957.

INDEX

Adams, Henry, 156n
Aestheticism: Ford's use of term
  with Pre-Raphaelitism, 16n; assumption justifying point of view
  and time-shift, 24-35
Arnold, Matthew, 18, 27
Ashburnham, Edward (character),
  156-158 (and 149-201 *passim*),
  278, 280, 281; early models of,
  114-122
Ashburnham, Leonora (character),
  154-155, 187 (and 151-201 *passim*),
  277, 280; early models of, 124-125
Austen, Jane, 21n, 23, 39, 57
—*Pride and Prejudice*, 57

Balzac, Honoré de:
—*La Comédie Humaine*, 24
Benefactor, The, 76, 83, 118-119,
  127-128, 136n, 143, 145, 147, 278,
  280
Bennett, Arnold, 22, 46
Bergson, Henri, 30
Biala, Janice, 42n
Blackmur, R. P., viii
Bowen, Stella, ix, 107-108

Brown, Ford Madox, 1, 3, 4, 9, 10,
  11
Brown Owl, The, 3
Browning, Robert, 18, 19
Bunyan, John, 52
Burke, Edmund, 215-216
Burne-Jones, Sir Edward, 1, 16

Call, A, 77, 109-113, 124, 137, 146-
  147, 153, 223, 277, 280, 295
Carlyle, Thomas, 43, 86
Character: Ford's theory of, 60-61;
  range of, in Ford's novels, 79-80.
  See also major characters indexed
Chateaubriand, Francois René, 23
Chekov, Anton, 59n
Cinque Ports, The, 71
Cobbett, William, 64
Collected Poems (1914), 15
Conrad, Joseph, viii-xi *passim,* 5,
  23, 25, 29, 32-33, 34, 133, 213, 254,
  280, 281n, 282, 293; collaboration
  with Ford, 4, 9, 14, 20-21, 35-36,
  128; his relationship with Ford
  and James, 23n; working with

303